DATE DU

822

ALAN BENNETT

Studies in Modern Drama
Kimball King, *Series Editor*

ALAN BENNETT

A Critical Introduction

Joseph H. O'Mealy

Routledge
New York & London

Published in 2001 by
Routledge
29 West 35th Street
New York, NY 10001

Published in Great Britain by
Routledge
11 New Fetter Lane
London EC4P 4EE

Routledge is an imprint of the Taylor & Francis Group

10 9 8 7 6 5 4 3 2 1

Library of Congress Cataloging-in-Publication Data
O'Mealy, Joseph H., 1948–
    Alan Bennett : a critical introduction / by Joseph O'Mealy.
      p. cm. — (Studies in modern drama ; v. 27)
    Includes bibliographical references and index.
    ISBN 0-8153-3540-7
    1. Bennett, Alan, 1934—Criticism and interpretation. I. Title.
II. Series.
PR6052.E5 Z8 2001
822'.914—dc21   00-065301

Printed on acid-free, 250-year-life paper.
Manufactured in the United States of America.

For Ryan, Michael, and Katherine

Contents

Abbreviations

Acknowledgments

My debts to friends, colleagues, and family extend over two continents and several states. In England, I am especially indebted to Olwen Terris of the British Film Institute, a fellow Bennett enthusiast, for helping me gain access to videos of Bennett's plays; to Ken Budge for regular gifts of Bennett books and videos; and to Tony Bodinetz and the late Allison Trumpy for their gifts of videos, books, and the address of Alan Bennett's agent. In California, I received much-appreciated help and encouragement from Kathleen Namphy, who sponsored my research at the Stanford University Library; from Peter Smith and Helen Pellegrin, who listened and offered valuable advice; from Barbara Kalhammer, another Bennett enthusiast, whose generous reading of an early draft of the book encouraged me greatly; and from Katherine Wright, whose editing skills make this book look good, despite its author's failings. In Hawai'i, I have profited enormously from the judgment of my friends in the English department of the University of Hawai'i at Manoa. I am particularly indebted to Nell Altizer, Miriam Fuchs, Craig Howes, and Kathy Phillips for their reading of the whole manuscript, and for suggestions for improvement that are gratefully incorporated throughout the book. I am also grateful to Bruce Bruschi for bringing the Alec Guinness material to my attention and for getting me a hot-off-the-press copy of the play version of *The Lady in the Van* and to Alan Holzman, who collected the reviews and found me hard-to-get tickets to *The Lady in the Van*. Special thanks go to Cornelia Moore, who as dean of the College of Languages, Linguistics and Literature gave me released time to pursue my research and writing, and to her successor, Ricky Jacobs, who allowed me to put the completion of the manuscript at the top of my duties as acting associate dean. In my office, June Nakaki and Michelle Aquino have earned my gratitude for their uncomplaining assistance with the final preparations of the manuscript. Dave Carter deserves special mention for his many years of encour-

xi

agement and his faith that I had at least one book in me.

Last but far from least, I would like to acknowledge Alan Bennett's role in all this. Though he declined my request for an interview, he did give this project his usual equivocal blessing. On the back of a postcard of Degas's *The Rehearsal* from the Frick Collection in New York, he wrote:

> I'm hopeless at talking about my own stuff and have always avoided it—if I could talk about the plays I wouldn't have written them. This isn't meant to be rude. I've said everything I want to say in the various introductions. . . . I hope this doesn't seem ungrateful and I much appreciate your interest. Treat me like a dead author and make it up—no-one will know.

Despite Mr. Bennett's advice, in the pages that follow I haven't made anything up, so far as I can tell, although I have speculated where the evidence seems to warrant it. And I am certain that I have not treated Alan Bennett as a dead author. On the contrary, I have tried to present him as a vital presence in the contemporary theater, ever ready to surprise, instruct, and delight.

Introduction: Who Is Alan Bennett?

When I began writing this book and mentioned its subject to American colleagues and friends, I was almost always greeted with polite silence as they mentally tried to fit the name to a body of work. Assuming they had misheard me, and grasping at a familiar Bennett, some would ask, "*Arnold Bennett?*" English colleagues and friends, on the other hand, knew immediately who I meant. They didn't need to read the dust jackets of Alan Bennett's books to know that he is "one of the country's best loved writers," or even "England's best-loved playwright"(*CTSU*, 1)—a national favorite.[1]

Bennett's ascension to household word status in England did not, however, occur overnight. Though he has been in the public eye since the early 1960s, his most lavish popular successes have come only in the last decade or so. The Royal National Theatre staged three of his plays in rapid succession—*Single Spies*[2] (1988), his adaptation of *The Wind in the Willows* (1990), and *The Madness of George III* (1991). *Writing Home*, his 1994 collection of diary entries, prefaces to plays, and book reviews, was a number-one bestseller in Britain, selling more than 200,000 copies in hardcover,[3] and revivals of his stage plays *Habeas Corpus* (1973) and *Kafka's Dick* (1986) were successfully mounted in the West End in 1996 and 1998, respectively. *Talking Heads* (1988), a highly acclaimed TV series consisting of six dramatic monologues, and *Talking Heads 2* (1998), a follow-up series of six more, have become his signature pieces among a certain portion of the English viewing public, achieving almost cult status. In late 1999, the announcement that Bennett was dramatizing his story *The Lady in the Van*, with Maggie Smith in the title role, caused a virtual stampede at the box office, with advance ticket sales of over one million pounds.

Despite its flattering sound, the title of "England's best-loved playwright" has become a double-edged sword for Bennett. It conjures up a warm and cozy link with the reading and viewing public similar to the sentimentalizing cults that once dominated appreciation of Jane Austen and Anthony Trollope.⁴ At its embarrassing worst, this lovable image has given one English journalist license to dub Bennett "the National Teddy Bear."⁵ At its misleading best, it has obscured or distorted Bennett's considerable gifts and placed him off limits for critical scrutiny and serious analysis. Although the quality British newspapers—the *Financial Times*, the *Independent*, the *Guardian*—have usually reviewed his plays as serious works written by an important playwright, until very recently few literary critics have given them more than a glance. To date, only two full-length studies of his work have appeared.⁶ Few surveys of contemporary British drama mention Bennett. He doesn't merit even a line, for instance, in Christopher Innes's *Modern British Drama, 1890–1990*, which devotes dozens of pages to Harold Pinter, Tom Stoppard, Caryl Churchill, and Alan Ayckbourn, to name only Bennett's most conspicuous contemporaries.⁷ This would not surprise him. In his diary entry for January 2, 1997, Bennett ruefully notes that Waterstone's *Literary Diary,* which records the birthdates of contemporary literary figures, has left his birthdate blank, except for the note: "The first British self-service launderette is opened on Queensway, London, 1949."⁸

To some sympathetic commentators, the fault lies not with Bennett but with critical fashion. "In many ways, he seemed set fair to rival John le Carré as the finest imaginative social historian of the post-war years," Lachlan Mackinnon writes, "but it is notable that during those years the mimetic function has increasingly been relegated to what are now perceived as minor genres. Doubts about Bennett's own literary status have derived from that displacement."⁹ It is not surprising then to see that an influential view of Bennett among the literary critics pigeonholes him as "a minor figure" whose sole claim to attention is his "immortalisation of the lonely, elderly woman."¹⁰

Yet to see Bennett as merely an old-fashioned realist is also to underestimate the protean nature of his gifts and his appeal. Ask any of Bennett's admirers what they like about his work, and they invariably cite his wit, the respectful treatment he offers the socially marginal, and the familiarity of his characters and their speech. Some rate his comic gifts most highly, like Sir Peter Hall, the eminent stage director, who claims that Bennett's "wit . . . puts him in the Oscar Wilde, Noel Coward, Harold Pinter league."¹¹ Others emphasize the dark edges that surround all of his work. "Bennett territory" for John Lahr is "the landscape of loss and retreat. . . . He makes a patchwork of his winded society from scraps of anecdote and overheard conversation."¹² Still others find in the combination of wit, pessimism, sympathy, and close observation the outlines of an imaginative world that has come to be called Bennett Land. In a review of one of the most recent television plays, the *Times*'s critic sighted (and cited) all of its familiar geographical features: "Patricia Routledge is only a couple of minutes into the monologue and you know it is by Alan Bennett. The style and tone are unmistakable. The acute ear for the banalities of everyday speech, the unerring social detail, the wry humour and the underlying sadness all evoke the singular Bennett world."[13]

Being "best-loved," nonetheless, has its rewards. The unveiling of his portrait at the National Portrait Gallery in London in 1993 and the accompanying television documentary, *Portrait or Bust*, indicate Bennett's elevation to an even higher position in the English celebrity pantheon. At a glance, Tom Wood's portrait (a detail of which is reproduced on the cover of this book) reveals Bennett in a disarmingly eccentric light. He looks off to the left, away from the viewer, chin resting on one hand, seated at what appears to be a counter. In front of him lie a brown paper sack with the end twisted shut (holding a modest lunch? sweets?) and a three-pronged appliance plug and wire (for an electric kettle?). A ceramic mug (for tea?) rests in his right hand. If Renaissance portraiture usually depicted the sitter surrounded by the marks of his status and wealth, then the iconography of Bennett's portrait, replete with these objects of working-class domesticity, wittily suggests his identification with his roots in Leeds as the son of a butcher and a homemaker— the homemaker apparently predominant. Another image, the black-and-white photo on the cover of *Writing Home*, shows Bennett in profile, hands folded in his lap, eyes slightly downcast, slouching in a straight-back chair, looking for all the world like a parody of *Whistler's Mother*.

These two portraits of the artist as self-effacing, harmless, and retiring are of course part of Bennett's public charm. Disarming the usual suspicion of the artist as superior, he reminds his audience instead of his ordinariness. *This* writer is not going to sneer at you and your values, these images say. To some, it's a calculated act. "Bennett's public role happens to be one the British adore," Ian Buruma writes, "the most successful playwright of his time as a *nebbish* with bicycle clips."[14] To others, it's strength of character. Seeing Bennett enter the posh Berkeley Hotel in May of 1996, "wearing a sports jacket, blue shirt with a crumply collar and twisted string of a tie," Alec Guinness writes in his diary, "I rejoice that he brings Yorkshire and Camden Town with him wherever he goes."[15] False or genuine, this disarming public image complicates Bennett's work in ways that are at least as interesting as those in which a macho persona informed Hemingway's work. One theater critic has noted the utility of Bennett's public image: "Alan Bennett is nothing like the cosy donnish figure he is so often mistaken for. But the disguise superbly suits his often subversive purposes."[16] And yet, as Bennett has said on a different occasion, "Really? And how would you know?"(*WW*, xi).

The American picture of Alan Bennett is less elusive simply because he barely registers on this side of the Atlantic. We don't have access to the same iconography, and our acquaintance with his work is rather spotty. Much of Bennett's best writing has been done for British television, not all of which has been shown in the States, and his best-known stage work either flopped on Broadway, as did *Habeas Corpus*, or had only a brief and limited national tour, as did *The Madness of George III*. Perhaps some remember him as one of the four actors in *Beyond the Fringe*, which had a successful eighteen-month New York run between 1962 and

1964. But the stage performer of sketch comedy bears only a passing resemblance to the mature playwright, and to think of the two as synonymous is to miss the real Bennett almost entirely. In recent years, the successful film version of *The Madness of George III*—retitled *The Madness of King George* so that historically challenged Americans would not dismiss it as a sequel—has brought attention to a wider range of Bennett's work. Stephen Schiff first turned the spotlight on Bennett for a large American readership in a lengthy essay in *The New Yorker* in 1993, just before the Royal National Theatre's production of *George III* played a short season at the Brooklyn Academy of Music. In his analysis of Bennett's works and personal character, Schiff dubbed Bennett "the poet of embarrassment," a writer whose divided awareness reminds us that "whatever we pretend to be on the outside is a deception; that underneath we are all weak, noisome, and, if we could only see it, deeply embarrassing."[17] This word has stuck to Bennett like mud to a shoe. Ian Buruma's appreciation of the George III play and film in *The New York Review of Books* a year and half later was entitled "The Great Art of Embarrassment"; it tried to explain to American readers how Bennett the man, an "ostentatiously diffident and private playwright[,] has turned himself into a public act."[18] Apparently taking its cue from Schiff and Buruma, in the winter of 1997 the Boston Museum of Fine Arts held a retrospective of some of Bennett's TV films. The series was called "Britain's Alan Bennett: The Poet of Embarrassment."

This emphasis on embarrassment, with its connotations of minor social blunders, blushes, and awkward encounters that amount to little if anything, looks at only a tiny slice of Bennett's output, mostly his earliest work. It brings us back to the old territory of the cozy—the realm that he has been allowed to inhabit without much challenge. Bennett has, however, produced a large body of exceptional work for which neither cozy and lovable nor embarrassing is the proper adjective. The man may be beloved in his native land, but it would be wrong to look at his work as anodyne.

Over the last thirty years Bennett has written ten stage plays, three screenplays, eight television documentaries, and over thirty plays for television, his preferred and perhaps most artistically satisfying medium. His stage and television plays tend to fall into three categories. The first is dramas and comedies set in the north of England. On the whole, these plays are naturalistic studies of ordinary people, written in what Bennett calls his "provincial" voice (*WH*, ix), which draws on the idioms and attitudes he grew up hearing and observing in Leeds. As Bennett puts it, "Brought up in the provinces in the forties and fifties we learned early on the valuable lesson that life is generally something that happens elsewhere" (*TH*, 13). And in these plays he corrects that imbalance as best he can by paying attention to marginalized, usually unheard voices. Duncan Wu has said that Bennett possesses "one of the most humane voices in contemporary theatre," a humaneness that comes through most clearly in his depiction of ordinary people.[19] But his humanity is not flabby. Bennett observes his characters with a rueful as well as a sympathetic eye; their pettiness and foolishness do not go unnoticed. Those perfectly captured locutions, tones of voice, and odd obsessions, sometimes harmless, sometimes malevolent, which remind readers and viewers of their relatives and acquaintances—the qualities that most endear his characters to his audience—may have begun in Bennett's reported habit of jotting down overheard conversations. But he is more than an eavesdropper. John Lahr has praised him for his ability to capture place and class through language. "As a performer and a playwright," Lahr writes, "Bennett strikes a deep chord in English life not so much by the stories he tells as by the voice he tells them in. . . . He is a master of mood and social detail, the Turgenev of the English lower-middle class."[20]

The second category of plays, written in his "metropolitan" voice (*WH*, ix), deals with larger political, literary, and social topics. In addition to historical figures, Bennett's subjects are often writers and spies, whom he tends to see as kindred spirits—both watching and recording in secret, both without deep loyalties except to the task at hand, both equally treacherous. Here Bennett complicates the theme of surveillance that resides just below the surface in so much of his work. The officious social workers and clergymen in the northern plays, whose surveillance of ordinary people is part of the background noise of the English welfare state, give way to the writer and the spy whose very professions depend on surveillance. Bennett's ambivalence toward his own role as a writer, a writer praised for his close and accurate observation of his subjects, comes out clearly in his treatment of these writers and spies, who watch others while resisting being watched, and of public figures in general, who must learn that the price of modern celebrity is perpetual exposure to surveillance. He has written a play about Proust, two plays about Kafka, a screenplay about Joe Orton, a play and a screenplay about George III, and three plays about upper-class traitors like Guy Burgess and Anthony Blunt. In these works, Bennett examines the artist's role in society, the identity performances of public figures—George III, for instance, is judged cured of his madness when he has "remembered how to seem"—and the paradoxical nature of national loyalties and national identities. Here he is at his most incisive as a social critic, with an urbane wit added to his usual dark sense of humor.

The third category is the dramatic monologue, an increasingly important genre for him. Beginning with *A Woman of No Importance*, a monologue he wrote for Patricia Routledge in 1982, Bennett has continued to deepen and refine his approach to this genre. He gave his first series of six highly celebrated dramatic monologues in 1988 and his second series of six a decade later the general title of *Talking Heads*, a self-deprecating borrowing of the dismissive term for British news readers (he calls it "a synonym in television for boring"), and he has even apologized for the directness and "simplicity (not to say crudity) of the form" (*OA*, 34). This is, however, false modesty. In important ways these monologues are Bennett's greatest achievements. Bennett has described the experience of viewing them as "closer to reading a short story than watching a play" (*TH*, 7), which has led some to compare him to Anton Chekhov, that Russian master detailer of small lives caught at small moments.[21] Actually, Bennett's "talking heads" derive more clearly from the English poetic tradition of the monodramas and dramatic monologues of Charlotte Mew, Alfred Tennyson, the Brownings, and T. S. Eliot. But as drama, they seem most connected to perhaps the greatest dramatist of the second half of the twentieth century—Samuel Beckett. Bennett's mastery of the dramatic monologue for the theater places him squarely in the tradition of such great works as *Happy Days*, *Krapp's Last Tape*, and *Not I*. Those solitary voices, lost in a desolate landscape, seem to be what Bennett heard as a young man when his mother, as she descended deeper into the delusions that marked her bouts of depression, would beg his father to leave the living room and join her in the pantry because someone was watching them. Thinking back on this painful scene, he sees it as an avant-garde drama: "A play could begin like this, I used to think—with a man on-stage, sporadically angry with a woman off-stage, his bursts of baffled invective gradually subsiding into obstinate silence. . . . Or set it in the kitchen, the empty room between them, no one on-stage at all, just the voices off" (*US*, 11). Bennett has yet to write a play quite like that (*Enjoy* probably comes closest), but the empty space, the words sent but not received, the dark humor, and the ultimate lapse into silence are all motifs familiar from Beckett's work. In the *Talking Heads* monologues, as well as in some of his northern plays, Bennett has domesticated the absurdist vision of Beckett's greatest plays by placing his characters not in a mound of dirt up to their armpits, or immured in urns, but buried alive in comfortable chairs in provincial, middle-class living rooms in towns with names like Leeds, Bradford, and Scarborough. The frantic banalities of Winnie in *Happy Days*, for example, are cheerfully repeated in the characters Bennett has created for Patricia Routledge. Like Winnie, Irene in *A Lady of Letters*, Peggy in *A Woman of No Importance*, and Miss Fozzard in *Miss Fozzard Finds Her Feet* natter on about the trivial events of a trivial life to keep the awful truth of their empty existence at bay. By situating the commonplace characters of the north in sophisticated and complexly ironic dramatic structures, these monologues serve as bridges across the provincial/metropolitan divide Bennett traces through his work. And not surprisingly, the more Bennett works in the form, the more his vision of existence becomes like Beckett's.

Another lens through which many of the plays must be viewed is the performance theory of the American sociologist Erving Goffman, whose "writings have had a profound influence on most of the social sciences."[22] Though Goffman is perhaps best known today for "frame analysis," Bennett's interest in Goffman's ideas centers on his earlier work, in particular his classic 1959 study, *The Presentation of Self in Everyday Life*, which uses a dramaturgical model to analyze the structures of social encounters. "Life itself is a dramatically enacted thing," Goffman has famously said. "All the world is not, of course, a stage, but the crucial ways in which it isn't are not easy to specify."[23] In a 1981 review of Goffman's *Forms of Talk*, Bennett expresses his longstanding appreciation of this theatrical view of human behavior. "As with all the best books, I took Goffman's work to be somehow a secret between me and the author," Bennett confides. "Individuals knew they behaved this way, but Goffman knew *everybody* behaved this way, and so did I.

Only we were keeping it secret" (*WH*, 303). One of Bennett's rare admissions that he uses Goffman's performative models in his works comes in a commentary on the screenplay of his George III play. Describing the final scene of the movie, when the newly recovered king stands on the steps of St. Paul's to receive the cheers of his subjects, Bennett remarks that "the King urges his family to smile and wave and pretend to be happy, because that is their job. This scene would, I hope, have rung a bell with the late Erving Goffman, the American sociologist whose analysis of the presentation of self and its breakdown in the twentieth century seems just as appropriate to this deranged monarch from the eighteenth century" (*MKG*, xxi).

That we are all actors let loose upon a stage without a script except one of our own improvising is not, of course, a new idea. Shakespeare says it, Pinter insinuates it, and Stoppard jokes about it. Goffman would suggest, however, that if we haven't been handed a full script, we at least are aware of a few plot points that will guide our performance in the social arena. Foremost among them is the need for "impression management"—to present ourselves in such a way that we define the social situation, which often amounts to no more than making the right impression on our audience. The very presence of an audience creates "regions" separating the performer from the others. The front region is where the two interact. Backstage is where the performer relaxes with other members of the team (a key concept in Goffman, though teams are usually absent in Bennett). With this need to control the definition of the social situation, however, comes the warning that all performances are subject to disruption, since they depend on both the skill of the performer and the goodwill of the audience. If Goffman has a Law of the Everyday Performative, this may well sum it up: "Whatever it is that generates the human want for social contact and for companionship, the effect seems to take two forms: a need for an audience before which to try out one's vaunted selves, and a need for team-mates with whom to enter into collusive intimacies and backstage relaxation."[24]

Goffman has been criticized for cynicism and inconsistency in his view of social interaction, and in his later work he seems to move away from the dramaturgical metaphor for social interaction.[25] But Bennett, who has been a performer both on stage and off, structures his plays so often around this imperative of performance, with its accompanying fragility, that it obviously speaks deeply to him as a man and as an artist. From his earliest play, *Forty Years On*, to his most recent dramatic monologues, *Talking Heads 2*, Bennett has created situations for characters who, whether they acknowledge it or not, perform their often idealized identities for an audience, whether the viewer/reader or another character, as well as for themselves. His most recent stageplay, *The Lady in the Van*, takes the question of staged identity one step further by dramatizing two Alan Bennetts, the public writer and the private citizen, each with a need to perform himself.

Performance in Bennett's works is therefore both literal, since it involves professional actors, and rhetorical, since the characters' persuasive powers are being exercised. Comic or pathetic, and sometimes both, these performances always seem inevitable. In Bennett's 1990 adaptation of Kenneth Grahame's iconically English

The Wind in the Willows for the National Theatre, for example, a central message of the play is the notion of performance as social necessity. Mr. Toad, whose impulsive desires for excitement and instant gratification lead him into disaster after disaster, and whose conversion to mature self-control is one of the messages of Grahame's book, doesn't really change in Bennett's version. "He just learns to keep it under," says Bennett. "'Keeping it under' is partly what *The Wind in the Willows* is about. There is a Toad in all of us, or certainly in all men, our social acceptability dependent on how much of our Toad we can keep hidden. Mole, by nature shy and humble, has no trouble fitting in; Toad, with neither of these virtues, must learn to counterfeit them before he is accepted" (*WW*, xxi).

Like Beckett and Pinter, whose skeptical views of the human condition he seems to share, Bennett finds most of his characters' performances amusing and/or poignant. Loath to condemn their need to present themselves in the appropriate light for the given audience, Bennett seems to have adopted Goffman's nonjudgmental attitude toward the everyday performative. Goffman's account of the social masks worn and discarded by the staff of a Shetland Islands hotel in the 1950s, as they "interact"—a term popularized by Goffman—does not judge, but instead appreciates the skill with which ordinary people shift almost effortlessly from role to role to maintain the right public persona. Goffman thus sees performance as a profoundly and multiply social act, as does Bennett. His characters not only need to strike the right impression for an audience, but also long for backstage companions with whom they can chatter and compare notes as they take off their makeup. In most of Bennett's work there's the first but not always the second. Though everyone is performing his or her act, even when the stage is full it's very often a monologue.[26]

As this study progressed, I realized that I would also have to address the autobiographical relationship between Bennett and his work, although this was not my original intention. For years Bennett has cultivated the reputation of an intensely private man, whom a journalist once dubbed "the Garbo of Primrose Hill"[27] because of his insistence on preserving his personal life from public discussion. It is a stance I respect. Yet when I read the introductions with which he prefaces his published plays, or the excerpts from his diary published annually in the *London Review of Books*, I was drawn to the nearly opposite conclusion: here is a man who doesn't mind exposing himself to the glare of public scrutiny, as long as it can be done on his own terms. Despite the fact that the diaries are unfailingly discreet, and the introductions reveal only anecdotal and piecemeal connections between the writer's work and his life, I began to detect two Alan Bennetts at war with one another. One is the Alan Bennett who teases his readers with autobiographical tidbits, and the other is the Alan Bennett who presents himself as the staunch defender of "the ramparts of privacy" (*LV*, 15). Most recently, with the stage production of *The Lady in the Van* and the first installment of a memoir entitled "Untold Stories," the two sides of Bennett seem to be converging for a dialogue, literally so in the stage play. The personal information about his mother's mental illness and his own domestic arrangements that Bennett reveals in these works, although still fragmentary, casts a revaluative light on some of his earlier work. Nonetheless, any autobiographical connections made in this study are tentative and speculative by design. Bennett seems determined to continue along this more openly autobiographical path, and when more is known, more can be said.

A dozen years ago, I happened upon a screening in south London of *Green Forms*, Bennett's one act play about office workers, with Prunella Scales and Patricia Routledge playing the roles of Doris and Doreen. The sheer pleasure of hearing the author's naturalistic comic dialogue put to the service of a dark and witty parable won me over and marked the beginning of my serious appreciation of Bennett's great talents. By examining in this book nearly all of Bennett's more than forty stage and television plays, roughly in the order of their composition, I hope to bring the considerable pleasures and insights I have received from Bennett's work to a wider audience and support my belief that Alan Bennett is as distinctive and valuable a voice in contemporary theater as his more celebrated colleagues Harold Pinter, Tom Stoppard, Alan Ayckbourn, and Caryl Churchill. A close look at the body of his work will reveal, I hope, Bennett's distinguishing marks, which one critic has perceptively defined as his expression of "moral seriousness . . . in loopy, curmudgeonly humour and fastidiously understated feeling."[28] While extremely funny in his depiction of human foibles and absurdities, Bennett's particular brand of comic pessimism does not flinch from the harder truths of modern life. Although never as heartless as Nell in *Endgame,* who says that "Nothing is funnier than unhappiness,"[29] Bennett has created a tragicomic vision of life that is distinctly his own. I hope this study will establish that Alan Bennett is not the cozy, comfortable writer whom publicists like to promote and whom some readers and viewers seem to prefer. Bennett may draw in his audience with satirical humor and familiar portraiture, but his complex, often astringent view of life is what makes his work deserving of fuller critical attention.

NOTES

1. The first phrase appears on the dust jacket of Bennett's *Writing Home.*

2. *Single Spies* consists of two one-act plays: *An Englishman Abroad,* which was originally written for television, and *A Question of Attribution,* which was later adapted for television.

3. *New York Times,* Oct. 19, 1995.

4. Ironically, Bennett is suspicious of "fans," calling them "a great deterrent," and points to Austen's and Trollope's popularity as examples of excessive fandom. *WW,* x–xi.

5. Quoted by Stephen Schiff, "The Poet of Embarrassment," *The New Yorker,* Sept. 6, 1993, 92.

6. Daphne Turner, *Alan Bennett: In a Manner of Speaking* (London: Faber and Faber, 1997); and Peter Wolfe, *Understanding Alan Bennett* (Columbia: University of South Carolina Press, 1999).

7. Christopher Innes, *Modern British Drama 1890–1990* (Cambridge:

Cambridge University Press, 1992), 279–97; 312–24; 325–348; 459–70.

8. Alan Bennett, *London Review of Books*, January 1, 1998, 3. Professional theater people take a different view of Bennett, however. Richard Eyre has said that "There's Beckettian and Pinteresque. And I think there ought to be an adjective dedicated to Bennett as well," quoted in Nicholas de Jongh, "In Search of the Garbo of Primrose Hill," *Guardian,* Dec. 13, 1990, 24.

9. Lachlan Mackinnon, "Life on a Sunday Afternoon," *Times Literary Supplement*, November 13, 1998, 20.

10. Ronald Bergan, *Beyond the Fringe . . . and Beyond: A Critical Biography of Alan Bennett, Peter Cook, Jonathan Miller and Dudley Moore* (London: Virgin, 1989), 192, 187.

11. *Independent*, November 14, 1999.

12. John Lahr, "Madjesty," *Light Fantastic* (New York: Delta, 1997), 189.

13. *Times* (London), October 6, 1998, 50.

14. Ian Buruma, "The Great Art of Embarrassment," *New York Review of Books*, February 16, 1995, 15.

15. Alec Guinness, *My Name Escapes Me* (New York: Viking, 1997), 177.

16. Charles Spencer, *Daily Telegraph*, 12 June 1996.

17. Schiff, 92.

18. Buruma, 15.

19. Duncan Wu, *Six Contemporary Playwrights* (New York: St. Martin's Press, 1995), 32.

20. Lahr, "Madjesty," 189.

21. Turner, xiii; Wolfe, 9-10.

22. Philip Manning, *Erving Goffman and Modern Sociology* (Stanford, Calif.: Stanford University Press, 1992), 6.

23. Erving Goffman, *The Presentation of Self in Everyday Life* (London: Penguin, 1990), 78.

24. Goffman, *Presentation of Self,* 201.

25. Manning, 44.

26. As is only appropriate for a study of this kind, discussion of Bennett's plays will include references to the performance of the piece, as well as analysis of the written text. This is often possible because so many of Bennett's works have been filmed for television and are archived at the British Film Institute in London.

27. De Jongh, 24.

28. John Peter, *Times* (London), December 12, 1999.

29. Samuel Beckett, *Endgame* (New York: Grove Press, 1958), 18.

ALAN BENNETT

CHAPTER ONE

Early Stage Works: From *Beyond the Fringe* to *Habeas Corpus*

Beyond the Fringe (1960–63)
Forty Years On (1968)
Getting On (1971)
Habeas Corpus (1973)

Alan Bennett was born on May 9, 1934, in Leeds, the manufacturing and mercantile heart of Yorkshire since the nineteenth century, though economically much depressed in the twentieth. Situated only two hundred miles from London, Leeds is nonetheless quintessentially "north" in the English geographical imagination, a world apart from the sophistications and prosperity of the cosmopolitan south. Alan was the second son born to Lilian and Walter Bennett. His father was a butcher, placing the family in that awkward "not poor, not well off"[1] status that straddles the upper-working and the lower-middle classes. This ambiguity undoubtedly contributed to his parents' social discomfort in public places, which rubbed off on their sensitive son. Bennett did well in school, eventually winning an open scholarship to study medieval history at Exeter College, Oxford, but not before putting in two years' National Service during the Korean War, studying Russian. Among his fellow would-be interpreters was Michael Frayn, who would also make his mark as a playwright (*Noises Off*, *Benefactors*, *Copenhagen*). Both men performed in service revues, writing their own satirical material. At Oxford, Bennett continued these short forays into performing and writing, attracting a small amount of attention with his amusing entries in the Junior Common Room Suggestions Book. Bennett recalls:

> As a repository of actual suggestions, the Suggestions Book was useless, but it served besides as a college newspaper, a diary, a forum for discussion, and a space in which those who were so inclined could attempt to amuse and even

paddle in the direction of literature. The result was a volume (in time a succession of volumes) that was parochial, silly, and obscene, but to me, and
possibly to others, of a particular value. A family atmosphere, captive audience and a set of shared references are good conditions in which to learn to
write, and I think it was through my contributions to the JCR Suggestions
Book that I first realized I could make people laugh and liked doing it. (*WH*,
18)

The end-of-term smoking concerts gave Bennett an opportunity to perform some of
his material, and, from these "uproarious drunken affairs," as he recalls in *Writing
Home*, emerged his first notable comic piece, the mock Anglican sermon. He
reports that "it took me half an hour to put together, and since it later figured in
(indeed earned me my place in) *Beyond the Fringe*, it was undoubtedly the most
profitable half-hour I've ever spent" (18). In 1959, two years after receiving his history degree from Exeter College, Bennett performed in a revue put on by the
Oxford Theatre Group on the fringe at the Edinburgh Festival. "Our contribution . . . was a great success," he recalls, "to the extent that the official Festival took
note and the following year decided to put on a revue of its own, inviting Peter
Cook and Jonathan Miller from Cambridge and Dudley Moore and myself from
Oxford to write and perform it" (19). The rest, as Bennett has said, "is history.
Except that in my case the opposite was true." The would-be medieval history don
had now gone over to show business, so "what it had been was history. What it was
to be was not history at all" (21).

Beyond the Fringe (1960–63)

This four-man revue began its life at the Edinburgh Festival in 1960 as a late-night
show at the Royal Lyceum Theatre, ran for nearly four years in various editions in
the West End and on Broadway, and helped shift the boundaries of theatrical comedy in Britain and America. It also introduced Alan Bennett to a national and then
an international audience. The hyperbolic title signaled a tongue-in-cheek avant-
garde claim. Plays not considered mainstream enough for the main festival were traditionally relegated to smaller venues dubbed "the fringe," but here was a revue
claiming to be *beyond* the fringe, even though it was part of the official Edinburgh
Festival offerings.[2] *Beyond the Fringe* captured the attention of a public whose
appetite for a new kind of comic irreverence called "black comedy" was growing.
In Britain, the premiere in 1955 of Beckett's *Waiting for Godot* and in 1956 of
Osborne's *Look Back in Anger* had opened up theatrical possibilities for a darker
presentation of the human condition. *Beyond the Fringe* connected Beckett's comic
absurdity with Osborne's antiestablishment politics in a way that resonated with a
British public far enough past the privations of the postwar period to be weary of
the Tory party's complacent reminder, "You've never had it so good!"
    Success in Edinburgh meant that a London run was worth a gamble, and the
revue opened there on May 10, 1961, at the Fortune Theatre. Bernard Levin's

ecstatic review expressed "gratitude that there should be four men living among us today who could come together to provide, as long as memory holds, an eighth colour of the rainbow. . . . The satire then is real, barbed, deeply planted and aimed at things and people that need it." Levin's review didn't hurt at the box office, as Ronald Bergan points out. But it was Kenneth Tynan, the dominant critic of the day, whose imprimatur made the difference, even if his praise was more cautious. "It can justly be urged against the show that it is too parochial, too exclusively concerned with taunting the accents and values of John Betjeman's suburbia: *Beyond the Fringe* is anti-reactionary without being progressive. It goes less far than one could have hoped, but immeasurably farther than one had any right to expect."[3]

In America, the satirical comedy of Lenny Bruce, Mort Sahl, and Mike Nichols and Elaine May had prepared the way for this particular quartet of English lads (the Beatles followed eighteen months later). Even though its premiere coincided with the tensest moments of the Cuban Missile Crisis, which perhaps added to its air of daring, the New York critics welcomed the show with open arms in the fall of 1962. *The New York Times* approvingly called the Broadway version "envenomed," cutting "painfully close to the bone."[4] A more working-class audience read in *The New York Daily Mirror* that the show possessed "needle-pointed jibes" and a "lethal sense of humor," even though "for us, God and religion are not subjects for levity. . . . nor our policy toward Cuba."[5] Though the four obviously hit a nerve with some critics, others were charmed by the subtlety of the satire, preferring it no doubt to Bruce's and Sahl's more acerbic homegrown version. One critic hoped that *Beyond the Fringe* would provide a more civil model for American satire: "England's government gets quite a treatment; if only American comics could be so devastating, mild and merry about ours."[6]

What was most striking about *Beyond the Fringe* then, and remains so today, was its refusal to ignore the elephant in the cold-war sitting room: the impending doom of worldwide nuclear destruction. The show opens with a jokey depiction of three naive Englishmen (Bennett, Cook, and Miller) trying to win over a Soviet spy (Dudley Moore) who repeatedly plays "God Save the Queen" on the piano and who subverts them instead. It ends with a pseudo-Biblical prophet waiting with his disciples for the end of the world. Of course, it doesn't occur at the moment he has predicted, but he knows that eventually he will get it right: "Never mind, lads, same time tomorrow, we must get a winner one day."[7] Apocalypse Soon. The appeal of laughing at the spectre of nuclear annihilation, a fate that seemed almost inevitable in those days of the Berlin Wall and the Kennedy administration's standoff with the Soviet Union over missiles in Cuba, depended upon allowing the audience to whistle past the graveyard of its deepest fears. The quartet mercilessly mocked the illogicalities of British and, by implication, American nuclear policies based on "deterrence" and mutually assured destruction. In one inspired instance of bureaucratic thickness, a panel of Civil Defense experts faces a question posed by a concerned member of the British public: "Following the nuclear holocaust—could you tell me when normal public services will be resumed?" The reassuring answer is better than

the question: "Following Armageddon, we do hope to have public services working fairly smoothly pretty soon after the event. Though I feel in all fairness, I should
point out to all of you that it must needs be something in the nature of a skeleton
service" (36).

The targets the four Oxbridge graduates aimed at went beyond cold war politics
to include most of the great comic taboos: religion, sex, and the royal family. Prince
Philip, the Archbishop of Canterbury, Lord Beaverbrook (the Rupert Murdoch of
his day), and the lord chamberlain (the theatrical censor) are all treated in varying-
ly disrespectful ways. Although not all of the two dozen sketches, which were
revised, deleted, or added on during the four-year run of the show in London and
New York, reached their intended targets with maximum impact, those that did
caused even some of the cast members to squirm. Especially sensitive was Bennett,
who felt "embarrassment"[8] when Harold Macmillan, the Tory prime minister, came
to see himself parodied by Peter Cook in a savage send-up of Conservative Party
attitudes toward the poor. "Well, let me say right away, Mrs. MacFarlane—as one
Scottish old-age pensioner to another—be of good cheer. There are many people in
this country today who are far worse off than yourself. And it is the policy of the
Conservative Party to see that this position is maintained" (25–6). Bennett also
experienced "squeamishness" when the queen attended a performance and he had
to say "erection." Committed as he was to maintaining and even strengthening the
satirical edge of the revue, he "priggishly refused" to delete it because of her presence, a hard line he later regretted.[9]

Bennett's scruples marked him as the odd man out even in that odd little troupe.
Looking back, he views his contributions skeptically, as less funny "and more
earnest than the rest." Unlike Dudley Moore and Peter Cook, who regularly
upstaged him, he "never made the band laugh"—much to his regret (*WH*, xi, 177).
Clive Barnes's review of the 1975 Broadway production of Bennett's *Habeas
Corpus* dismissively identified him as "a member of that *Beyond the Fringe* quartet—he was the one who was not Jonathan Miller, Dudley Moore or Peter Cook."[10]
Yet two of his solos in the show, even if they were received indifferently at the time,
now seem to be seminal pieces in Bennett's development as a writer. The first was
a monologue by an addled vicar, preaching words of consolation and wisdom on
the least promising verse in Genesis, "But my brother Esau is an hairy man, but I
am a smooth man." Arising from Bennett's firsthand experiences as a devout youth
exposed to an excess number of well-meaning but boring clergymen, the sermon
delights in the absurd non sequiturs of the speaker while still respecting his obvious
sincerity—a balance that is quintessential Bennett. The second is a monologue
added to the 1964 edition in New York and spoken by an elderly Yorkshireman on
the anniversary of his daughter's death. Even though Bennett reports that the
"English Way of Death" was greeted with six months of "stunned silence" by New
York audiences and "embarrassment" by his fellow performers (*WH*, xii), and the
New York Times referred to it as "long, macabre, only occasionally funny,"[11] it
pointed in the direction his future work would take him:

Still I can see in it now the germ of the television plays I went on to write ten years later. The margins of humour were beginning to interest me too. I wanted to try my hand at material that was sad as well as funny. There was no place for this in *Beyond the Fringe* but in my first stage play *Forty Years On,* which was part play, part revue, I did try and combine comedy and nostalgia and found the result more satisfying than anything I'd done in *Beyond the Fringe.*[12]

Forty Years On (1968)

After Bennett ended his run in *Beyond the Fringe,* he spent several years wondering where his talents should lead him. He returned to Oxford for a while, but decided that, after the considerably brighter lights of show business, life as a history don wouldn't do. He acted in other people's plays, wrote for other people's television shows, and in 1966 wrote and starred in his first television comedy series, *On the Margin.* Only six episodes were filmed—all now lost thanks to the BBC's economical erasing of the tapes— but the mixture of satirical sketches, poetry readings, and film clips of old music hall performers indicated the revue-like direction Bennett would take when writing his first stage play.

Although it is hard to imagine a play less germane to their northern working-class experiences and taste, *Forty Years On* is dedicated to Bennett's mother and father. It is set in an elite public school, Albion House, where a play is being staged to celebrate the retirement of the conservative Headmaster, played by John Gielgud in the original production, and his replacement by the more liberal Housemaster, played by Paul Eddington. The changes facing Albion House are of course small versions of those facing the greater Albion itself, and the play's tone and structure grow out of the "Aftermyth of War" sketch in *Beyond the Fringe,* which satirized the nostalgic memoirs of homefront life by upper-class twits and of battlefield action by modest war heroes. Bennett has said that it "rankled" him that he wasn't given enough credit for his part in the writing of *Beyond the Fringe,* because "I did have a hand in some of the best stuff in the Aftermyth of War and the Civil Defence sketches, both of which helped to give the revue its topical, not to say . . . 'satirical' flavour."[13] For example, Bennett's absurdist voice is instantly recognizable in the following passage from "Aftermyth": "I do remember that black, black day that rationing was imposed. My wife came out to me in the garden, her face a mask of pain. 'Charlie,' she said, 'rationing has been imposed and all that that entails.' 'Never mind, my dear,' I says to her. 'You put on the kettle—we'll have a nice cup of boiling hot water.'"[14] But in lines such as "It's the end of our world, Nursie. They are rolling up the maps all over Europe. We shall not see them lit again in our lifetime," *Forty Years On* complicates such absurdist resignation with a parodic allusiveness worthy of the history scholar Bennett had once hoped to become (*FYO,* 39). Performed for the visiting parents at Albion House, the play is called "Speak for England, Arthur," and it's really not much more than an excuse for a parodic look at English history in the twentieth century, especially life as it had been shaped by the two world wars. Noel Coward's *Cavalcade,* with its sentimentality and snobbish reverence for the upper classes, is an obvious satirical target.

Bennett has written that his major problem with *Forty Years On*, which was rejected by the National Theatre but found an independent West End producer, "was the struggle there'd been finding the play a shape." This struggle arose largely because Bennett had not conceived the play as an organic whole, but as a series of sketches akin to those in *Beyond the Fringe.* He later confessed that "most of the parodies in the play I'd written separately and stockpiled, hoping vaguely to put together a kind of literary revue" (7). As a result, different scenes spoof national icons like Lawrence of Arabia, Bertrand Russell, and the Bloomsbury group or stand as pastiches of Oscar Wilde's aphorisms and John Buchan's snobbish spy thrillers. As Bennett himself admits, "the play is stiff with quotations" (9), which gives it the feeling of a clever undergraduate revue. And finally, the play responds to the recent abolition of the lord chamberlain's censorship office by cramming in so much sexual innuendo of the "nudge, nudge, wink, wink" variety that Bennett later described the play as "an elaborate life-support system for the preservation of bad jokes" (8).

Yet *Forty Years On* had a fair degree of success. *The Guardian* thought it the funniest play of 1968, and it ran in the West End for more than a year.[15] The play is most amusing to those who recognize the English originals it parodies, making it probably the least accessible of any of Bennett's plays to Americans, even though its fondness for the lost pastoral world of the Edwardian great house might appeal to those reared on the Anglophile productions of "Masterpiece Theatre." The play's wash of nostalgia, marked by choruses singing the Eton Boating Song and the Anglican Doxology and by reminiscences of upper-class young men listening to nightingales in Kent on the eve of the Great War, is counterbalanced by the constant mockery of Tory privilege—perhaps nowhere more harshly than in the excoriation of Neville Chamberlain as a leading example of the fatally deluded gentleman politician who thinks good breeding alone can prevail in a postpastoral world. Yet as Daphne Turner points out, "parody allows a writer to have it both ways: he can love that which he mistrusts and mocks,"[16] and Bennett takes full advantage of this ambivalence. The play ends on an elegiac note for an England not already lost, but being lost inch by inch as the audience sits and watches. In the Headmaster's words: "Country is park and shore is marina, spare time is leisure and more, year by year. We have become a battery people, a people of under-privileged hearts fed on pap in darkness, bred out of all taste and season to savour the shoddy splendours of the new civility" (95).

Early on, Bennett recognizes that the decay of language is intimately connected with the decay of a culture. His nostalgia for a world that neither he nor his parents ever knew is therefore more rhetorical than personal, more willed than experienced, though undoubtedly deeply felt. In its ambivalence and ultimately its confusion about the loss of old England, *Forty Years On* disguises with bad jokes and clever caricatures those concerns for loss, change, and alienation that time and many more plays show to be Bennett's true subjects.

Getting On (1971)

After the intermission in *Forty Years On*, the Headmaster recommences the play within the play with a prayer that not only parodies the language of such invocations, but also introduces a dramaturgical metaphor that figures more prominently in Bennett's next play and increasingly will come to dominate his work:

> O God, who has given unto each of us a part to play in this great drama we call life, help us so to sustain our roles that when the lights of life go down and the last curtain falls we may put off the motley of self and the raiment of sin and take our place at last in that great chorus line of saints ever more praising Thee around the glassy sea. (70)

Of course, in a play about actually putting on a play, the characters are performing for us, and this parody is only one in a hailstorm of jokes. But in the more naturalistic framework of *Getting On*, this sense of life as a performance affects our perceptions of the characters' behavior in a more serious way. In fact, the Headmaster's performance metaphor in Bennett's first play may be one of the few visible links to the second, a cursory summary of which might suggest two different writers, or at the very least a writer who has changed his conception of theatrical form and subject.

Getting On is a character study with a very casual plot. The title suggests such themes as career advancement, growing old, and social compatibility. Its central figure is a Labour member of Parliament, George Oliver, who is getting on in his career, getting on in years, but not getting on with people. The stage directions describe George as "deeply misanthropic" (*FYO*, 103) Unlike Timon of Athens, who rails against the corruption of his times, George Oliver rails against the bad taste of his own, for instance, cars with "dangling dolls, jokey notices, scatter cushions . . . . What I want is an Austin Ascetic, a Morris Monk, or a Triumph Trappist" (146). Played by Kenneth More, who was cast against type, George possesses a biting wit that casts everything in a dark light. He is good with words, but that may be all he is good with. His relationship with his family is an arm's-length affair. Almost as if they were a reported act of violence in a Greek tragedy, his two younger children are kept offstage. We hear them clamoring for George every now and then, but he rarely goes upstairs to comfort them. He barely notices his second wife, Polly, who has given up a university career to care for him and their children and seems reduced to tidying, recycling, and washing up. When she begins an affair with a young handyman, George doesn't catch on, although everyone else in the family seems to. His relationship with Andy, his seventeen–year-old son from his first marriage, becomes the focus of the second act. Here the values of the two generations come into open conflict. The father upholds work as the great good; the son is content to drift. George envies what he imagines to be Andy's sexual liberation—another symptom of the younger generation's freedom from responsibility. But George is wrong about Andy, who is still a virgin and who must remind his father that shy people still exist: "How is it easier to reach out and touch someone for the first time? Why is it easier for me now, than it was for you then, whenever that was?" (181).

This blindness to Andy's reticent personality, so obvious to any perceptive viewer, fits in neatly with George's general self-absorption. Though he is a socialist in politics, his concern for others is clearly programmatic, not personal. When he rehearses for his wife a television speech delineating his political beliefs, we note that though he says all the right things, the effect on the listener is very calculated. Take for example this apparently spontaneous laugh, thrown in at a dramatic moment:

George: I believe that some people are better than others, better not
         because they're cleverer or more cultivated or God knows—(*He*
         laughs)—because they're better off, but—
Polly: Are you going to do that?
George: What?
         (*Polly imitates his mid-sentence laugh.*)
         I might. Why?
Polly: Oh, nothing. (113)

Though we all know that politicians rehearse their speeches and employ rhetorical flourishes to make an impact, we don't usually witness the behind-the-scenes preparations. Placing the audience in that Goffmanian backstage region where only insiders are allowed, Bennett lets us evaluate the sincerity of George's message, that "the best society—I think a socialist society—is one in which fewest people are wasted" (113), in light of that rehearsed spontaneous laugh (which does in fact appear during the broadcast). His convictions about socialism seem to be merely rhetorical. George the "deeply misanthropic" MP is performing a socialist conscience, not living it.

Nearly everything else in George's life is performed with an eye to an audience as well. He envies a Tory colleague's dress sense, marveling at the ease with which his clothes fit him:

It looks like it's grown on you, that suit. I want something like that, bred in the bone, without anybody thinking I've paused before the mirror and chosen it. I want an honest suit of good broadcloth . . . whatever that is. I want to look like Sir Kenneth Clark or a well-to-do solicitor in a Scottish town or the head of an Oxford college. Such a suit as Montaigne might have worn, had he lived, or Marcus Aurelius. (118)

Not unlike the efforts of a wardrobe mistress to find just the right hat or cape to define a heroic actor's role, George's search for the right costume extends to the decoration of his home. Part of his self-disgust comes from knowing that he is complicit, for reasons he can't fully comprehend, in the creation of an artificial lifestyle. He complains to his down-to-earth mother-in-law that his household furnishings are theatrical props, chosen to evoke a class and style that everyone aspires to:

> I wish sometimes we could just go out and buy something when we need it, without all this performance of consumer's guide and best buy. I tell you. We bought that gas oven last year. There was that much consultation and consideration we might have been getting a divorce. Your house, you see, Enid, isn't like this. This isn't a house. It's a setting we've devised for ourselves. We're trying to get something over, though God knows what it is. . . . This is scenery. It's been dropped in from the flies. (133)

Perhaps the most unsettling example of this calculated creation of a "look" comes with Polly's latest shopping coup, a Victorian cemetery headstone that she wants to use as a piece of furniture and undoubtedly as a conversation piece. George sardonically addresses the name on the headstone: "Joseph Banks, now lying in some nameless grave, patiently awaiting the Resurrection. Well, this is it, Joseph. Everlasting life as a coffee table in Highgate" (135). Monuments to the past become decorative touches in the dwellings of the upwardly mobile. Even death supplies props for the chic.

Bennett has complained that the original production of *Getting On* was "clumsily cut without my presence or permission and some small additions made: jokes were largely left intact while the serious content of the play suffered" (101). The culprit, it seems, was Kenneth More, who had built his career on playing decent, heroic types. Rapidly discovering during tryouts in Brighton that the audience didn't warm up to George—in fact it found him distasteful—More "felt lost" without his viewers' affection and called a rehearsal to cut the play in a way that would emphasize the comedy and make George more attractive. Bennett was barred from the theater and "in fact never saw the play in its entirety from that day until it closed in the West End eight months later." The George that Kenneth More created, "all nice and palatable with no ambiguity" (14), bore little resemblance to the George that Bennett had conceived, a man "so self-absorbed that he has a diminished sense of the existence of others" (15). For example, More, "finding it unbearable that he should be playing a character who doesn't care that his mother-in-law may be dying," inserted the line, "I'll go and see her doctor tomorrow" (15).

To attempt to create a good impression with an audience is, however, within George Oliver's nature as Bennett actually conceived him. Perhaps another way of looking at this painful experience is to view it as an instance of a veteran performer giving the novice playwright a lesson in how deeply ingrained the impulse toward impression management truly is. Oddly enough, *Getting On* won the *Evening Standard* award for Best Comedy of 1971; when he accepted it, Bennett bemusedly remarked, "it was like entering a marrow for the show and being given the cucumber prize" (17).

Bennett now says that *Getting On* was "far too long, too wordy, and probably reads better than it performs: a good part but a bad play" (17). Nonetheless, the play does have its virtues: several characters are unusual for the mainstream stage in 1971. Neither bisexual Geoff, who sleeps with George's wife as well as his best friend Brian, the Tory MP, nor George's flirtatious socialist mother-in-law, Enid, are caricatured or condescended to. Even more bravely, Bennett creates sympathy for Brian as an unstereotypical homosexual blackmailed out of his parliamentary seat. (Of homosexuality, George angrily asks, "What is it in this particular sin?" Lies, bribery, and gross heterosexual carnality don't end the careers of other politicians [176].) When the supporting characters are more interesting than the main figures, however, there may be a problem, and perhaps George isn't "a good part" after all. His caustic humor wears thin after a while. Like most misanthropes who can strike only one note he becomes a bore. George may make moving speeches about the "leftovers" of society, but since we know that he cares nothing about anyone but himself, we soon stop listening (113). A look ahead to the most characteristic of the later works reveals that, at his best, Bennett doesn't allow authority figures such as George to talk about the "leftovers" of society, but lets them talk for themselves. For all the trouble it caused him, then, *Getting On* may have served a useful purpose by helping Bennett move closer to his real subjects as a dramatist.

Habeas Corpus (1973)

In a classic essay, Eric Bentley writes that "Farce is a veritable structure of absurdities" in whose presence "we enjoy the privilege of being totally passive while on stage our most treasured unmentionable wishes are fulfilled."[17] *Habeas Corpus* is Bennett's attempt at farce and his third stylistic experiment in as many plays. Even though he once claimed that he couldn't write about sex until after his father's death in 1974,[18] in this 1973 play Bennett does not shy away from what Bentley identifies as farce's stock in trade: transgressive obsessions with sexual misconduct and the absurd misunderstandings arising from it. What Bennett has dispensed with is the traditional stage furniture of multiple doors and beds. In a stripped-down version that perfectly fit the absurdist styles of Beckett and Ionesco, the original production starring Alec Guinness got by with three chairs on a bare stage. It ran a year in the West End. Irving Wardle in *The Times* gave the play a lukewarm review, regretting that Bennett had not yet found the "kind of play which would sustain his wry, oblique talent," but conceding at the same time that "*Habeas Corpus* strikes me as his most successful experiment so far."[19] Michael Billington in *The Guardian* was more generous, praising it as "a gorgeously vulgar but densely plotted farce" and concluding with a pun designed to match the tenor of the play: Bennett "clearly knows his farce from his elbow."[20]

The Broadway production two years later was radically redesigned to look like the traditional Feydeau farce. Opening to almost uniformly negative reviews, it closed in less than three months. *The New York Times*, whose influence outweighed that of all the other newspapers combined, was perhaps the harshest in its assessment. Clive Barnes called the play "slight and boring" and "a lemon," but did not blame the cast and the director. "Rarely can a dead play have been so cleverly embalmed."[21] Howard Kissel, who gave the play its only positive review in New York, was more understanding, reminding his readers that farce "is an enterprise whose esthetics are not always appreciated by the undiscerning."[22] Bennett himself prefers to blame the New York failure on the redesigned staging, which showed a misunderstanding of the play and its aims. "There is just enough text to carry the performers on and off, provided they don't dawdle. If they have to negotiate doors or stairs or potted plants or get anywhere except into the wings, then they will be stranded halfway across the stage, with no line left with which to haul themselves off" (*FYO*, 17).

This concern with the mechanics of staging, the actors' comfort, and the audience's reception probably arises from Bennett's unhappy experience of losing control of *Getting On*. The turn from a "serious" play to a non-naturalistic farce is part of his continuing search for the best vehicle to express his complex ambivalence, "material that was sad as well as funny." Though he now regards *Habeas Corpus* as "a favourite of mine"—partly because it is non-naturalistic and partly because "it is the only one of my plays to be done regularly by amateurs"—Bennett has not attempted the farce form again (*FYO*, 18).[23] On the surface, the reason may seem to lie in another insight of Eric Bentley's, who asserts that "melodrama and farce are both arts of escape and what they are running away from is not only social problems but all other forms of moral responsibility" (255). But, as much as Bennett cherishes transgression and absurdity, he puts both to the service of moral responsibility, not escapism. For all its foolishness, for all its smutty double entendres, *Habeas Corpus* is really about the age-old puzzler: How should we best live our lives, knowing that we must die? So, "it's not altogether farce" (18), as Bennett is the first to admit, and the literal translation of the title—"You should have the body," from Middle Latin—points the way to Bennett's philosophy.

Habeas Corpus wears its debts to Oscar Wilde's greatest farce proudly. Staged a year ahead of *Travesties*, Tom Stoppard's more famous appropriation of *The Importance of Being Earnest*, Bennett's *Habeas* Corpus offers a much darker version of Wilde, though at least one critic finds Bennett's appropriation of Wilde "far more entertaining and penetrating than the even more punilinguistic 'intellectual farces'" of Stoppard.[24] Lady Rumpers and her daughter, Felicity, are sexualized versions of Lady Bracknell and her daughter, Gwendolyn. Bennett's women have become pregnant out of wedlock and need to find unsuspecting men to marry them. The linguistic echoes also twist Wilde's absurdity into something more sinister: the hypochondriac son's excited discovery that he has a fatal disease, "I always said I had Brett's Palsy" (254), echoes Jack's "I always said I had a brother." But *Habeas Corpus* owes another debt to *What the Butler Saw* and Joe Orton, a playwright Bennett admired, though more for elements of Orton's plot than for his anarchic dionysian mood. (Bennett's screenplay of John Lahr's biography of Orton, *Prick Up Your Ears*, is discussed in chapter 7.) While Orton approves of satisfying all the body's appetites, Bennett adds a dose of skepticism about the body and its drives. He tries to walk a narrow line between the libertine and the ascetic—acknowledging both but trying not to embrace either one exclusively.

As a result, we witness in *Habeas Corpus* the collision of the two great opposing forces in English culture: Puritan asceticism and the Cavalier *carpe diem*. The characters are caught in the vise created by English middle-class subscription to the respectable public virtues of sexual continence and fidelity and to the denial of their corollary, the body's impulses to polymorphous perversity. Arthur and Muriel Wicksteed, who obey all the social commands to live irreproachably and to live comfortably (in Hove, the posh section of Brighton), have long since stopped having sex (with one another). He lusts after other women, to whom as a medical doctor he has easy access. She hides her frustration in trivial domesticities like cake decorating classes. Arthur's younger sister, Connie, is also frustrated sexually, and, as a flat-chested spinster of thirty-three, despairs of ever finding sexual fulfillment. Nor do the attentions of the local clergyman, Canon Throbbing, promise her the kind of passion she is looking for. The farce engine kicks into action when Connie orders a set of padded breasts (discreetly called "an appliance") through the mail. The first in a series of mistaken identities occurs when Mr. Shanks, the "fitter" from the "appliance" company, comes to the door and, mistaking Muriel for Connie, gropes her breasts to adjust the fit. Muriel, so long starved for sexual attention, responds passionately and pursues the terrified Mr. Shanks. (Like Canon Throbbing and Felicity Rumpers, nearly all characters are suggestively named.) Mr. Shanks's attempts to find his real customer, and the overlapping liaisons set up for "Thursday at 2:30" by several of the other characters will be the source of continual confusion for the characters, and delight for an audience whose "most treasured unmentionable wishes" are being acted out on the stage. By placing the phrase "This must be what they mean by the Permissive Society" in the mouths of three different characters as they face unfamiliar but relatively tame sexual situations, Bennett mocks the favorite cliché of the late '60s and early '70s moralists.

Amid all this titillation, we hear other voices of prudish restraint. Several of the characters expend great amounts of energy loudly protesting against the claims of their own bodies, even inveighing against physicality itself. No one does so more than Dr. Arthur Wicksteed, who says he is revolted by what he sees in the course of a day's work: "I am glued to every orifice of the body like a parlour-maid at a keyhole. . . . They parade before me bodies the colour of tripe and texture of junket. Is this the image of God, this sagging parcel of vanilla blancmange hoisted day after day on to the consulting room table?" (196). Connie complains as well, "You want to say: look, this body doesn't really suit me. Could I move into something different?" (199). Overseeing all this revulsion as a sort of quiz show emcee, with the characters as "contestants" (191), is Mrs. Swabb, the charlady—the part Bennett himself played in the latter stages of the London run. With her fondness for both doggerel—"in all that passes, I represent ye working classes" (191)—and olympian commentary—"I am Fate" (194), Mrs. Swabb as self-appointed guardian of public morality and relentless snoop makes a powerful case for the pervasive force of sexual prudery throughout English society. Her take on the body is just as dismissive as Wicksteed's. She addresses the audience in one of her many asides:

> Quiet, isn't it? Gone quiet. It won't last. It will not last. Give them five minutes and they'll be in and out of here like dogs at a bazaar. Sniffety sniffety sniff. On the fruitless quest of bodily pleasures. And it is all a waste of time. After all as I tell my husband what is the body but the purse of the soul? What is the flesh but the vest of the spirit? Me, I don't bother with sex. I leave that to the experts. (208)

Like Nursie in *Forty Years On*, Mrs. Swabb is a moral juggernaut who never loses an opportunity to hammer out absolute moral pronouncements with unselfconscious conviction. Wicksteed, however, cannot sustain his nauseated response to the physical. At one point he launches into another diatribe—"We're all pigs, pigs; little trotters, little tails. Offal. Show me a human body and I will show you a cesspit"—only to be wrenched out of it by the appearance of the beautiful Felicity Rumpers—"I eat every word"(200–1).

With the exception of Mrs. Swabb, this disjunction between public virtue and private lubricity is common to all the characters, even though everyone tries to perform the role of Outraged Innocence. The moralistic urge to proclaim one's purity and then brandish it as a weapon in the face of other characters' peccadilloes is nearly universal. Muriel, for instance, relishes the power her "innocence" gives her over Arthur once his attentions to Felicity have been exposed—until Shanks stumbles onto the stage, trouserless, sees Muriel, and pleads with Arthur to protect him from her debauchery. For Lady Rumpers and Sir Percy Shorter, president of the British Medical Association, the grander their public positions, the more likely they are to perform the role of Virtue and the less virtuous they are likely to be. Sir Percy's public image of moral probity is destroyed when he attempts to expose Arthur's interfering with his female patients. Sir Percy's obsessive desire to gain revenge on Arthur for winning Muriel away from him years before proves his undoing. Unmasked as the apprentice doctor who impregnated Lady Rumpers during the Blitz in Liverpool, he is exposed not only as a hypocrite but also as Felicity's father. Hypocrisy is so familiar a Puritan response to sexuality that Bennett wastes no time railing against it. It's old news. Better to welcome the hypocrite into the ranks of the Cavalier realists than to ostracize him and drive him deeper into denial and self-pity. So when Sir Percy tries to claim injury in his exposure, "It's not fair. Why is it always me?" (252), Arthur embraces him instead: "How extraordinary! So even you, Percy, are human. Just like all the rest of us, the world over. Each one of us walking the world because someone somewhere happened to bring their body and lay it against another body" (252).

By the end of the play, Wicksteed has come to terms (ambivalently of course) with the inescapable fact of the body. In the final scene, he matches Mrs. Swabb's grisly moralizing with some advice of his own.

Mrs. Swabb: The body's an empty vessel,
The flesh an awful cheat,
The world is just an abattoir,
For our rotting lumps of meat.
So if you get your heart's desire,
Your longings come to pass,
Remember in each other's beds
It isn't going to last.
The smoothest cheek will wrinkle
The proudest breast will fall.
Some sooner go, some later
But death will claim us all. (256–7)

In response to this cheery philosophy, Wicksteed offers the all-important "Yes, but . . .":

Wicksteed: But on those last afternoons in the bed by the door.
Do you think that you think
Of the things that you did
Or the things that you didn't do?
The promise broken, the meeting you missed,
The word not spoken, the cheek not kissed.
Lust was it or love? Was it false or true?
Who cares now?
Dying you'll grieve for what you didn't do.
The young are not the innocent, the old are not the wise,
Unless you've proved it for yourselves,
Morality is lies.
So this is my prescription: grab any chance you get
Because if you take it or you leave it,
You end up with regret. (257)

As Wicksteed speaks his final couplet, "Whatever right or wrong is / He whose lust lasts, lasts longest" (257), he begins a dance in top hat and tails to a carnival organ. He then dances until he can no longer move. Bennett, recalling that Alec Guinness suggested this dance as a coda to the play, calls it "a real dance of death" that "slowly shudders to a halt as the spotlight dwindles." He adds in admiration of Guinness's skills, "I can't imagine anyone else bringing off that dance, or how to describe it in a stage direction. I imagine most amateur productions turn it into a knees-up, which is very different but no bad way to end" (18).[25] Is the final dance macabre or celebratory? Bennett seems to think it can go either way, and his ambivalence fits the tone of the play and of the widely varying responses of critics who have admired it. Michael Billington sees it as "a downright celebration of sex and the human body,"[26] while Ronald Bergan sees it as "rather more a wake than a celebration" (161). The truth for Bennett apparently lies somewhere in between, "because if you take it or you leave it / You end up with regret." Since regret and death are inevitable, it seems only sensible that pleasure should compensate you at some points along the way. In Bennett's *Habeas Corpus*, that "should" in the English translation of the title ("You should have the body") reads more like a hortatory: you *must* have the body. The Puritan wishes it were different, but the body can't be denied.

NOTES

1. Bergan, 75.
2. Bergan, 3.
3. Bergan, 21–2.
4. Howard Taubman, *New York Times*, Oct. 29, 1962.
5. Robert Coleman, *New York Daily Mirror*, Oct. 29, 1962.
6. Norman Nadel, *New York World Telegram and Sun*, Oct. 29, 1962.
7. Bennett, et al., *Beyond the Fringe* (New York: Samuel French, 1963)56. All references to the text of *Beyond the Fringe* come from this edition.
8. Bergan, 34.
9. Bergan, 10, 34.
10. Clive Barnes, *New York Times*, Nov. 26, 1975.
11. Howard Taubman, *New York Times*, January 10, 1964.
12. Alan Bennett et al., *The Complete Beyond the Fringe*, ed. Roger Wilmut (London: Methuen, 1987), 156.
13. *Complete Beyond the Fringe*, 154.
14. Bennett, *Beyond the Fringe*, 31.
15. John Bull, *Stage Right: Crisis and Recovery in British Contemporary Mainstream Theatre* (New York: St. Martin's Press, 1994), 6. Bull analyzes the even greater success of the play's 1984–85 revival as a symptom of a return to a more conservative strain in English audiences during the Thatcher years. The ambivalence of Bennett's attitude toward the Headmaster's values are less noticed now and the nostalgia for a lost Golden Age more readily embraced. Knowing Bennett's disdain for Thatcherism, I can only view this shift as an irony worthy of Bennett himself.
16. Turner, 20.
17. Eric Bentley, "Farce," *The Life of the Drama* (New York: Atheneum, 1965), 244, 229.
18. Bergan, 161.
19. Irving Wardle, *Times* (London), May 11, 1973.
20. Michael Billington, *Guardian*, May 11, 1973.
21. Clive Barnes, *New York Times*, November 26, 1975.
22. Howard Kissel, *Women's Wear Daily*, November 26, 1975.
23. Even though *Habeas Corpus* is Bennett's only pure farce, elements of farce appear in later plays such as *Enjoy* and *Kafka's Dick*.
24. Bergan, 162–3.
25. Alec Guinness must also regard this "dance of death" as a singularly memorable piece of stage business, since he chose a photograph of himself as Dr. Wicksteed doing this "little solo dance" to illustrate the cover of the third volume

of his autobiography. Alec Guinness, *A Positively Final Appearance* (New York: Viking, 1999), 2.

26. Billington, *Guardian,* May 11, 1973.

CHAPTER TWO

Early Television Plays: 1972–1979

A Day Out (1972)
Sunset across the Bay (1975)
The Writer in Disguise (1978–79)
   Me, I'm Afraid of Virginia Woolf
   Afternoon Off
   All Day on the Sands
Office Suite (1978)
   A Visit from Miss Prothero
   Green Forms, aka *Doris and Doreen*

Between 1972 and 1979, Alan Bennett wrote ten plays for television, nearly all set in the north of England. To the American mind this area of England conjures up two conflicting images: the "dark satanic mills" of Victorian Manchester and Liverpool, or the moors of Emily and Charlotte Bronte, windswept and romantic in a bleak and bracing way and populated by the ghosts of Heathcliff and Cathy, Rochester and Jane Eyre. The north for Bennett is neither romantic nor tragic. The Brontes, for instance, don't merit any distinction in his pantheon other than as "those three ailing and unconvivial sisters," whose names have been appropriated for all-purpose meeting rooms in every Yorkshire hotel, "venues for discos and parades of beachwear, demonstrations of fire-fighting equipment and new lines in toiletries" (*WH*, 38) Alan Bennett's north is populated by minor players in the pageant of civilization, men and women living on the social margins due to their class, age, or intellectual abilities. As Daphne Turner describes it, "Bennett's northern characters are mainly lower middle and working class. . . . His north is an intensely respectable world, conservative in dress and moral attitudes, often peopled by characters much older than Bennett. Small refinements are important. . . . It is a world of small snobberies and shames and social awkwardness."[1] It is in

19

many ways the world that Bennett himself experienced growing up and that he has remembered and elaborated on in these early plays.

In 1988, Alan Bennett wrote and narrated a documentary for the BBC about the Crown Hotel in Harrogate, Yorkshire, a hotel with a reputation for gentility. His introduction to the published transcript explains that though *Dinner at Noon* "was meant to illustrate some of the work of the American sociologist Erving Goffman," the result owed more to autobiography than to sociology per se (*WH*, 30). However, it's clear to any reader of the script that Goffman's dramaturgical framework provides the underpinning for the commentary. When Bennett describes the role that hotels played in his youth, he calls them "theatres of humiliation" (32) because of his family's sense that they were trespassers—not moneyed or "educated" enough (his mother's explanation) to execute the mannered rituals of hotels and their attendant restaurants. He recalls some of these initial childhood experiences as formative lessons in not belonging, of never having the proper script for the part he is attempting to play outside the safe confines of lower-middle-class Leeds:

> When I was little my parents didn't have much money, and when we went into cafes the drill was for my Mam and Dad to order a pot of tea for two, and maybe a token cake, and my brother and me would be given sips of tea from their cup, while under the table my mother unwrapped a parcel of bread and butter that she'd brought from home, and she smuggled pieces to my brother and me, which we had to eat while the waitress wasn't looking. The fear of discovery, exposure and ignominious expulsion stayed with me well into my twenties, and memories of that and similar embarrassments come back whenever I stay in a hotel. (32)

What Bennett calls his parents' "drill" is the kind of protective covering of respectable behavior that we find in many of Bennett's northern plays. Characters cling to tried-and-true formulas of acting that shield them from a world they suspect, usually correctly, is hostile to their ordinariness, or at least prefers to ignore them as if they were embarrassments. The Bennett family motto, he tells us, was "let's pretend we're like everyone else" (40). In other words, don't let on that we don't share the scripts that all other families supposedly model their actions on.

With the passage of time, and the accumulation of experience and observation, the adult Bennett realizes that "every family has a secret, and that secret is that it's not like other families" (35). The northern households in Bennett's television plays, however, operate under the older dispensation. Because these households sense that they were somehow absent the day the rules for social ease and interaction were handed out, they close ranks against the outside lest their inadequacies be exposed. This of course reinforces their insularity and their differences, making them both comic and poignant in their efforts to justify themselves and their ways in a changing world. Bennett's special talent is to make us see these relics, these exasperating leftovers, as our fellow creatures and not merely as sociological samplings of a passing culture.

I. STARTING OUT: 1972–75

A Day Out (first broadcast December 24, 1972)
Sunset across the Bay (first broadcast February 20, 1975)

Ian Buruma warns that "to call [Bennett] nostalgic would be to misread him. . . . However much he plays up his north country roots, in his work and his public performances, he does not wish to go back."[2] True enough. Yet though Bennett may not want to "go back" himself, he realizes what a privilege it is to have a choice in this matter, and one of the overriding concerns in his television work is with those who don't have that option—those who can't "go back" because they have never left. Bennett's first efforts at depicting his native region are therefore marked by an affectionate sense of melancholy and loss that in the later plays would gradually be married with satire. Directed by Stephen Frears, the first television play, *A Day Out*, depicts a world on the verge of extinction, with Bennett acting as its sympathetic historian. Set in Halifax, Yorkshire, on a Sunday in the summer of 1911, and colored by the romanticizing of a lost place and time that Daphne Turner calls Bennett's "pastoral of the north" (9), the play "was intended as a gentle Edwardian idyll with intimations of the war to come" (*OA*, 136) *A Day Out* is unusual in Bennett's canon in that its characters are nearly all male and its subtext is their bonding across class and occupation. A cycling club composed of a cross section of the men of Halifax takes a day trip to the ruins of the Cistercian monastery at Fountains Abbey. Bennett's subtle use of language and dress to signal the characters' class standings and differing political affiliations, and the ironic contrast he explores between the peace and beauty of the day and the viewer's knowledge that in only three years the horrors of the First World War await these men, are strong points in a script otherwise too symbolic and schematic to be moving or even particularly engaging.[3]

Three years later, in his second TV play, *Sunset across the Bay*, the historian's distance gives way to the observer's personal proximity.[4] We suddenly find ourselves on the outskirts of genuine Bennett territory—not in the realm of history but of contemporary life. Also directed by Stephen Frears, *Sunset across the Bay* begins with an ironic prologue as a female singer and a piano accompanist perform a florid version of Ivor Novello's "We'll Gather Lilacs in the Spring Again," the woman dressed in the style of the 1940s—red dress, red hair, with a spray of flowers across her chest. The next scene introduces us to the main characters: an older married couple who were probably young and hopeful enough in the 1940s to believe the promise of Novello's song. The husband is retiring from his job that day, and the changes he and his wife will undergo multiply as the story progresses. Urban renewal in Leeds is tearing up old neighborhoods and forcing long-term occupants to move. Displaced from their home of twenty-seven years, this couple has decided to move to Morecambe, a summer resort on the western coast where, if there are no lilacs to gather, at least they will presumably escape the decay and upheaval of "mucky Leeds," where the most destructive vandals, the politicians and developers, are reducing the place to "a battlefield."

Once at Morecambe they soon settle into a life of routine boredom, with the husband perhaps more frustrated than the wife. ("I had six men under me" is his plaintive reminder of a lost purpose.) They try an Italian restaurant, but order only Welsh rarebit, tea, and bread and butter. They decide against all food novelties— "we can't be branching out into yogurt at our ages"—and they quarrel about such trivial things as whether to go to the movies in the middle of the day. Their only social connections are a chatty widow they meet at a bus stop and the pensioners at the club, whom we see singing "I'm H-a-p-p-y," which clearly belies their real feelings and conditions. Much like the elderly couple in a later play, *Say Something Happened*, our couple finds this "mix in-join in" atmosphere not to their liking. The one bright spot in their dislocated new life is their son's visit from Australia. He's a successful businessman who urges them to emigrate as he did, little thinking how much more dislocating Australia would be than Morecambe. On a trip to the Lake District with their son, the mother surprises everyone, even herself perhaps, with an impromptu recitation of Wordsworth's daffodil poem ("I wandered lonely as a cloud"), remembered from her school days of fifty years before. A sunset shot of the three of them in silhouette on the strand at Morecambe is perhaps the only lyrical image in the film, but the golden light is shortlived. The son returns to Australia; the father dies of a stroke soon afterward. The final image is of the wife walking alone along the strand. Seeing the chatty widow at the bus stop, she waves to her, forming a small connection between one loneliness and another.

The wife is the first in a long line of Bennett's signature northern housewives who are obsessed with cleaning, hygiene, and outward appearances. As they abandon the house in Leeds to the wrecking crew, she worries that she should have "washed down" the house better. On the bus ride to Morecambe, she struggles over whether to use the toilet at the back of the bus because "everyone will know." After much thought and discussion she decides to use it, reasoning that they are off to a new life where the "spirit of adventure" should reign. And besides, they don't know anyone on the bus. This fastidiousness takes a less comic turn, however, when at the end of the play her husband suffers a stroke in a public restroom while she waits outside for what seems like hours. Unable to bring herself to enter a men's lavatory, she must wait until a male stranger passes by before she can mount a rescue of her husband. But then it's too late.

The husband also foreshadows a familiar type in Bennett's later TV work. He's the quiet, stoical partner of the more outgoing wife, a man whose entire self-presentation has been wrapped up in his job. He's most frequently called "Dad," just as his wife is usually called "Mam," although we rarely see them as parents. Their children are usually long grown and gone. Whether we see him in retirement, as in *A Visit from Miss Prothero* and *Say Something Happened*, or as unemployed, as in *All Day on the Sands*, Dad is usually more invested than Mam in preserving the past, a time when his occupation gave him an identity. His current status as a man without work leads to a melancholy that he finds hard to articulate. In *Sunset across the Bay*, one of the most poignant moments comes when Dad enters the public restroom to "shed a tear," a northern euphemism. These are his last words before his stroke, and they suggest a depth of unspoken sorrow that perhaps even he cannot fathom.

Sunset across the Bay contains in embryo many of the concerns of the later television plays of the late '70s and early '80s. Set in the landscape of the aging and changing north, it offers us people on the margins being pushed farther off the map, away from the Wordsworthian romantic sublime of a world saturated with daffodils and lilacs and toward Matthew Arnold's modern world, dominated by the "unplumb'd, salt, estranging sea."

II. *THE WRITER IN DISGUISE* AND *OFFICE SUITE*: 1978–79

Me, I'm Afraid of Virginia Woolf
Afternoon Off
All Day on the Sands
A Visit from Miss Prothero
Green Forms aka *Doris and Doreen*

Bennett wrote six plays for London Weekend Television in 1978. Four are set in the north: *Me, I'm Afraid of Virginia Woolf*; *Afternoon Off*; *All Day on the Sands*; and *Green Forms*, first broadcast under the title *Doris and Doreen*. The other two, *The Old Crowd* and *One Fine Day*, are set in London. All are collected in a volume Bennett entitled *The Writer in Disguise* except *Green Forms*, which was paired with another play from 1978, *A Visit from Miss Prothero*, in a collection entitled *Office Suite*. They were written at the height of the long economic recession of the middle and late 1970s that brought Margaret Thatcher and the Conservative Party to power in 1979. Economic failure is a keynote of many of them: the unemployed father in *All Day on the Sands*, the office workers threatened with dismissal from comfortable jobs in *Green Forms*, the deserted northern seaside town and idle factory workers in *Afternoon Off*, the vacant office building in *One Fine Day*. Even in the least political of the plays, *Me, I'm Afraid of Virginia Woolf*, the main character's job as a polytechnic lecturer is admired because his income is "indexed to inflation."

That Bennett should collect several of the plays under the title *The Writer in Disguise* is puzzling, as Daphne Turner points out, since none of the characters is a writer. However, she notes that some of the male characters in these plays (especially Hopkins in *Me, I'm Afraid of Virginia Woolf* and Lee in *Afternoon Off*) exhibit "many similarities to the persona that Bennett presents to the public" (89). Identifying Bennett's own public persona of abashed observer as a vocational marker of the writer—who is also "passive, dejected, at odds with [himself]" (*WD*, 9)— and linking it to that of his characters is tempting because the fragility of vocational self-presentation is a prevalent theme in these plays. Writers under the skin or not (and very few of them qualify for even that loose a connection), the characters in these plays from the economic hard times of the late '70s are deeply conscious, almost self-conscious, about the connections between work (or its absence) and worth, whether self-worth or their worth to the world.

Me, I'm Afraid of Virginia Woolf (first broadcast December 2, 1978)

Trevor Hopkins is one of Bennett's most concentrated portraits of the entrapping nature of conventional self-presentation. Confused and ill at ease with himself, Hopkins is a lecturer in English literature who suffers from depression, sexual awkwardness, and, if we believe his interfering mother, constipation. His personality is certainly clogged up. We first see him in a doctor's crowded waiting room. Once the crowd begins to thin, we hear him mentally agonizing over whether the woman he's been seated next to will interpret his moving to an empty seat as hostility. If he remains, will she think he is being unduly familiar? This situation is analogous to the one Bennett uses to illustrate the essence of Goffmanian "impression management" in his essay "Cold Sweat":

> I am waiting in an office for an appointment. A secretary sits at the desk. I shift in my seat and the leather upholstery makes a sound that could be mistaken for a fart. I therefore shift in my seat again, two or three times, making the same sound deliberately in order to demonstrate that I have not inadvertently farted. The secretary looks up inquiringly. She may just be thinking I am uncomfortable. She may, on the other hand, be thinking I have farted, and not once but three times. (*WH*, 302)

Afflicted with a general malaise—his fears of conveying the wrong impression being only one symptom—Hopkins consults the doctor more for psychological counseling than for physical healing: "I'm not happy. I'm uneasy, uncertain of myself. People make me uneasy. . . . I don't feel the same as everybody else. . . . I'm always wondering what people think" (*WD*, 36) The doctor's medical-student observer floats the suggestion that Hopkins's problem may be sexual in nature, but neither the doctor nor the patient wants to entertain publicly such an embarrassing possibility. On the bus ride home, we see Hopkins reenact his earlier panic. By involuntarily moving to make room for a large black woman, he feels compelled to explain himself: "When I made room for you on the seat, did you notice, I sort of shifted, budged up a bit. Well, that was all I was doing, making room for you. I mean, I wasn't moving away because you were bla . . . I'd have done the same for anybody, that's what I mean. I was just giving you more room." The large black woman, who is undoubtedly used to having fellow passengers move aside to give her more room, doesn't understand what he's concerned about. "What's troublin' you there, man," she says (38).

Whatever is troubling Hopkins may not be clear to him, but we see a man weighted down by a hygiene-obsessed mother—"Life for Hopkins's mother was a canopy slung between three poles. Dirt, Disease and the Lavatory" (40)—and by his "girlfriend," the yoga teacher Wendy, whose language is the mellowspeak of late '70s posthippiedom—"the real you wanting the real me"(48)—and who can't eat her muesli without getting her hair in it. Teaching comparative literature in a Yorkshire polytechnic, at night, to a class full of mostly middle-aged women there for an evening's diversion, isn't any more satisfying. The only bright spot is a young male student, Skinner, with a working-class confidence that Hopkins envies. The narrator, who is Bennett himself, tells us, "Skinner was wearing an ear-ring. Hopkins longed to wear an ear-ring but he knew he could never carry it off. Skinner carried it off beautifully. Hopkins hated Skinner and longed to be him" (52).

For Hopkins, Skinner seems to live outside the code of impression management that afflicts Hopkins and most middle-class people. Skinner doesn't care what other people think. He speaks his mind, sometimes sardonically, as he comments on the moral outrage felt by the rest of the class when posters of Virginia Woolf and E.M. Forster have been defaced, and sometimes angrily, when he barks at the custodian who complains about the untidy state of the classroom: "Look. This is a lecturer in Comparative Literature. His job is throwing ideas about. You are a caretaker. Your job is straightening up the chairs afterwards. That's his work, this is your work. So stop chuntering because if each one of us does our work and rejoices in it we shall all achieve salvation. Correct?" As his contribution to the dialogue, the ever-polite, ever-guilty (secretly delighted) Hopkins murmurs a conciliatory middle-class "Sorry" to the custodian (62–3).

Goffman might suggest that Skinner is himself playing a part in a familiar class and sexual drama—like the working-class men in Forster's *Maurice* and Lawrence's *Lady Chatterley's Lover* who melt the social and erotic reserve of the upper-class English—but Hopkins doesn't see this. Thus the viewer probably concludes long before Hopkins himself "that this has been a love story" (71). The homoerotic clues, which have been there all along, range from the ludicrous—Hopkins's mother insisting that she had lesbian experiences during the blackouts in World War II by merely sharing a bed with her sister—to the literary—Woolf, Forster, and the Bloomsbury Group, with their active pursuit of bisexual and homosexual relationships, are the subjects of that week's class discussion. Unlike Martha in Albee's play, Hopkins fears Virginia Woolf not for the seductive example of her suicide, but for the apparently unattainable model of her casually bisexual life. Add to these allusions the medical student's early diagnosis of sexual dysfunction; Hopkins's reply, "I'm nothing, Mam," when his mother asks him if he's "That," her euphemism for the male equivalent of lesbian (44); and a funny scene in a restroom when Hopkins's inability to urinate in front of another person causes the other man to interpret his delay as solicitation —"This toilet is only a stone's throw from the West Yorkshire Constabulary. You're playing with fire" (64), he warns him. We don't really need to hear Rodgers and Hammerstein's "I'm in Love with a Wonderful Guy" sung over the final freeze-frame of Skinner's and Hopkins's smiling faces.

Bennett has written here a coming-out play that not only explores a troubled sexual identity, but also depicts breaking the chains of conventional self-representation, which is bound up tightly with the roles demanded by class, gender, education level, and parental expectation. Skinner's love seems to offer Hopkins a way out of that morass, but of course we never see beyond the moonstruck epiphany that both characters share. Bennett doesn't suggest how either of them will construct their new lives or present themselves to an inevitably hostile world in conservative, working-class Halifax—to say nothing of how they will explain themselves to Hopkins's mother.

Afternoon Off (first broadcast February 3, 1979)

Bennett uses the simple action of this play—a foreign waiter wanders through a Yorkshire resort town on his afternoon off—to illustrate some key Goffmanian principles of social interaction. The play begins with an allusion to Goffman's classic study of the behavior of the staff in a Shetland hotel dining room and kitchen.[5] Like the islanders, the staff in this Yorkshire resort hotel take diametrically different postures toward the customers/guests depending on whether the staff is in the dining room serving them or in the kitchen out of their sight. In a nearly deserted dining room, the two waiters and the maître d' maintain a facade of respectful patience as the father of a small family, the last remaining customers from the lunch service, performs the florid role of the jokey, ironic paterfamilias for them, extending their working hours with his self-important grandstanding. He favors hyperbolic and archaic locutions ("my lady wife"), mixed with cutting insults about his children ("my children are pigs") and pretentious dollops of Italian (*"senza crema per favore"*) (WD, 225). Back in the kitchen, one of the waiters does a devastating imitation of the pompous father: " 'Two cups of your excellent coffee and we shall have the courage to face the world.' (*Addressing the swing doors*) You pillock. It's half-past bloody two. I shall be on teas in five minutes" (226).

This opening prepares us for the main body of the action, which involves the quest of an immigrant waiter, Lee, whom Bennett has variously described as Chinese, Cambodian, or North Vietnamese (9, 225), in search of a woman named Iris, who he's been told fancies him. In the course of the afternoon Lee wanders through the town and "in a series of comic vignettes"[6] encounters many English types just as obnoxious as the father in the dining room. We see repeated examples of casual racism, xenophobia, and ignorance as Lee takes on different roles in the eyes of the locals, as if they were all stage managers casting him in a play of their own, based on their own idiosyncratic scripts.

To the billiard hall players he's a member of a visiting delegation of Chinese; to the art gallery attendant he's a potential "Kamikazi" terrorist; to the flower arranger in the church he might be a Buddhist like her recently deceased best friend; to the shoe shop manager he's Iris's suspected accomplice in pilfering from the store; to the old-age pensioners listening to a performance of "Pedro the Fisherman," Lee is Pedro himself when he wanders onstage; to the office workers in a factory (Bennett plays one of them) he's a South Korean businessman; to Iris's father he's her hated pimp; to the self-satisfied ladies in the tea shop he's surprising proof that Asians can show emotion; and to the women in the hospital ward, where he finally abandons his quest, he's a foreign exchange student performing good deeds by visiting the bedridden and lonely. When Lee finally meets Iris she's in bed with his fellow waiter, Bernard, who had originally sent him on the quest. Her response at meeting Lee casts him once again as the Asian "extra" in someone else's script—"I think they're creepy."

Lee, the tabula rasa, has been inscribed on by everyone he meets and the graffiti they leave says a lot more about the English in this northern town than it does about him. However, Bennett's point is not that the average citizen of Yorkshire is a bigot. As the immigrant outsider who speaks almost no English, Lee cannot control, as Goffman terms it, "the definition of the situation which the others come to formulate."[7] Lee's situation reminds us that dramaturgical interaction is a collaborative effort among people with shared cultural values and tools, language being chief among those tools. Bennett the writer knows that, without language, Lee cannot correct or intervene in the creation of these several scripts. He will remain a terrorist, a pimp, a thief, an exchange student, whatever, as long as he is unable to formulate a counter identity and present it to his audience. By being so innocent of the prevailing cultural imperative to define himself before others do it for him, and by being so helpless in the face of it, Lee demonstrates the powerful connection between the calculations of self-presentation and successful social interaction.

All Day on the Sands (first broadcast February 24, 1979)

The Coopers, a lower middle-class family of four from Leeds, are forced to take their seaside holiday at Morecambe in Lancashire this year instead of in Spain because the father has been laid off from his job. The parents try their best to act as if nothing has changed—after all, they are on holiday, even if it isn't Marbella or Minorca—but the children's boredom and the tension of keeping up appearances among their fellow vacationers bring only unhappiness to everyone. The plot is slight, turning on the restless twelve-year-old son's attempt to retrieve his sister's sandal, which he has thoughtlessly dropped out the window in a bored effort to knock over a bottle. But from a small detail like a missing sandal Bennett creates a comedy of frustrated self-presentation and loss of face.

When the mother chastises the girl for her supposed carelessness, we learn the family's deep secret: "Where do you think we find money for new sandals now we've naught coming in? It doesn't run to new sandals, Social Security" (*WD*, 83) She warns both Colin and Jennifer not to "let on . . . You know. About your Dad" (83). Mrs. Cooper's fears of embarrassment would not be so urgent were it not for the pretensions of the hotel they have chosen. It is in fact barely more than a boarding house with dreadful food, regimented hours, and inflated standards of propriety reinventing itself as a Mediterranean villa—The Miramar. Naming the dining room the Portofino Room in order to acquire that "Riviera feel" (104) is one of its pretensions; another is the proprietor's obsessive use of a public address system to convey oily morning greetings and make pompous meal announcements. In the kitchen, just as in *Afternoon Off*, the staff has a more contemptuous message they'd like to send to the guests, whose consumption of sauce insults the cook's pride in her own skills: "it's not as if my cooking needed sauce. . . . I wouldn't care but they go at the salt and pepper like mad things. You'd think they'd never seen a cruet in their lives. Pigs. Pigs' tea. Pigs' toast. Pigs' marmalade" (80).

In the dining room, however, the tyranny of strict etiquette prevails. Every action must uphold middle-class values of refinement. The family's greatest fear is of being exposed to ridicule when others discover that they no longer belong among the respectably employed. Jennifer is reminded by her mother to keep her feet under the table so that no one will see she's barefoot; Colin's efforts to switch the menu around to have both "flakes and segments," when the rules state you have to choose one or the other, are met with scorn from the waitress and disapproval from his mother. "You two, you do show us up" (84) is her catchphrase whenever the children threaten the family's protective self-image of perfect middle-class decorum. The danger of making a mistake, of being "shown up," increases exponentially in the company of the Thorntons, a smug couple the Coopers meet at breakfast. The Thorntons are quick to congratulate themselves for vacationing in May because "it gets a bit common" (84) in July. They counter the Coopers' namedropping of Minorca as their last holiday site by replying, "it's overrated, is abroad" (90). As bad luck would have it, the Thorntons overhear Mrs. Cooper being corrected by the proprietor's wife for letting Jennifer eat breakfast barefoot. In her embarassment the mother can only hiss at Jennifer, "you don't half show us up" (87).

The Coopers, while desperately eager to preserve their own pretensions, are not blind to the pretensions of the hotel. Appropriating the insinuating language of mass advertising, the proprietor solemnly intones through the public address system: "Those patrons who have ordered lunchboxes will find them waiting for them now in the Marbella Lounge. Weight-watchers are recommended to try our slim-line lunch pack specially selected to form part of your calorie-controlled diet" (87). Of course the product doesn't live up to its promotion. What the Coopers discover are plastic boxes with "Your Eats" inscribed on top, mysterious meat fillings for the sandwiches ("Ham, I think," says Dad), the odd addition ("There's a broad bean in mine," Dad complains), "one scrutty apple," plastic forks, knives, and spoons, and individual salt and pepper. Mam cuts to the heart of this shallow presentation of elegance:

> It's all to do with airlines. . . . All this plastic cutlery. Little salt and pepper. It's pretend we're on an aeroplane. . . . Like trains. They have this voice telling you how fast you're going and there are buffet-car facilities available on this train. It's all splother. All of a sudden everything has to be such a performance. (97)

It's ironic of course that Mam can dissect the hotel's pretentious performance so

expertly but remains so deeply committed to the family's own decorous performance. When Colin gets caught trying to use a stolen fishing line to retrieve his sister's sandal, he not only shames the family but also blurts out their secret.

The play ends with Dad breaking into Colin's room in a rage of shame and
anger, striking him, while Mam "waits on the half-landing below, hearing but not
seeing."

> Mam: Dad, Dad. Don't hit him on his head, Dad.
> Dad: Showing us up. I'll give you fishing line. Why didn't you say? All
>   you have to do is say. The sandal dropped out of the window. Full
>   stop. Can we get it? Full stop. Stead of which you go pinching fish-
>   ing lines, and spreading it around I'm unemployed. Well, I'm
>   employed now, doing something useful for a change. (109–10)

To the newlywed man who comes out of his room to check on all the commotion,
Dad offers some bitter advice: "Just got married, have you? Magic, is it? Bliss?
Well, take a good look, because you'll come to it before you know where you are"
(110).

This is not a comic ending, of course. Tears and frustration seem to be commonplace for the Coopers. But Bennett is making one small comic point: children
disrupt the performance of middle-class decorum. They make life, as Dad charges,
"more complicated" (110) and make it harder to keep up the act. Of course that is
the Coopers' first mistake—not having children, but attempting to keep up appearances, trying so hard to avoid being "common" that they cannot be happy being
themselves. On a deeper level, then, Bennett is exposing one more example of the
northern working class's pervasive inferiority complex, which usually manifests
itself in the desperate impulse to ape the genteel affectations of the class just above
it. Trapped in a depressed economy that has forced them onto the dole and has
knocked them several pegs down the social ladder, yet determined to maintain allegiance to standards of appearance that they can no longer live up to, the Coopers
are almost predestined to being "shown up."

A Visit from Miss Prothero (first broadcast January 11, 1978)

In *A Visit from Miss Prothero*, we see the triumph of malice disguised as caring, the
kind of performance Bennett often accused the Tories and Mrs. Thatcher of. Miss
Prothero, played by Patricia Routledge, visits her retired boss, Mr. Dodsworth, to
keep him abreast, ostensibly, of the latest news from the office. This includes gossip about illegitimate births and interdepartmental transfers, and musings about the
age and unnatural hair color of co-workers. Miss Prothero wears the mask of sober
propriety and sororal concern. But her propriety is really prudery and her concern
is really prurience. For example, she reports to Mr. Dodsworth that when she was
shown the photos of a co-worker's illegitimate baby, "I didn't know where to put
myself." In other words, she was embarrassed, not so much for herself but for the

young woman who didn't know enough to be ashamed (*OS*, 45). Modesty doesn't play much of a role, however, in her prying questions to her former boss about the condition of his "waterworks" and whether he still wears an "appliance" (47).

Her real purpose in visiting is not, however, just to deliver disapproving gossip. She turns up uninvited to tell Mr. Dodsworth that all the efficiency reforms he inaugurated, and looks upon as his legacy, have been overturned. A new manager has wiped away Dodsworth's contributions with his own, which are even more efficient. Dodsworth knows enough not to trust Miss Prothero's motives for visiting; early on, when she leaves the room "to pay a call," we hear him mutter, "Then get off home you bad, boring bitch. (*He goes over to the birdcage.*) What does she want to come on round here for in the first place. We're quite happy, aren't we, Millie?" (47). After working with her for many years, he knows her methods well enough to suspect that she's up to no good. Yet, even though he sees through her performance and surely doesn't believe her when she claims, "I didn't want to tell you all this but you would drag it out of me" and "Well, we always had a soft spot for one another you and me, didn't we?" (56), he falls into her trap. He must know more about the changes, cruel though the knowledge may be that his monument has been dismantled and his legacy will soon be forgotten. By the end of this short play he is completely in her power. He almost begs her to return. She promises to show him on her next visit "how the procedure works, and that'll set your mind at rest" (56). That's hardly likely, as the narrator tells us: "Mr. Dodsworth stands in his sitting-room feeling his whole life has been burgled. . . . Next time Miss Prothero will tell him more; and he will have less" (57). A psychologist might call Miss Prothero a classic example of a passive-aggressive personality; Bennett would probably ascribe the source of her behavior to the malice that maiden ladies can get away with because their power comes from their apparent powerlessness. Or perhaps Miss Prothero's rhetoric foreshadows the kind of political cant that came to dominate the Thatcher years—ruthless discipline administered for one's own good by a government that cared.[8] However Miss Prothero is understood, Bennett knows that a lot of damage can be done in the name of caring.

Green Forms, aka Doris and Doreen (first broadcast December 16, 1978)

If Miss Prothero's performance somehow manages to succeed despite its fragility, Doris and Doreen's fails despite its apparent security. In richly comic portrayals, Prunella Scales (Doris) and Patricia Routledge (Doreen), luxuriating lazily in their sinecures, attempt to preserve the illusion of work in a massive bureaucracy—without success. They are the Laurel and Hardy of office workers—smug when everything goes smoothly, panicked and ineffective when trouble arises. Change is coming for them as it did for Mr. Dodsworth, and unemployment is the likely result. We see them on what appears to be a typical day, chatting over coffee and the newspaper about the trivial details of their lives—Doris's mother's health, Doreen's husband's vegetable garden—while the work piles up around them. The pink forms were due back in Personnel last Monday, but they sit untouched. Doris offers the thought, "I suppose I ought to look through them. Though I don't see why we should break our backs for Mr. Cunliffe. What have Personnel ever done for us? Except make our lives a misery" (*OS*, 17). The only misery we know about is Personnel's suspected role in purloining their wash-basin plug, which has led to a feud between the two offices.

The missing basin plug may be a hint from their coworkers, since Precepts and Invoices is a clogged drain that needs unblocking. Though Doris and Doreen pretend to be overworked, the empty Out tray provokes sarcastic remarks from other workers: "Right hive of bloody industry this is" (22). This particular day is proving to be an especially upsetting one because they keep receiving a series of PS104 forms, requisitions for single items like a light bulb, a lampshade, and a rubber plant. Doris is indignant: "That's three hours' solid work. Three PS104s. I think a cigarette is called for" (17). After a while it dawns on them that all these PS104s (they soon number more than half a dozen) are coming from the same source—RB/57/212/X—a personnel identification number. Some of the best comedy in the play comes from the two women's increasingly panicky attempts to unravel this tangled skein of impersonal letters and numbers to discover the identity and motives of this mystery person. Once they have her name, Dorothy Binns, they learn that she is an efficiency expert who has regularly been brought in by upper management to wind down operations earmarked for closure. As Doreen notes, "everywhere she's been, Doris, a trail of redundancy" (30). Slowly it dawns on them that each of the items Dorothy Binns has requisitioned is an item that their own office is sorely in need of. Their sleepy existence is coming to an end. Doreen laments, "Nobody's ever been interested in us before, have they? The annual inspection, that's all. Otherwise you'd hardly know we were here. . . . I know why. I know. It's redundancy, Doris. It's the cutbacks. Like in the *Bulletin*. Goodbye to Leeds Cardigan Road. Smiles and sadness at simple ceremony" (29).

Doris decides to adopt a work ethic—better late than never—in order to distinguish herself from Doreen, in case only one of them is destined to be fired. She starts typing those long-overdue pink forms for Personnel, refusing to share them when Doreen asks her to send some work her way. Self-preservation turns the two women against one another. Doris orders Doreen to clean up the office; Doreen threatens to join the trade union. Their facade of comradeship has crumbled. Some bitter truths that have been carefully repressed for years are spoken. But it's all too little too late. Dorothy Binns is already among them, as they discover when they jimmy open the third desk in their office. They hadn't seen her earlier because they didn't show up that morning until, in Doreen's words, "half-past nine-ish," which probably means ten o'clock. As Doris recognizes, "That'll stop" (36).

Green Forms is a scathingly funny portrait of bureaucratic lassitude and inefficiency plotted as a horror movie with Dorothy Binns as Nemesis, whose shadow cast across the office door is the last thing we see on the television screen. Bennett plays to all our stereotyped suspicions of complacency, pettiness, and waste in massive office operations such as this one. Here the surveillance is richly deserved, and the implied punishment fits the crime. He will return to this theme and setting eight years later with his television play about Kafka, *The Insurance Man*, in which the vagaries of the bureaucracy aren't so funny and the horror cuts much deeper. Yet, despite their more farcical dilemma, Doris and Doreen inhabit their own little corner of hell in the existential captivity of the office, playing out an endgame that will produce no winner. Only Bennett's scathing wit and his delight in human folly distract us from the bleakness and emptiness of their lives.

NOTES

1. Turner, 5.
2. Buruma, 17.
3. Daphne Turner analyzes *A Day Out* in some detail for what it shows about Bennett's view of "pastoral," 8–14.
4. As of this writing, no published text of *Sunset Across the Bay* exists. This discussion is based on the videotape archived in the British Film Institute.
5. Goffman, *The Presentation of Self,* chapter 3.
6. Turner, 90.
7. Goffman, *The Presentation of Self,* 15.
8. In his diary entry for August 23, 1990, just after the Iraqi invasion of Kuwait, Bennett compares Saddam Hussein's posing with children for public relations purposes with the Tories' own attempts to project a "'caring' image . . . and with about as much truth in it": *WH,* 191.

CHAPTER THREE

Deeper North: *Enjoy, Objects of Affection*, and *A Private Function*

Enjoy (1980)
Objects of Affection (1982)
   Intensive Care
   Our Winnie
   Say Something Happened
A Private Function (1984)

B ennett's early television plays, even at their most nostalgic, contain a pronounced streak of melancholy. The economic failures of the 1970s—high unemployment, labor unrest, an annual inflation rate of twenty-five percent by 1975, capped by the 1978–79 "winter of discontent" [1]—color all of Bennett's work from that period. The prolonged economic slide of that decade affected no part of England more destructively than it did the north, with its reliance on heavy industry and coal mining. By 1980 unemployment had crested above two million, a postwar record. Yet nothing prepared Bennett's fans for the savage darkness of many of his works from the early '80s. The rueful, more naturalistic comedy that marked Bennett's view of northern life had given way to an absurdist comic perspective on his familiar territory.

Bennett's diary entries for the early '80s suggest a few reasons for his continuing and deepening distress with the state of the nation, especially the northern half. Foremost among them is the return to power of the Conservative Party in 1979 with Margaret Thatcher at the helm. As a northerner himself, whose class and region had perhaps been helped the most by the social welfare reforms of the Labour party, Bennett instinctively opposed Thatcher's dismantling of the social and economic policies that had governed Britain since World War II, in particular her privatization of national industries and her hard-line resistance to the trade unions. Thatcher's jingoistic exploitation of the British public during the 1982

Falklands War, not only to gain support for a questionable foreign policy but also to gain re-election, even though she couldn't produce an economic recovery with her programs, especially disgusted him. In the diary entry for June 9, 1983, he succinctly punctuates years of growing frustration: "On the day that Mrs.Thatcher is elected for a second term I spit blood" (*WH*, 129) Bennett knows it's only a mild case of bronchitis, but he can't resist this melodramatic flourish.

Bennett's writing from the early '80s, for stage, screen, and television, profits from this hyperbolic impulse. The five works discussed in this chapter represent some of his boldest work to date—yet also perhaps his least appreciated. He sharpens his already well-developed instincts for satire, taking the merciless wit he employed in *Green Forms* and the bleak social vision implicit in *All Day on the Sands* to produce a view of northern life that disturbs and unsettles even as it amuses. *Enjoy* is clearly his masterwork from this period. It shocked West End audiences with its absurdist depiction of a severely dysfunctional Yorkshire family earmarked for a heritage museum that preserves the customs and culture of the northern working classes. Produced four years later, Bennett's first screenplay, *A Private Function*, employs a lighter touch than *Enjoy*, although its satire of petty class snobberies and social ambitions in a small Yorkshire town doesn't offer any prettier a picture of human nature. The tone is marginally less bleak in the three 1982 television plays set in the north—*Intensive Care, Our Winnie, Say Something Happened*—and collected in the volume entitled *Objects of Affection*, although the subjects are no laughing matter, ranging from mental retardation to the marginalization of the elderly. *Say Something Happened*, which seems to be a reworking and a tamping down for a wider audience of some of the more outrageous and offensive elements of *Enjoy*, can stand alongside the best of Bennett's television plays for its complex blend of sympathy and satire.

Enjoy (1980)

After nearly twenty years of sometimes modest but steady success, Bennett faced his worst critical and popular setback with *Enjoy*. It opened to generally hostile reviews and lasted only seven weeks in the West End, which made the New York production of *Habeas Corpus* seem like a smash hit. Most of the reviewers found its picture of life among the elderly in the working-class north unrelievedly dreary and sordid. But the reviewers for *The Times* and *The Guardian*, even if they responded equivocally, respected Bennett's attempt to do something seriously different. *The Times* characterized the mood of the play as "barbed with quiet rage" and perceptively noted that "the first act which has more than a touch of vaudeville . . . ends rather like Samuel Beckett in a back to back."[2] Michael Billington, writing in *The Guardian*, admitted that "parts of it seriously misfire," yet "by the end, Bennett's sanity and tough compassion for the old had almost entirely won me over."[3] Joan Plowright, who played Mam in this production, publicly defended the play on the grounds that it was "about love and death and cruelty and age and hypocrisy and forgiveness and language and the twentieth century and things like that. It's also very funny." Her husband, Laurence Olivier, had his say in a letter to the newspapers, pronouncing it "a dazzlingly brilliant work and we know that dazzling brilliance is often blinding to some critics."[4] The exaggerated claims of the Oliviers' rebuttals suggest how much trouble the production found itself in.[5] A brief plot summary may explain what all the fuss was about.

Mam and Dad live in Leeds in one of the last back-to-back houses, soon scheduled to be torn down. Unlike the couple who faced a similar dislocation in *Sunset across the Bay,* Mam and Dad have made no plans for their future. She is losing her memory; he is retired and disabled. They snipe at one another from too-long familiarity. Dad welcomes the bulldozers and talks warmly about his daughter's globe-trotting career as a private secretary. Mam laments change and thinks nostalgically of their long-missing son, who Dad insists is dead because he's a "nancy," or homosexual. A stranger, Ms. Craig, comes to the door, sent by the local Council to study "traditional communities." She takes up her station as a silent observer, another in the long line of snooping bureaucrats who populate many of Bennett's plays. Mam and Dad attempt to be "typical" and act "normally" in front of her, but ugly truths about their marriage and their children begin to surface. Dad has been physically abusive to his wife and sexually abusive to his daughter, Linda, who is not a private secretary but a prostitute, and Ms. Craig, who is obviously a man in drag, turns out to be their son, Terry, now called Kim. S/he has engineered this bizarre observation period to determine if Mam and Dad are suitable candidates for a heritage museum that will preserve them, and their house and furnishings, as examples of pre–World War II working-class life. As one of her/his associates says, "We plunge through the rain forests of the Amazon to protect a few lost tribes. But it's here, Mrs. Craven, now. This is the disappearing world. Leeds, Bradford, Halifax. A way of life on its last legs" (*FYO,* 322).

Bennett admits that "there are things wrong with the play," not least among them the son in drag, "since it persuaded some critics that I cherished a shamefaced longing to climb into twinset and pearls." For the critics, the play's major failing was that Bennett abandoned his naturalistic treatment of the north. They dismissed the play for being, in Bennett's words, "far-fetched, expressionistic even. A back-to-back in a museum! I was told in future to stick to the particularities of dialogue and the niceties of actual behaviour that I was supposed to be good at, and leave social comment to others" (19). Ironically, one of Bennett's inspirations for the play came from a newspaper account the year before that a Victorian school in Yorkshire "was to be taken down stone by stone and re-erected in Bradford Museum, where it is to be visited by, among others, patients suffering from Alzheimer's Disease, in the hope, one presumes, of jogging their memories" (18). In recent years, the restoration of Paul McCartney's childhood home in Liverpool to its authentic 1950s condition with all the accurate indices of poverty, including "the linoleum floors, brown wallpaper and Spartan furnishings typical of British post–World War II life,"[6] makes Bennett's supposed flight of fancy in *Enjoy* seem more like prescience.

But *Enjoy* displays even more audacity than Bennett is properly credited with. *Enjoy* presents everyday people as performers, players upon a stage that is both literal and figurative. It is one thing to show us public school types performing in a play within a play in *Forty Years On*, or self-dramatizing politicians turning their habitat into a stage set in *Getting On*, but to suggest that dear old ordinary Mam and Dad in a fusty back-to-back in Leeds are performing their own lives too is to exempt no one from the burdens of everyday performativity. Performance is in everyone's blood. And the defining performance in *Enjoy* is Mam and Dad's impersonation of the traditional nuclear family, with Mam starring as the self-sacrificing, houseproud mother and Dad as the breadwinning, dominant father. The roles of the son and daughter are less clearly defined but will conform to the parents' desires, or so the parents imagine.

The opening stage directions set the tone Bennett wants. He urges the production to eschew naturalism even as it seems to embrace it: "There should be something not quite right about the room . . . Is it that the furniture is too far apart . . . ? Or is it islanded in the centre of the stage with space round it . . . a stage upon a stage? Perhaps it's just that the room is too real" (265). The staginess of this apparently solid reality is underlined once again at the conclusion of the play when the entire set and its contents are dismantled right under the noses of the characters, to be re-erected in the heritage theme park.

On this "stage upon a stage," it's easy to see that Ms. Craig, a man in a woman's dress, is role playing with gender. Her/his presence is the most obvious sign of the performative and as such s/he serves as something of a red herring in the play, allowing both characters and audience to assume that they are "normal" while s/he is somehow the only role player. But Bennett has other ideas. Ms. Craig is the proverbial mote in the eye that prevents others from seeing their own performative behavior. Mam and Dad, the names Wilfred and Connie Craven consistently call one another, are constructed identities too. Even though there are no young children in the house and mounting evidence shows that they have not succeeded in their roles as mother and father, Wilfred and Connie are always Mam and Dad. It's an identity that flatters them, lost as they are in the mists of denial about Linda's real profession (she even dresses like a tart and brings customers home) and the real reasons for their son's disappearance. Dad can boast about Linda, relish his clearly erotic attachment to her, and never have to face up to his responsibility for her corruption. Mam can reminisce fondly about their long-lost son, idealizing the bond that once existed between them, while forgetting that she passively allowed him to be alienated from the family.

In front of Ms. Craig, Mam and Dad try to put on a good face. This is simple impression management, and Mam and Dad are working as a team to present themselves in a favorable light to their observer. But Mam and Dad are not a good team. Mam is more worried about being a gracious hostess and a tidy housekeeper. "Don't start yet," she tells Ms. Craig, "this isn't typical yet. I'm sorry the place is upside down, I haven't had a chance to get round this morning, that's not typical either" (273). Dad is less interested in being typical; he wants Ms. Craig to know that "I had six men under me" (274) and that his daughter is "a grand girl. Everything a father could wish for" (275). Dad is also hostile to Ms. Craig (at the end it becomes clear that both Mam and Dad know Ms. Craig is their son, although it's unclear when they discover it). He belches, he says "piss" and "fuck," while Mam tries to excuse his aggression with mollifying remarks like "he wouldn't say that normally" (278). Ironically, she claims that Dad's rudeness is "all a perform-ance. For your benefit. We don't live like this. Granted we have the occasional dif-ference but when it's just the two of us we get on like a house on fire" (280). Brutally contradicting her, Dad strikes Mam when she insists on talking about their son. His defense is that Ms. Craig's silent presence "eggs you on," and Mam excus-es him by agreeing. "You aggravate matters, you distort things, watching, sitting there," she tells Ms. Craig (283). Linda, their daughter, also knows that surveillance alters the performer's actions. She tells Ms. Craig, sitting silently taking notes, how her presence titillates her. "Stay if you want, sweetheart, I never object to onlook-ers, once in a while. . . . Brings out the actress in me, if you see what I mean. Course it's all acting really, isn't it?" (285).

Being a successful whore is being a good actress, but Linda's remark that "it's all acting" has a wider application, and its full meaning comes clear when Anthony, the green-haired punk, and Mrs. Clegg, the helpful neighbor, make their entrances in the second act. Anthony is a sixteen-year-old street tough straight out of *A Clockwork Orange.* He has his own observer, Gregory, who silently shadows him and takes notes while Anthony pounds on Dad's door, urinates through the letter drop when Dad refuses him entrance, taunts Dad with pornographic photos of Linda (which Dad pretends to have no interest in), and finally bashes Dad so hard on the steel plate in his head that it seems he's killed him. Anthony explains his actions this way: "I had to do that. I have to act normally. I'm not supposed to behave. It's not like probation. I do what I want. Unless I do just what I want, it's useless. Isn't it, Gregory?" (302). Here is one case where surveillance incites the per-former to give the audience what it expects, even to exceed its worst expectations. Ironically, in the presence of Anthony's operatic performance, Dad's performance goes in the opposite direction—it becomes cautious. When he refuses to look at the pornographic photos, we have to agree with Anthony that Dad is playing it con-servatively for Ms. Craig's sake. "I hope you're taking note of this carry-on," he says to Ms. Craig. "Under ordinary circumstances he would have no hesitation. This isn't the real him. You're making him shy" (303).

Dad's apparent death exposes another piece of role playing: Mrs. Clegg enters to help Mam lay out the body. Mrs. Clegg has her "pretensions to refinement" (306), but instead of mimicking the high born, Mrs. Clegg, who is also accompa-nied by her own observer, Adrian, has taken on the part of a traditional working-class housewife, one who still does everything the way her mother and grandmoth-er did. Observers from the Council, like Adrian, encourage the following of tradi-tional ways—which seem to be mostly the habits of the poor and uneducated with

limited options—so Mrs. Clegg tries to give Adrian what she imagines he is looking for. When forgetful Mam asks her what their observers actually want from
them, Mrs. Clegg is quick to remind her that "survivors [are] what they're looking
for. People who haven't gone under. I don't think I disappointed them" (308). She
enjoys being brisk and helpful in a crisis like Dad's apparent death: "The first thing
to do is to lay him out in the customary manner, wash the body and dress it in the
clean clothes traditionally set aside for this purpose" (307). But Mam is confused
and not even sure Dad is dead. "Till I know I'm not sure what to do," she tells Mrs.
Clegg. "Should I be showing grief? Do I mourn or what? I don't want to jump the
gun. Isn't there somebody at the Council we could ring? . . . Is this death? I'd like
an official view" (307). Mam has lost her script and she's doubtful about the one
Mrs. Clegg, who has no such doubts, is following. Mrs. Clegg pontificates for
Adrian's benefit a sentimental line on old-fashioned values: "when death occurs in
the home, tragic though it is, we should try to think of it as a privilege. So many of
the fundamental experiences of our lives have passed beyond our personal control.
Passed into the hands of doctor, social workers, nurses and the like so we are denied
that contact with birth, sickness and death, with poverty, with suffering and all
those areas of human experience" (310).

Rude low comedy immediately undercuts this lofty cant, with its echoes of the
Thatcherite call for a return to "Victorian values." Dad gets an erection as soon as
Mam touches him with the wash cloth, much to her horror and dismay. She blames
Mrs. Clegg and her piety about the traditional ways for this embarrassing develop-
ment. "You would wash him," she tells her. "You would make out that's what it is
we do. Traditionally. Normal procedure. For their benefit. Folks don't wash the
dead and lay them out. Not in this day and age. It's what my mother used to do.
This is the twentieth century. You call in an expert" (311–2). Dad isn't dead, but
Mam certainly speaks for most in the audience when she asks to be excused from
such supposedly authentic folk customs.

Ms. Craig's attitude toward her/his parents is oddly ambivalent. S/he seems
mostly a passive observer, although it's hard not to be suspicious about the motives
behind this surveillance. For instance, why does s/he encourage Mam to revel in her
role as mother-martyr?

Mam:	Was I a good mother? A capable housewife?
Ms. Craig:	Down to the last detail.
Mam:	I never let you go short?
Ms. Craig:	With you self-sacrifice always came first.
Mam:	I sound to have been a perfect mother. (323)

The result of Ms. Craig's observation of the family seems to be the reinscription of
Mam's domestic entrapment in the heritage museum. The roles and appurtenances
of working-class life that s/he remembers from childhood will be preserved forever.
"It'll be exactly like it was when I was little," she more than a little selfishly admits

(323). Ms. Craig, while not literally "the writer in disguise," may embody for Bennett well-meaning outsiders like himself who do damage when they return to watch and take notes in order to recreate a world that once was and that time and memory have made dim. S/he may be Bennett's own guilty admission of the price that the past has to pay for the nostalgic impulses of autobiographical writers.

The price of nostalgia is high in *Enjoy*, which satirizes the sentimentalizing of "heritage" when it means nothing more than preserving the least-admirable aspects of the past, in this instance the culture of male brutishness represented by Dad— he's so awful "we must have him" (325), one of the team of experts whispers—and of female submission represented by Mam. Daphne Turner has described *Enjoy* as "scathing about the northern way of life" and suggests that it might even be a play "that rejects the north" (14–5). Scathing it certainly is, but rejection of the north may not be what Bennett had in mind. He seems instead to be saying that a national climate that views the past—its "heritage"—as a commercial opportunity for entrepreneurial gain, that overlooks the ugliness and the deprivation that actually constituted the lives of the people in that place and time, is an absurdity deserving only scorn and derision. The transformation of history into a theme park where the shadows are brightened and the inequities and cruelty are toned down so that visitors—another euphemism for paying customers—have an uplifting experience is really what Bennett is rejecting. Almost needless to add, the Thatcher years saw the promotion of England as a heritage museum rise to the top of the national agenda.

OBJECTS OF AFFECTION (1982)

Intensive Care
Our Winnie
Say Something Happened

These three plays are among five broadcast in the fall of 1982 on BBC2, the other two being *Rolling Home* and *Marks*. The collective title Bennett has given them— *Objects of Affection*—though unglossed by Bennett himself, is appropriate. The portraits of a son facing his father's death, two elderly women caring for a retarded adult child, and a novice social worker meeting a recalcitrant "at risk" couple have a layered richness of text and subtext that is new to Bennett's television work. These plays offer a more internal appreciation of their characters, with a deeper sympathy for their psychological as well as social alienation, than did Bennett's earlier television treatment of northern life. Yet these characters are familiar at the same time, speaking a language we have heard before. Advice like "have a tablet" is offered frequently to the nervous and depressed. Astonishment at offspring who can "choose from a menu without turning a hair," and accusations that someone is trying "to show us up" are phrases and situations that are part of the fabric of Bennett's north. This is the language spoken by people driven by the desire to make a good impression, but doubtful about their ability to carry off the performance.

Intensive Care (first broadcast November 9, 1982)

Alan Bennett plays the lead role of Denis Midgley, a repressed, worried, thirty-nine-year-old schoolteacher trying to act the dutiful son to a dying father. In the first scene, he is holding his hands in front of his face, prompting the questions, is he tired? protecting himself from some unpleasantness? adjusting his mask? The first words we hear are a voice-over that ominously begins, "On the many occasions Midgley had killed his father, death always came easily" (*OA,* 172) Although Midgley is only guilty of imagining the manner of his father's ultimate demise, not plotting it literally, Bennett the playwright knows that the former involves a little of the latter. This comic ambiguity at the start of the play enriches the portrait of a man trapped by what he thinks convention expects of him, yet unable to decide what he would really like to do.

Intensive Care is set mostly in a hospital, which is a natural venue for playacting and anxiety about playacting—the English don't call operating rooms "theatres" for nothing. Receiving the long-expected news that his father is finally dying, Midgley, who isn't particularly close to his father, is faced with a performance dilemma. What is the proper tone to adopt at the hospital? cheerfulness at the hope of recovery? solemnity in the face of possible death? stoical acceptance? dignified grief? rage? Midgley is convinced that selfless attendance at the bedside is his duty. As he leaves for the hospital, he promises his wife, "I'll make it right. I'll be there when he goes. I'll hold his hand. I shan't let him down" (180). All those *I*s call into question the selfless element in his hospital attendance. His father's dying seems an excellent opportunity to advance his self-estimate as a son, to compensate for his guilty indifference or hostility to his father while he was alive. From this transformative experience of selfless devotion, he believes he will become a "different person," one who can "Live. Start!" (180).

As the rest of the family gathers at the hospital in Bradford, each one reveals his own idiosyncratic agenda, though concern and grief are of course on everyone's lips. Aunty Kitty is the dying man's only sister and something of an ambulance chaser. She gets there first and stays, taking up residence in the waiting room, leading her other brother Ernest to remark on seeing her, "where no vultures fly" (185). Once we become acquainted with her need to know the intimate business of everyone in the hospital and witness her careless gossiping about it, all in the name of caring, we agree with Ernest's assessment: "It's a wonder to me how your Aunty Kitty's managed to escape strangulation so long" (196). Aunt Kitty is no worse than other hospital visitors who put on equally transparent performances. Midgley's cousin's family, who trot in to pay their respects, are dressed for a night out at an expensive restaurant: wife in a coat with a fur collar, father and son in suede jackets, and daughter with elaborate blond curls and pink chubby sweater. The parents' expressions of solicitude compensate somewhat for their inappropriately grand attire, but the two children, as in *All Day on the Sands*, are less practiced and slip up several times, undermining the parents' performance. The most telling example occurs when the daughter, observing her mother's assumption of a sad demeanour, asks,

Elizabeth:	Are you crying, Mam?
Jean:	Yes.
Elizabeth:	There aren't any tears.
Jean:	You can cry without tears
Elizabeth:	I can't. How do you do it, Mam?
Jean:	I'll give you such a smack in a minute, your Uncle Denis's father is dying.
	Elizabeth starts to cry.
Jean:	There, love. It's all right. He doesn't feel it.
Elizabeth:	I'm not crying because of him. I'm crying because of you.
	(188–9)

Like her daughter, the mother is confused. She reads her daughter's tears in light of socially prescribed behavior at a hospital: she thinks that Elizabeth is learning how to make an appropriate impression. On the contrary, the daughter is frightened when her mother suddenly drops the mask of social grief and replaces it with the controlling and threatening parental persona.

Midgley's performance of the dutiful son is even more disturbing. People begin to question his odd need to stick around—even Aunty Kitty goes home at night. On the phone he insists to his wife, "I must be here when he goes." She tells him, "You've done all that's necessary. Nobody would blame you." When he refuses to come home, she drops the supportive tone: "I understand you. It's not love. It's not affection. It's yourself" (191–2). Both the hospital matron and the doctor on duty tell him, "You've done your duty" (194, 198), as they try to ease him out of the hospital. Uncle Ernest puts it even more bluntly to Midgely and his own son: "I'll not come again. Again and again. It gets morbid. . . . There's no need to go through all this performance with me, you know. Come once, and have done. Mind you, I'll be lucky if you come at all" (196).

Bennett's stage directions tell us that as Midgley watches his uncle and his son spar, "it is like a play within a play of his relations with his own father" (197); most likely, the play in question is *Oedipus Rex*. Midgley's oedipal struggle with his father comes out clearly in a dream that reads like a parody of D.H. Lawrence (Midgely is an English teacher, after all). He is a young boy again, sitting with his mother in a green field on a picnic cloth, she dressed in immaculate white. A slag heap rises behind them in the distance. A loud noise suddenly breaks the idyllic mood and a man covered in soot and coal dust comes running toward them and embraces his mother, soiling her pure whiteness. Midgley's barely submerged hostility toward his father's sexuality surfaces again when he disputes the opinion of Valery, the night nurse, that many women would have found his father attractive: "Women didn't go for him. Only my mother" (197). He has to revise that idea however, when Alice, the mistress Midgley didn't know his father had, shows up at the hospital. She's warm and blunt, and a rich widow, someone his Aunty Kitty will enviously describe later as "a real common woman" (209). She deconstructs some of the mystique that has built up around his father and that has stunted Midgely's own sense of self-worth all these years:

Midgely:	He was good. Everybody says how good he was.
Alice:	He always had to be the one, did Frank. The one who did the good turns, the one who paid out, the one who sacrificed. You couldn't do anything for him. I had all this money, he wouldn't even let me take him to Scarborough. We used to sit in Roundhay Park. Roundhay Park! We could have been in Tenerife. (208)

Used to hearing his own wife tell him that he'd never be half the man his father was, Midgley finally meets the first person to tell him that his father was no paragon of perfection. Alice has singled out his father's insistence on sacrifice, usually read as his greatest virtue, and seen it for what it really is, a puritanical weakness so prevalent in Bennett's north: the denial of pleasure for fear of what others might think. Inspired partly by Alice's advice, "don't you be like your Dad" (209), Midgley decides to seize what small chance at pleasure he can, so he asks Valery to sleep with him. Despite this bold move, he tries to balance duty and pleasure by insisting that he be called if his father's condition should change. Valery deliberately takes the phone off the hook, and by the time it is reconnected, it's too late. His father awakens from his coma, looks around, asks, "Is our Denis here," and dies. It's almost too neat an irony. Midgley concedes the victory to his father: "Of course he's smiling. He's won. He's scored. In the last minute of extra time." When asked what he was doing during his father's crucial last minutes, he remarks only that he was "living" (212).

Back home he has lost whatever bravado his encounter with Valery gave him. He sits at the kitchen counter, hands open like a martyr waiting for the nails to be driven in, not much changed by his liberation through death and adultery. He chastises his son and his girlfriend for showing affection to one another so soon after granddad has died, guilty perhaps about his own night with Valery. His wife winks at the young couple, urging them, "Take no notice . . . It's only your father" (214). Her words diminish further his own obsession with doing his duty by his father. If a father is so easily discounted, then all his fuss has been pointless. Back at school, he smokes a cigarette as a sign that his experience of death has altered him, but it's a shallow gesture. Perhaps a more reliable index of his condition is offered by the school secretary who, when asked where she will go on that world cruise she has promised herself when her mother dies, replies "Bridlington," a seacoast resort in Yorkshire. She has no illusions about escaping from her world and neither, according to Alan Bennett, should Midgley.[7]

Our Winnie (first broadcast November 12, 1982)

On the surface, this play seems a simple exercise in sentiment and irony. Two elderly women, Cora and Ida, take Cora's grown daughter, Winnie, who is retarded, to visit the grave of Winnie's father. At the cemetery, they meet a young woman, who is a photographer, and a young man, who is sketching. The photographer, who has been unsuccessful in capturing genuine dignity and emotion among the crematorium workers, takes candid shots of the three women without their knowledge or permission. The male artist sees it as exploitation; the photographer defends it as respectful attention. She wins a prize for her photograph of the three women.

The complex interweaving of several strands of conflict—the two northern lower-middle-class women over the proper presentation of themselves and Winnie; the photographer and the crematorium workers over what constitutes an authentic performance of grief; and the university-educated photographer and the sketcher over the proper role of the artist toward his/her subject (as well as Bennett's own complex attitudes to all these characters)—makes this short play of shrewdly observed comedy and muted pathos an excellent example of how Bennett has complicated and enriched some of the familiar themes and techniques of his northern plays.

Cora and Ida are women we have already met many times in Bennett's work. They are not formally educated beyond a certain rudimentary literacy, they haven't seen much of the world beyond their own neighborhoods, they often have not had careers outside their homes, they are widows or spinsters, and their children, if they have had any, are usually absent or unavailable for support. Yet these women are no shrinking violets. They have strong opinions, sometimes shading into prejudices. They like to manage other people's lives, and they take great pride in their respectability, which includes the proper way to dress, speak, and act. Above all, they have enormous respect for their social betters. In short, they perform all the expected rituals that establish their middle-class pretensions, if not credentials.

Our first sight of Cora emphatically establishes her interest in appearance, both her own and her daughter's. As she helps dress this fully grown woman she remarks to her, "Fasten your buttons. . . . There. You can look really nice if you want to. It's done well has this coat. Your hair'll want cutting in a bit" (*OA*, 12) In the second scene, we see them walking down a street of well-kept semidetached houses on their way to meet Ida. Cora comments critically to Winnie on the changes that she's witnessed in the neighborhood: "This is where Doctor Handley used to live. He delivered you. Flats now. His wife died. Right refined woman. Always used to speak. Kept that garden lovely. Somebody's chucked a mattress out. It's a right tip [garbage dump] now" (12). Her disdain for the current state of her neighborhood doesn't quite match what we see, marking Cora as one of those Bennett women obsessed with hygiene and the old order that prevailed when they were young.

Ida, on the other hand, is slightly less interested in social conventions and niceties. She refuses to accept Cora's sympathy for her spinsterhood: "I didn't want a man. . . . It's something you've never understood, you" (15). And she's not fooled by Cora's nephew's excuse that he can't drive them to the cemetery because of his scuba lessons. She puts him on the spot:

Eric: We haven't actually got into the water yet. To date it's all been theory.
Ida: Oh. I thought you'd have been a fully qualified frogman by now.
Eric: These things take time.
Ida: Put paid to our little jaunts anyway. It was nice, the Capri. (14)

Later, while waiting for the bus, Cora and Ida are approached by a woman conducting a survey on bus ridership. Cora immediately informs the interviewer, "we wouldn't ordinarily be using this bus. My nephew used to run us up." Ida undermines Cora's genteel act:

Interviewer: Now, you say you have access to a car.
Cora: Yes.
Ida: No, we don't. Not since he started doing this . . . silly diving
             thing.
Cora: It'll pass. . . . Put down occasionally.
Ida: Very occasionally. (16)

Their attitudes toward social expectations color their feelings about Winnie. Her mother is easily exasperated by her failures to act normal and is self-conscious about her difference, telling the interviewer "you'd better not put Winnie down" in the survey. "We never do. She's not right" (16). When Winnie goes astray in the cemetery, it's her mother who disciplines her with a smack across the legs while "Aunty" Ida wipes away her tears and comforts her: "It's all right, love. Your Mam and me are here. You're not lost" (23). When her mother gets upset with Winnie for getting mud on her shoes and punishes her by making her sit on a bench, Ida defends her: "You expect too much of her. . . . You ought to give her responsibility, not take it away" (26). Cora retorts that Ida doesn't know what it's like to have to put up with Winnie's difference day after day. Ida insists, "She's company. . . . It's a person. Someone there, choose what you say. You've two plates to put out. Two cups. Someone to follow." Cora falls back on conventional wisdom to remind Ida that her loneliness is her own fault: "You've no right to complain. It's what I say. You should have got wed" (27).

At the end of the day, back home, the two women look at old photos, and Cora reminisces about the time when Winnie's retardation could no longer be denied:

Once we knew for certain, I didn't go out. Didn't go anywhere. I wouldn't take her out. Dad had it all to do. Dad and you. The housework. The shopping. Everything. It was long enough before I came round. Still, life has to go on, I suppose. Folks stare. They look at her and don't realise. Then when they do realise, they look away. You don't want them to stare, and yet you don't want them to look away. I don't know. (30)

Cora's fear of what other people will think, her shame, and her confusion about her appropriate role as the mother of a retarded child have altered her sense of her family's place in the community, have made her feel she doesn't belong and must set herself apart. Ida, who has gone against the grain of what was expected of her, first by learning to drive a truck during the war and then by not marrying (we sense she might have married Cora's Frank if she'd been asked), is less uneasy with ambiguity. She replies to Cora's speech with a simple but telling platitude: "It's a good job there's love." As she speaks the line, the camera focuses on Winnie eating cream-filled tea cakes with her fingers. She looks up in Ida's direction and smiles.

Bennett avoids the dual sentimental pitfalls of the cemetery setting and mental retardation by counterbalancing the story of these three women with another triangular relationship, that of the photographer with the crematorium workers and the artist. While performance was a muted subtext in Cora and Ida's lives—how best to perform middle-class respectability in the face of having to take the bus or how to present a dignified front when your grown daughter acts like a three-year-old—performance is central to this subplot.

Liz, the photographer, is first seen trying to get a photo of the crematorium attendant turning the page of the Book of Remembrance. Kept in a glass case, this book contains the names of those who've died on that particular day. The turning of the page is undoubtedly meant to be weighted with ritual significance, perhaps even with emotion. But Liz doesn't seem to be getting what she wants from the attendant's actions. Her presence has made him self-conscious, and a fellow attendant, who would clearly love to be in the photo himself, keeps offering advice and criticism that only flusters him further. "You do it reverently," he advises him. "Course I do it reverently. I'm not doing it reverently now because there's nobody here. If it's just me I come in and do it. I don't make a big performance of it. Only if there are any bereaved about I make it a bit more ceremonial. A bit more . . . military" (18).

It seems that Liz is looking for something unperformed, something that the Second Attendant calls "the genuine article," proof that "the camera cannot lie" (21). She certainly doesn't get it from Ivy, another crematorium employee, who is called in to substitute for the attendant in the shot. If he was too casual, she is too histrionic, offering what the stage directions call "a parody of grief," hanky to nose (20). Ivy can't concentrate on her performance because she's still disappointed that her request to wear a trouser suit to work has been turned down by the management, which decides it "smacked too much of leisure wear" and suggests instead "a plainish frock." Her retort that "if it's genuine grief it doesn't matter a toss what I wear" (21) carries little weight with the funeral directors who know that grief in these situations and establishments is often performed ritually, not felt emotionally. Appearance and attitude are inseparable to them. Later they will banish Liz from the premises for wearing pink trousers.

Liz's interaction with Cora, Ida, and Winnie takes place under the disapproving eye of the sketcher, Charles. While he copies a statue on a grave, she begins to follow the three women, sensing an opportunity for an unposed shot. He tells her, "You can't. She's retarded. It's not fair." She replies, "It doesn't matter. Does it?" (27). The question goes unanswered, although it's central to Bennett's concerns here and in *Enjoy*: What responsibility does the artist or observer have to his/her subject? When does the use of "material" for your own purposes shade into exploitation?

Liz decides that the only way to get the pictures she wants is by deceit. She asks permission to take a picture, but while Cora, ever in thrall to appearance, takes a minute to reapply her makeup (Ida just looks on), Liz is snapping away, catching all three of them in unguarded poses. Typically, Cora insists that Winnie be excluded from the posed picture, but her tears, along with Ida's urging, finally gain Winnie a photo of her own. Only Liz and Charles know of the candid shots, however. She tries to justify ingratiating herself with the trio in order to get the candid shot by making her photography into a work of charity: "You attend to people, that's all it is. You photograph people, you attend to them. Attention, these days, it's what people want" (28–9). Liz isn't completely off base in her assessment. Cora and Ida have enjoyed their day out because they have been noticed, their usual invisibility dispelled, if only for an afternoon, by those who seem to belong to the greater world they don't fit into. As Cora puts it, "We haven't done so bad to-day. We've been interviewed vis-à-vis the bus service. We've come in contact with the younger generation and we've had our photographs taken. They're quite nice some young people now, whatever you read in the papers. Those two were all right" (29).

Bennett makes sure that the ambiguity of the situation is not flattened by Cora's optimistic pronouncement. The final scene shows us a gallery with photographs displayed on the wall, and on the photo Liz has taken of the three women there is a ribbon marking it as a prize winner: Cora on the right looking into her compact and applying powder, Ida on the left with her eyes cast slightly downward, and Winnie behind them in the middle staring into the camera with her mouth gaping open. The stage directions tell us that "it is a heartless photograph, but a striking one. It is also the one that Liz said she had not taken" (30). Liz has created an image of undeniable voyeuristic power by catching these three women in Goffman's backstage region, especially Cora, before she can put on her socially prescribed face of middle-class female respectability. All the things Cora is so invested in protecting are now exposed for everyone to see. Her performance of normality has been upstaged by Liz's performance in the role of the artist in search of the "real" at all costs. Which performance, asks Bennett, deserves our allegiance more?

Say Something Happened (first broadcast December 17, 1982)

Bennett mines here the same vein of suspicion about the ubiquity of surveillance in contemporary English life that he exposed with such savage glee in *Enjoy*, but with a gentler irony suited to the more general audience of television viewers. When an inexperienced social worker visits an elderly couple, whom the Council deems "at risk" because of their age and isolation, they challenge her assumptions about their neediness with such skill that before long they seem to be interviewing her. We are in familiar Bennett territory: elderly, fiercely independent northerners lock horns with a "caring" bureaucracy that insists on snooping about and intervening where it can do little good. Looking at this richly ironic play in Goffman's terms we also see what happens when an inexperienced performer (June, the social worker) meets an audience (Mam and Dad) that can see through her act. But since Mam and Dad also have a performance of their own to maintain, they do not wish to disrupt it completely, displaying what Goffman calls "audience tact."[8]

The film opens with two immobile figures in a cluttered living room. Mam is standing looking out the window, Dad is sitting slack jawed in an easy chair. They are, in Goffman's dramaturgical universe, backstage before the curtain rises. They snap out of their lethargy when the doorbell rings and Mam spies a young woman on their doorstep. Despite judging her to be "educated" because of the briefcase she is carrying, they are reluctant to let her in, steeped as they are in gory cautionary tales from the tabloids. Later Mam will advise June that if she had been wearing something more businesslike, instead of a poncho, she would have been let in sooner: "If you want to come waltzing into people's houses you ought to get yourself a little costume. You'd look heaps better in a two-piece, and you'd find people much more forthcoming" (*OA*, 118) Mam's sensitivity to the importance of a prop like the briefcase and a costume like the two-piece solidifies the theatrical sense established in the opening frozen tableau. The curtain has risen on their dramatic interaction with their visitor.

June is so naive about what she's doing that she fails almost from the start to sustain her role as the authority figure representing the local government. When Dad confides to her that he has no objections to a poncho, she weakens her "team" by giving Dad a peek at their backstage strategy: "Mr. Farquarson tells us not to dress up. Otherwise we get into an 'us' and 'them' situation" (119). When Dad asks her about the purpose of the questionnaire while Mam is in the kitchen preparing tea, June reads aloud her instructions from her manual. Clearly, this is going to be a very rough run-through. In fact, June doesn't seem to know any of her lines, but as she reads verbatim from her manual Mam seems to know exactly what's coming next: "Hypothermia. (*June stops.*) Is that it? Hypothermia? Not us. We've got a Dimplex. Background heating." When June presses forward, asking more questions, Mam resists: "This is old people. It's not us. . . ." June counters, "Hang on," and reads aloud, "'The refusal to recognise the approach of old age and the possibility of infirmity is entirely natural . . . and in its way commendable'" (122).

When they see her jotting down a note, Mam challenges her to disclose what she has written. June is forced to admit that as a newcomer to Social Services (with those ominous initials S.S.), having only recently taken a "sideways jump" from Transport, she needs to learn on the job. June once again gives away her "team's" strategy. "Mr. Farquarson said that the survey," she confesses, "would be a chance for us to do a little ad hoc assessment. Part of our training. You know, fieldwork. Only I'm not supposed to tell you that" (124). In this light, Mam characterizes herself and Dad as "guinea pigs," but if they are, they soon take charge of the experiment. They turn a social work cliché like "at risk" back onto June when she faults them for not mixing socially:

Mam:	What about you, do you mix?
June:	I tend to run across people at work. I'm not at risk. I'm not old.
Mam:	Old, old. There's risk with youth. You might commit suicide. That's snowballed.
Dad:	Mam.
Mam:	Well. How old are your parents?
Dad:	Nay, they've split up, haven't they?
Mam:	Split up? Are you married?
June:	No.
Mam:	Where do you live?
June:	Kirkstall.
Mam:	They've knocked most of it down. Is it a flat?
June:	A bedsitter.
Mam:	A bedsitter? Child of a broken home, living in a bedsitter in one of those inner city areas: you're the one that's at risk. You want to get yourself on a register. Coming around telling us. (125)

Mam's defensive and ruthless use of logical deduction demonstrates the formidable power of an uneducated northern housewife to intimidate the unwary and unprepared.

Mam's tart common sense, however, places June's performance in dire jeopardy. She becomes so unnerved that tears fill her eyes: "I've gone wrong somewhere . . . it's my fault . . . we're in a confrontation situation now . . . well you shouldn't get into a confrontation situation, Mr. Farquarson says, you get into a confrontation situation you've slipped up" (126). June's reliance on jargon ("confrontation situation") can be overlooked, but the imminent collapse of her performance as a representative of authority cannot. If June is unable to rescue herself, then "saving the show" is up to Mam and Dad. Luckily for her, there is a mechanism in social interaction that impels onlookers to "help the performers save their own show" and makes special allowances for novices. "When the performer is known to be a beginner," Goffman writes, "and more subject than otherwise to embarrassing mistakes, the audience frequently shows extra consideration, refraining from causing the difficulties it might otherwise create."[9] Mam feeds her scones and Dad reassures her, "you're doing champion," placing the blame for the disruption on themselves: "We're not good at interviews, probably, are we, Mam?" (126). After a while, Mam tells June, "You've got your poise back now, love, haven't you?" (130).

Their motives for rescuing June are related to the fragility of their own self-presentation. The information they volunteer about their daughter, Margaret, who has left home for a career in London, reveals that she is not likely to be much of a support to them as they age, either financially or emotionally. But they insist they are proud of her career as the personal secretary to a man in ceramic heating tiles. "We get postcards from all over," Dad tells June. "I've got booksfull. If we had grand-children it would be a real geography lesson" (130). The postcards that substitute for visits—"Daughters, they used to live round the corner" (128), Mam com-plains—and the absence of grandchildren—"She's never been all that interested in the opposite sex, our Margaret" (128), says Dad—tell us all we need to know. Dad adds defensively, "I don't think you should expect it of your children" (132).

Both Mam and Dad support one another's interpretations of Margaret, even though to a sharper observer than June they seem to contradict their stories at sev-eral places. It's only when Dad leaves the room to find one of Margaret's postcards that their performance of the proud and contented parents is disrupted. Mam con-fides to June that Margaret is not their only child. "We've told a lie. We have two children. We had a son. After Margaret. Colin. Only he wasn't right. He's in a home near Otley. . . . We never talk about it to anybody. We never talk about it to each other. We ought to do, only he won't" (130). Like Cora in *Our Winnie*, Mam and Dad feel shame at their child's difference, as if it were a breach of middle-class deco-rum and respectability, but Mam's pain at abandoning even the mention of her son is much deeper than Cora's daily discomfort at Winnie's presence. Goffman says that on rare occasions,

> a moment in the performance may come when the separateness of the teams will break down and be momentarily replaced by a communion of glances through which each team openly admits to the other its stage of information. At such moments the whole dramaturgical structure of social interaction is suddenly and poignantly laid bare, and the line separating the teams momen-tarily disappears. Whether this close view of things brings shame or laughter, the teams are likely to draw rapidly back into their appointed characters.[10]

Goffman's "communion of glances" doesn't apply here because of June's confusion at the revelation. How should she respond? The instructions in her manual don't cover this kind of event. Mam has disrupted the performance of self-sufficiency, and real life has interrupted. "I don't know what to say," June stammers. "It's not to do with this, that. It's more . . . private" (131). "That"—she can't get any closer to Colin and the family's tragedy than with a demonstrative pronoun. The best she can do is to reciprocate with her own version of "audience tact," by promising not to let on to Dad that she knows and carrying on with the interview as if nothing unex-pected had been said.

June leaves them a placard reading HELP that they can put in their window in case of an emergency. She feels rather satisfied that Mam and Dad have "helped me with my course" (133), though the benefit to those who were supposedly in need is debatable. Mam looks at the HELP sign and says to Dad disapprovingly, "It's telling the whole street. We'll keep it, just in case. I'll put it in my drawer" (133), the fear of people knowing your weaknesses easily overpowering any practical con-siderations. In some ways, who can blame them? What has the social worker offered that will alter the inevitability that one of them will die before the other? How can she change their sad knowledge that their lives are bleak and empty, even with one another? The room grows darker as she leaves. Mam and Dad fall back into the torpor that prevailed at the start of the play—she frozen at the window, he seated in the chair, as if they are backstage once again after the curtain has fallen on an exhausting performance. The metaphor is made literal, as the camera shifts to the outside of the house and we see leaves falling and Mam closing the curtains.

The title of the play—*Say Something Happened*—becomes richer when we realize that nothing will happen to these people except the common fate of decline and death. Perhaps nothing has ever happened to them. Like Vladimir and Estragon in *Waiting for Godot*, about whom a wag once said, to account for the play's two-act structure, that nothing happens twice, Mam and Dad are the northern everyman and everywoman of a certain age and class. They have a comic toughness that derives from their performance of self-sufficiency, but when the curtains are closed we also know they are trapped. Bennett, like Beckett before him, knows how we perform our lives to fool others about that entrapment, and, if our act is a good one, even fool ourselves. It's a theme Bennett will take up again with the actress who played Mam, Thora Hird, in *A Cream Cracker Under the Settee* in the first series of *Talking Heads* monologues.

A Private Function (1984)

Bennett's first screenplay takes a more lighthearted view of the north than *Enjoy* does, though the satire is hardly less pointed. Set in 1947 on the eve of Princess Elizabeth's marriage to Prince Philip, when England was suffering through food rationing even worse than in the darkest days of World War II, *A Private Function* presents a small Yorkshire town's response to these two contradictory experiences: celebration and privation. The plot turns on the discovery by newcomers—a chiropodist and his wife—that the elite of the town are planning to celebrate the royal wedding by slaughtering a black-market pig. Gilbert and Joyce Chilvers, especially Joyce, want to be included in the dinner, and ultimately they use their knowledge to blackmail the town powers into inviting them. On this simple framework of social ambition taking aim at the entrenched class structure, Bennett has elaborated a complex and darkly comic web of interconnected ironies, many familiar from his earlier work.

Chief among them is the notion, central to *Habeas Corpus*, that the bourgeois social order is only a thin covering thrown over the naked carcass of animal appetite. This performance of decorum always attempts to disguise the bestial drives in human nature and is always vulnerable to disruption. These characters in food-scarce postwar England are hungry. Theirs is a literal hunger: long food queues turn violent when rations are cut and butcher shops closed. In the face of these hungry rioters, the police inspector can only shake his head in wonder: "These used to be ordinary decent people" (*PF*, 43) Their hunger is also metaphoric, directed to the acquisition or the maintenance of power, the kind that allows one group

social privileges over the others, in this case an invitation to an exclusive dinner—
"a private function." Bennett shows us "a society split between petit bourgeois and
Establishment,"[11] but beneath the surface of these class distinctions we see pretty
much the same impulses to beastly behavior. The undeniable connection between
the human and the animal in all of us is expressed most harshly when a moralistic
character retorts, in response to the admonition that we need to be more understanding of our fellow creatures' weaknesses because we're all only human: "when
people say they're only human it is because they have been making beasts of themselves" (38–9). *A Private Function* neither condemns this nor is shocked by it.
Instead, it finds all the comedy it can in a Darwinian competition whose prime
directive is eat or be eaten.

The comic irony in the situation arises from the order and gentility on the surface of this rapacious world that gives only lip service to the new socialist ideals that
the Labour Party began introducing in 1945. The opening scene of the film shows
us a mock Pathé newsreel tut-tutting at black-market smuggling and hoarding in
France. In England, where the weekly bacon ration has just been halved, the narrator piously intones that "fair shares for all" is the English way, implying that the
corrupt practices of the black market are foreign to English egalitarian values. Our
first encounter with the leading citizen of this Yorkshire town—the physician, Dr.
Swaby, "a thorough-going shit" in Bennett's own words (22), but a suave one as
played by Denholm Elliott—indicates that "fair shares for all" is not a motto he
subscribes to, as he decides the guest list for the special dinner. Swaby strikes one
couple from the list because their daughter was a six-months-pregnant G.I. bride,
which he maliciously reveals in a breach of professional confidentiality. He dismisses a second couple, by the name of Goodman, by making insinuating piglike
noises to remind his committee that Jews and pork dinners don't mix, "apart from
anything else" (24).

Like most bigots, Swaby wraps himself in the mantle of high moral standards to
justify his discriminations. He pontificates on the sacred national importance of the
occasion they are celebrating: "This is royalty. It's a pure and unspoiled couple"
(24). Swaby is especially prickly and overbearing because his sense of entitlement
as moral guardian and social leader of the town is threatened by Labour's new programs to promote social equity, the National Health Service being the one that will
most directly affect his status as a doctor. He reaches heights of indignation over
the new prospect of universal access to medical treatment: "God, it's a nasty piss-
stained little country now is this. It's like this new Health Service. Do you realize
that any little poorly pillock is henceforth going to be able to knock on my door
and say, 'I'm ill. Treat me.' Anybody! Me!" (90). But no amount of bullying can disguise the fact that this celebration of the purest by the best is founded on the illegal, and very noisome, raising of an unregistered pig for private consumption.
Everything in Swaby is sheer, blustery performance, and Denholm Elliott, renowned
for his ability to steal scenes from the most seasoned performers, is up to the task,
even when face to face with Betty, the pig.

The film belongs, however, to Maggie Smith as Joyce Chilvers, the socially ambitious wife of the chiropodist (Michael Palin). Bennett has described Joyce as "a distant relative of Lady Macbeth" (8), and we initially see her taking a seat in a movie theater as the Pathé newsreel ends. She tells her mother to get another seat because "I'm going up" (19). Indeed she is. She is the theater organist, who begins to play as the organ rises from the floor of the theater. But in another sense it's a prophetic wish, for Joyce would like nothing better than to join the "Town's Best" (107) at the top of the social tree. As Daphne Turner has noted, Maggie Smith signals the character's awkward ambitions to rise by choosing a voice and an idiom for Joyce that is "just not quite right . . . would-be genteel, the voice of one aspiring to leave her class and always marked as not belonging to the other" (41).

Joyce wants to believe that she is naturally destined for better things than marriage to a chiropodist. Sounding more like Margaret Thatcher, the greengrocer's daughter who took diction lessons, than like Lady Macbeth, she reminds her husband of her social credentials, in case he ever has forgotten them, which is unlikely. "My father had a chain of dry cleaners. We regularly used to drink wine with the meal as Mother well knows. . . . My father wore a carnation in his buttonhole every day of his life" (65). She imagines that she would be most at home in the elegant surroundings of a grand hotel, sipping tea and dancing. "You see this is where I belong, Mother. Get me in a long dress and surround me with sophisticated people, I'd bloom" (64).

Joyce's hunger differs from the cravings of her mother and husband. She's not eager for food, but for the social position that comes from power. Her husband can envy the steak he sees Dr. Swaby eat, but to Joyce, "it's not just steak . . . It's status" (37), just as she knows that possession of that contraband pig is "not just pork. It's power" (70). In the face of her husband's sentimental inability to slaughter the pig, once they steal it, she can urge him to "screw your courage to the sticking point" (her less poetic phrase is "kill your friend") and offer him sex—"do it for me"—but she finally has to take matters into her own hands. And not by wielding the butcher knife and chasing the flatulent, incontinent pig through her immaculately clean house, although she does try that. Joyce discovers instead that her real talent lies in hard bargaining. She can blackmail with the best of the men, that is with Dr. Swaby, when she learns who has been raising this illegal pig. In exchange for her silence she gets three invitations to the wedding dinner, and even if the seats are located next to the lavatories, she knows that "toilet or no toilet, we're in now. In ten years that'll be us" at the head table with Swaby and the mayor (109). Joyce and Swaby seem made for one another. At the dinner they dance together and she lets his hand wander from her waist, a sure sign of future collaborations.

Bennett gets his darkest comic effects in *A Private Function* from the juxtaposition of the animal and the human. That connection is made most tellingly in the way the elderly are looked upon as disposable items not unlike the pigs raised for slaughter. Joyce Chilvers's mother, for example, is always seen eating, just like Betty, the black-market pig. Whether it's stealing her son-in-law's lunch, or clandestinely devouring the cocktail nibbles intended for guests, this old woman never seems to satisfy her hunger. When the pig is sequestered in the Chilvers' home, and the neighbors complain of bad smells coming from the house, Joyce points to her mother. "She's getting a bit careless" (85), she explains, an extraordinary admission from a woman for whom keeping up appearances in front of the neighbors is paramount. But Joyce's mother is an easy sacrifice if the reward—status and power—is great enough. It's also no accident that when the pig has been slaughtered and needs to be removed from the premises they dress her in the old woman's hat and coat.[12] One benefit of Joyce's newfound alliance with Swaby is his offer to help find her mother a place in a rest home, since he's "on the board of several"—a fate the old woman has been dreading throughout the film. Joyce's response, fully within her mother's hearing, is an effusive, "Oh, how kind!" (106).

An even more callous example of this equation of the elderly with the disposable occurs during one of the several raids on butcher shops by the inspector for the Ministry of Food. While he finds half a pig hanging in a clothes closet, the other half, shoved under the covers of a pensioner's bed, escapes confiscation. The confused old man in the bed clutches the meat and tells his daughter, "your mam feels cold," to which she replies, "It's not surprising. She died in 1937" (29–30). Sentiment has no place in a world where everyone is "on the twist" and survival of the shrewdest is the order of the day.

A Private Function depicts an intensely physical world, but it's not a pretty picture. We see Gilbert Chilvers handling a lot of smelly feet, scraping off hard skin and clipping toenails to earn his daily bread, meager as it is. We see gross heaps of garbage hoarded to feed to Betty the pig, garbage that will inevitably be spilled occasionally on dignified people like Dr. Swaby (one of Bennett's cruder revenges on him). We see Betty wallowing in her filth, we hear her suffering from diarrhea and flatulence, and we witness the distress of everyone who must smell the results. Sex is mostly joyless physical exercise, whether it's Joyce terrifying Gilbert by methodically wielding an enormous contraceptive douche, or her bluntly announcing that "sexual intercourse is in order" (106) once the pig has been slaughtered and they have won their tickets to the dinner. Even the royal wedding of the "pure and unspoiled couple" (24) is deflated through its connection with the gross facts of physical reality. As the pig's throat is being slit and we hear her cries from the bathroom, Joyce is waxing lyrical about the ceremonial pageantry that England does so well. "Oh, England. It's like a fairy tale," she trills to Betty's dying cries (103).

"To take the edge off Betty's death" (10), Bennett and the director, Malcolm Mowbray, decided to add a coda to the film, a scene in which Gilbert and Allardyce, one of Swaby's crowd, both of whom had fallen in love with Betty and tried their feeble best to save her, are seen raising another piglet in secret. This addition works nicely in the film, giving it a more familiar comic ending with new life and proud parents. It doesn't wipe away the darker aspects of the film, just relieves a little the audience's uneasiness at being so amused by the often nasty proceedings.

We know, or should know, as Bennett says, that this "piglet too will be dead by now" (10), and that Gilbert and Allardyce's soft-heartedness will never overcome the ruthlessness of Swaby and Joyce. Still, in a world where most people are reluctant to face up to the bestial origins of so much of their behavior, Bennett and Mowbray know that most of their audience will welcome a brighter ending.

NOTES

1. See Kenneth O. Morgan, *The People's Peace: British History 1945–1990* (Oxford: Oxford University Press, 1990).

2. Ned Chaillet, *Times* (London), October 16, 1980. "Back to back" refers to terraced houses whose backs abutted against one another; they were designed for the working classes mostly.

3. Michael Billington, *Guardian*, October 16, 1980.

4. Bergan, 172–3.

5. Bennett's diary entry for July 10, 1982, puts the Olivier remarks in context: "Olivier is much given to excessive and almost laughably insincere flattery; he described *Enjoy*, I remember, as the best play he had ever seen." (*WH*, 124).

6. *New York Times*, July 22, 1998.

7. Bennett has recently published a prose version of *Intensive Care* entitled "Father! Father! Burning Bright," *London Review of Books*, Dec. 9, 1999, 17–26.

8. Goffman, *The Presentation of Self*, 224.

9. Goffman, *The Presentation of Self*, 207; 222; 225.

10. Goffman, *The Presentation of Self*, 227.

11. Turner, 40.

12. Another scene, in which the mother sits on the toilet and contemplates the dead pig in the bathtub, was cut from the film because "it seemed to hold things up," (*PF*, 10) according to Bennett.

CHAPTER FOUR

Spies and Writers: Burgess, Blunt, Kafka, and Proust

The Old Country (1977)
An Englishman Abroad (1983/1988)
A Question of Attribution (1988)
Kafka's Dick (1986)
The Insurance Man (1986)
102 Boulevard Haussmann (1991)

Notorious spies and famous writers figure in Bennett's work in the 1980s almost as prominently as anonymous northerners figured in his earlier work. As early as 1977, Bennett wrote his first play about treason and espionage—*The Old Country*. As recently as 1991, he wrote a television play about a famous literary figure—*102 Boulevard Haussmann*. But, in an extraordinarily concentrated outpouring between 1983 and 1988, Bennett produced four plays—*An Englishman Abroad, Kafka's Dick, The Insurance Man,* and *A Question of Attribution*—about spies and writers. With one exception, the central characters are not fictional creations, but well-known historical figures, objects of almost unceasing attention and speculation, whose biographies and psyches Bennett explores with idiosyncratic sharpness and ambivalence. Examined side by side, these six plays suggest interesting parallels between the motives and methods of spies and writers. They represent a further development in Bennett's already evident fascination with the performance of identity and its burdens.

Guy Burgess and Sir Anthony Blunt, infamous English traitors who spied for the Soviet Union in the early years of the cold war, and Franz Kafka and Marcel Proust, two of the most celebrated European fiction writers of the twentieth century, seem to share neither similar interests nor congruent behaviors, since the clandestine performances of the spy and the public performances of the writer appear to be so different. Yet in Alan Bennett's imagination the links between writer and spy are clear.

As Richard Eyre, who directed both *Kafka's Dick* and *The Insurance Man* has noted, "Alan's fascinated by the idea of spying: the idea of being outside a society and at the same time within it. There's the sense that as a writer he's a spy on his own world: it's certainly one of the characteristics throughout his work."[1] If in the Italian adage the translator is a traitor, then the writer in Bennett's scheme of things also practices a form of betrayal as real as the secret agent's. Spies and writers are secret sharers in a literal sense; they observe where often they shouldn't, and they pass along what they have seen, often to the distress of those they have observed. They work best in solitude and isolation. In Bennett's world, their loyalties are often only to themselves, rather than to any ideology. The writer expresses himself for the sake of self-expression; the spy transgresses for the sake of transgression.

Yet, in one of Bennett's most trenchant ironies, his writers resist the public scrutiny that comes with their success. Like the accomplished spy, they want their work to be admired but their private lives to be exempt from tabloid gossip and speculation. This have-your-cake-and-eat-it-too attitude is not surprising in Bennett's spies who, as members of the English upper classes, are ensured by virtue of their social standing access to circles of power that are closed to ordinary mortals, circles that will close around them and offer protection if they are caught *in flagrante*. In Bennett's view, writers share a similar privilege relative to the rest of society, albeit a privilege of a different kind. They write, and the writer's freedom from the physical labor that defines work for the vast majority of humankind has always made Bennett, the son of a butcher from Leeds, feel the need to apologize for his good fortune. During the filming of *The Insurance Man* in Liverpool in the summer of 1985, Bennett noted in his diary that the economic depression in that city seemed to reproach him personally. "Work though it is," he reminds himself, "a play, however serious, is play, and play seems tactless where there is no work" (P2, 119).

A performative link joins the Traitor Trilogy (*The Old Country, An Englishman Abroad*, and *A Question of Attribution*) with the two Kafka plays (*Kafka's Dick* and *The Insurance Man*) and the Proust play (*102 Boulevard Haussmann*). Whether it's Proust as the genius who must be coddled, Guy Burgess as the madcap homosexual whose eccentricity disguises his subversion, or Kafka, who, with his false modesty, asks that all his work be burned after his death, Bennett presents these characters as performers. Yet these performances have a rich ambiguity that signals the growing complexity of Bennett's interpretations. Anthony Blunt, when he argues for a more contextual reading of his own treasonous actions, reminds us of the difficulty of reading the signifiers of performance. Gentleman spy and eccentric writer, eccentric spy and gentleman writer, each inhabits a closed society of his own devising, worlds within worlds that Bennett portrays sympathetically, wittily, and not a little enigmatically.

The Old Country (1977)

Bennett employs his love of ambiguity and irony in the opening scenes of this play to enormous effect. At first, everything and everyone on stage seems comfortably familiar. An English couple in their sixties, Hilary and Bron, await luncheon guests on the veranda of a summer house. Their house is crammed full of books, and they are dressed in that casually shabby way that identifies them as upper-middle-class intellectuals. They exchange the kind of small talk born of long familiarity, neither quite following the other's train of thought. Bron seems to dread the arrival of their guests, but Hilary doesn't notice because he's caught up in reminiscing about World War II and deceased friends from the War Office. They and their situation seem very ordinary until Hilary asks, "Where would you say this landscape could be? Other than here" (*P2*, 202). He answers his own question by proposing Scotland in a John Buchan spy novel like *The Thirty-Nine Steps*, where the ordinary hides the sinister, no one is really as he or she seems, and the young hero is betrayed by the very people he has trusted. "It is a trap," Hilary says, "this haven: the place where they had meant him to end up all along" (203). When Bron goes into the house, Hilary waves to an unseen figure in the garden and shouts, "Hello! Where've you been hiding yourself? You're quite a stranger. Nothing amiss, I hope?" (203). Is he addressing a neighbor, or is something happening here that doesn't quite fit our initial assumptions about these two people and this place? Bennett has laid the clues before us, but few viewers anticipate his great *coup de theatre*. Midway through the first act we learn that Hilary and Bron are not in Wiltshire or Hampshire, but in a *dacha* in the woods outside Moscow. They had fled to the Soviet Union fourteen years earlier when he was about to be arrested by British intelligence as a spy. The man Hilary has waved to is assigned by the Soviets to spy on them.

The main action of the play consists of the visit from England of Hilary's sister, Veronica, and her husband, Duff, who holds a high position in the Foreign Office. Their stated purpose is social: fourteen years is a long time to be without family connections. The half-spoken purpose is to persuade Hilary to come home and face punishment, which with Duff's influence will amount to little more than a slap on the wrist. But the real purpose is to force him back to England as half of a spy swap. Hilary is no longer of any use to the Russians, but the English are willing to forgive and forget to get one of their own home again. Duff's exertions for Hilary do not extend, however, to another defector/spy couple, Eric and Olga. They don't fit the proper social profile. Eric was a draughtsman in the Portsmouth dockyard and Olga, vaguely middle-European and Jewish, isn't even English. Although Eric recognizes Duff as the man he had a sexual encounter with in his youth, class trumps a shared bisexuality. Eric and Olga are left behind while Hilary and Bron are hustled into the black embassy cars and returned to England.

The Old Country is a play bathed in irony: Russia mistaken for England, the once-celebrated spy now the object of surveillance, the English upper classes embracing a traitor from their own set. Bennett takes particular delight in foregrounding two of these ironies: Hilary in betraying his country has not betrayed his class, and the subterfuge associated with espionage is also the cloak of everyday behavior.

All the characters in the play are skilled performers. Just as the veranda serves as a stage for Alec Guinness and Rachel Kempson—Hilary and Bron in the original West End production—it serves also as a stage on which the two main characters perform different roles for different audiences: ideological stalwarts for the Soviet watchman, happily adjusted exiles for Veronica and Duff, supportive comrades for Eric and Olga, and moral amnesiacs for one another. The more we investigate the behavior of all the characters, the more we see that everything is staged—nothing is accidental.

No one is more adept at acting a part than Hilary, and irony is his favorite vehicle for self-expression.[2] He delivers perhaps the most resonant rejoinder in the play when his wife, exasperated with his mocking mention of English staples like Fuller's walnut cake for afternoon tea, admonishes him, "Oh stop it. Stop it. You've no need to keep it up now." He corrects her, "Nothing to keep up, as you should know by now. The best disguise of all is to be exactly what you say you are. Nobody ever believes that" (269). Hilary *is* nostalgic about afternoon tea, but his ironic stance allows him to hide his mawkishness under a veil of sophisticated dismissal. Irony, however, is more than just Hilary's personal tic. According to him, it's the English way: "In England we never entirely mean what we say, do we? Do I mean that? Not entirely. And logically it follows that when we say we don't mean what we say, only then are we entirely serious" (247). For the English spy in particular, irony is both culturally "inescapable" and absolutely necessary. "We're conceived in irony. We float in it from the womb," Hilary reminds Duff. "It's the amniotic fluid. It's the silver sea. It's the waters at their priestlike task washing away guilt and purpose and responsibility. Joking but not joking. Caring but not caring. Serious but not serious" (263–4). Irony allows Hilary to keep an emotional distance from the implications of his treachery. He mocks E. M. Forster's famous statement—"If I had to choose between betraying my country and betraying my friend I hope I should have the guts to betray my country"—as "nancy rubbish" (251) because "friend" is Forster's code word for homosexual partner. That kind of intimate loyalty unnerves Hilary. His defection arises from no emotional or intellectual commitment. When pressed, he resists subscribing to any credo, offering only that his treachery arose from a desire "to be on one's own. Alone. If for no other reason than to be one's own worst enemy" (255). But he isn't alone. He has dragged Bron along with him into their own Soviet *huis clos*. It's little wonder that when Duff quotes another famous Forster line, "Only connect," Hilary replies, "I never quite understood what that meant" (224).

Bron tries to break through Hilary's wall of ironic detachment by reminding him of some of the horrific consequences of his betrayals. "People died. And not merely died. Eventually died. Good people. Friends." He protests only mildly, "That is true. It isn't altogether fair, but it's true" (264). Bron isn't being fair, that is, keeping embarrassing truths to herself, but that's partly because she doesn't have an ironic bone in her body. Her directness, however, does not preclude a well-developed ambiguity of motive and meaning about herself. She confesses, for instance, that she had once looked forward to reaching the age of fifty so that she could assume the role of the "wonderful woman," a paragon, as she explains it to Veronica, that could be performed only in England:

> A wise, witty, white-haired old lady, who's always stood on her own feet until one day at the age of eighty she comes out of the County Library and falls under the weight of her improving book, breaks her hip and dies, peacefully, continently and without fuss under a snowy coverlet in the cottage hospital. And coming away from her funeral in a country churchyard on a bright winter's afternoon people say, "She was a wonderful woman." That's what I wanted to be. Only here there's nobody to be it for.[3]

"Character," Bron insists, "needs an audience or what are you? Here, who's watching?" (242). Hilary isn't watching Bron; he's too busy watching himself watch himself. That leaves the "brute in the garden" (243) as Veronica calls him. But, as a Soviet functionary, he doesn't possess the cultural acumen to recognize the nuances of Bron's performance of the upper-middle-class Anglican lady. All he can do is watch Bron "gardening, getting up in the morning. Hilary reading, feeding the birds." Still, she concedes he'll have to do. "At least he's an audience" (244). Just before the Act 1 curtain, Bron sets out a lunch tray for their watcher, whose nourishment is now subliminally linked to that of the theater audience as it files out to find its own refreshments during the interval between the acts. Perhaps Bennett is suggesting that, like the Russians, we too are ill-prepared to catch the subtle depths of Bron's performance, not as the Anglican old lady, but as the dutiful wife uprooted and forced into exile because of her husband's treachery. She is not the contented helpmate she pretends to be. Remarks such as "Wives are part of the betrayal. Wives are part of the selling-out. Wives are settling for something" (252) reveal a bitterness that counterpoints Hilary's suave ironies, a bitterness, in fact, fueled by his ironies. Bron's performance is all the more impressive for being so much more restrained than Hilary's, but it's a performance nonetheless.

The odd symbiosis between the secret societies that spies must belong to and the closed circles that constitute the English upper classes is one of Bennett's mordant ironies. All four Cambridge spies who betrayed the English to the Soviets in the '40s and '50s—Guy Burgess, Donald McLean, Kim Philby, and Anthony Blunt—belonged to the ruling classes. The security and privilege of their station were such that they were trusted with state secrets almost implicitly, despite their political views. Like them, Hilary never concealed his left-wing sympathies, his "Bolshy" leanings. His sister, who wants everyone to know that she hasn't had the wool pulled over *her* eyes, gushes, "I always knew you were a big Stalin fan" (255). Hilary never had to hide his politics because as a member of the upper class— with an apparent investment in the status quo—his ideological positions were assumed to be ironic, a form of posturing that didn't need to be taken seriously. What real spy would be so open about his heterodoxy? Duff, the representative of Her Majesty's government in the spy swap, a sexual hypocrite and apologist for treason who has recently been awarded a knighthood, represents the power of that upper-class circle to protect and forgive its members. The moral obtuseness with which he wields his power comes across most clearly when he assures Hilary that a return to England would be in his best interest:

> Now I can't quite say, 'Come home. All is forgiven.' There are still one or two people who feel quite strongly. Time dwindles their number but the fact remains, there were deaths, disappearances. People . . . died. Some of them first class. And I think you will probably be made to stand in the corner for three or four years. . . . Librarian pushing your trolley round. Rather fun, I would have thought. (253)

It's hard to say what is most odious in this speech: Duff's regret that some of the people who remember Hilary's treachery are still alive, the ellipsis that reluctantly connects subject and predicate, or the notion that Hilary's expiation will cost him so little and may actually be enjoyable. Those Olgas and Erics who do not have access to the ruling class perquisites that Hilary and Duff share, who are not born members of the exclusive club that ultimately smooths the way for Hilary's repatriation, will be left in exile. Duff's mission to retrieve Hilary proves that old school ties are stronger than political differences or personal misbehavior, bearing out Hilary's cynical boast that only the murder of children guarantees social ostracism nowadays, "because any other crime will always find you friends" (257), especially if you start from a position of privilege and can act the part.

During the run of *The Old Country* in London, Bennett reports that the *Daily Telegraph* correspondent in Moscow found himself sitting next to the defector Kim Philby at the Bolshoi opera—a real example of the polite Establishment-Traitor nexus to set alongside the fictional one between Duff and Hilary. Philby said he had heard about Bennett's play, but didn't think it likely that Hilary was based on him. "This wasn't surprising," Bennett writes, "since if I'd had anybody in mind when writing the play it was not Philby but W. H. Auden, the play seeming to me to be about exile, a subject that does interest me, rather than espionage, which interests me not a bit." Auden had been heavily criticized in England during the war for emigrating to America, an act that seemed, if not treasonous, at least unpatriotic. As a left-leaning homosexual Auden also belonged to a circle who jokingly referred to themselves as the Homintern. In America, Auden was apparently troubled by his exile from England and never relinquished his sense of himself as an Englishman abroad, a paradox similar to Hilary's own and one that Bennett exploits even more wittily in his second spy play. "Still," the rarely insistent Bennett finally concedes, "Philby or Auden, the play ran, and who was I to complain?" (*WH*, 209). If Bennett ultimately refuses to insist on Auden over Philby as the inspiration for Hilary, it's because *The Old Country* is at heart a meditation on the persistence of national identity, of Englishness, perhaps the one identity even a master spy cannot disguise or extinguish.

An Englishman Abroad (1983/1988)

Bennett's second play about an upper-class traitor, in this case Guy Burgess, finds us back on familiar ground where exile is the price of espionage, and the psychological relationship of the spy to both his new homeland and the old country he has betrayed is the playwright's major interest. Bennett raises some of the same paradoxical questions about what constitutes the English national identity that he introduced in *The Old Country*, but with a wit and a moral ambivalence that is missing from the previous play.

There are two versions of *An Englishman Abroad*, the one made for television in 1983 and a streamlined stage adaptation, which, combined with *A Question of Attribution*, debuted in 1988 at the National Theatre as the double bill *Single Spies*. The television and stage versions of *An Englishman Abroad* don't differ much. Both begin with Bennett's witty juxtaposition of dour portraits of Marx, Lenin, and Stalin with the voice of Jack Buchanan—the English equivalent of Fred Astaire—singing "Who stole my heart away?" Both asserting and poking fun at the romantic appeal of Communism, this opening establishes a tone of sympathetic yet ironic distance. The major change in the stage version, in addition to a few new jokes and a few clarifications, is the use of the main characters, the Australian actress Coral Browne and the English traitor Guy Burgess, as narrators who summarize for us some scenes that were acted out in the television version. The stage version has no way to duplicate the impact of the alien, exotic Russian cityscape we see in the film (footage actually shot in Dundee and Glasgow), and concentrates instead on hermetic interiors that point up Burgess's solitude amid the shabbiness of his surroundings. Either way Burgess comes across as a stranger in a strange land.

Bennett first got the idea for the play during the run of *The Old Country* when Coral Browne came to see the show. Afterward, over dinner, she told Bennett and Alec Guinness the story of her encounter with Guy Burgess in Moscow in 1958, when she was playing Gertrude and Michael Redgrave was Hamlet during the Shakespeare Memorial Company's cultural exchange tour of the Soviet Union. Burgess had come backstage to speak with Redgrave, but had become violently ill. Redgrave called on Browne to help him with Burgess, and the next day Browne received a note from Burgess inviting her to lunch at his flat. There he talked her into taking his measurements and ordering him a new suit from his tailor in London. From this odd, brief encounter Bennett has created one of his most witty and appealing plays.

Guy Burgess, as conceived by Bennett and played by Alan Bates in the television version, has a raffish appeal that Hilary's ironic bitterness can't compete with. From the very beginning we know he can't be trusted (he steals Coral Browne's cigarettes, soap, Scotch, and face powder when left alone in her dressing room), but, when he's confronted with his theft and he replies, "One should have asked. One is such a coward" (*OA*, 238),[4] his upper-class manners disarm even his victim. The dislocation between action and speech creates a comic, even absurd, effect. Here is a notorious spy and traitor reduced to petty theft. Burgess's larceny can be chalked up to the scarcity of basic goods in Russia, although his appropriation of these items can also be seen as an extension of his upper-class sense of entitlement. Regardless, Coral Browne never recants her first impression: "I liked him. For all he was sick in my basin. Bags of charm" (231). Part of this charm is Burgess's apparent indifference to his reduced circumstances. He is watched all the time, allowed to leave his dingy flat only with the permission of his handlers, and must make do without such amenities as the fashionable clothing, elegant toiletries, and well-fitting dentures that set an English gentleman apart from his low-born countrymen. All Burgess has left is his well-bred gentleman's charm.

As an Australian actress and an outsider to the English system of upper-class male privilege, Coral Browne is the ideal emissary between Burgess and us, to say nothing of her usefulness to him as a sartorial go-between. The English friends he wants to hear gossip about—Cyril Connolly, Harold Nicolson, W. H. Auden, John Pope-Hennessey—are only names to her, and to most of us. She asks instead the questions we might ask if we were to meet a notorious spy, mostly variations on Why? Burgess (or Bennett) can't come up with anything more riveting than Hilary's answer in *The Old Country*—"Solitude" (245). We can only suppose that his answer suffices for her; sympathy for the pitiable contrast between Burgess's alcoholic loneliness and his old Etonian good breeding finally persuades her to carry his measurements to his Jermyn Street tailor. But she isn't being completely sentimental. While she sees the failings of the English system that nurtured him—we witness her endure an excruciating interview with two upper-class twits at the British Embassy—she doesn't excuse his betrayal.

Bennett has written her a speech that tempers indignation with compassion, along with some shrewd analysis of the English character from an outsider's perspective, pitched beautifully to capture her great lady of the theater persona:

> Listen, darling. I'm only an actress. Not a bright lady, by your standards. I've never taken much interest in politics. If this is communism, I don't like it because it's dull. And the poor dears look tired. But then, Leeds is dull and that's not communism. And look at Australia. Only it occurs to me we have sat here all afternoon pretending that spying, which was what you did, darling, was just a minor social misdemeanour, no worse. And I'm sure in some people's minds much better than being caught in a public lavatory the way gentlemen in my profession constantly are, and that it's just something one shouldn't mention. Out of politeness. So that we won't be embarrassed. That's very English. We will pretend it hasn't happened, because we are both civilised people. Well, I'm not English. And I'm not civilised. I'm Australian. I can't muster much morality and outside Shakespeare the word treason to me means nothing. Only, you pissed in our soup and we drank it. So. Very good. Doesn't affect me, darling. And I will order your suit and your hat. And keep it under mine. Mum. Not a word. But for one reason: because I'm sorry for you. Now in your book . . . in your real book . . . that probably adds my name to the list of all the other fools you've conned. But you're not conning me, darling. Pipe isn't fooling pussy. I know. (244–5)

The inherently English need to appear civilized and not display vulgar emotions like moral disapproval or shock is borne out by Coral's experience with Burgess's tailor and haberdasher. The tailor agrees that "Moscow or Maidenhead, mum is always the word" (248) when it comes to the indiscretions of the upper classes. He refers benignly to Burgess as "One of our more colorful customers. . . . Always getting into such scrapes, Mr. Guy" (248). The hatter notes with some amusement that the initials on Burgess's hat block are the same as those of the nation: "G.B. (*He smiles.*) Great Britain" (249). Not every clothier to the upper classes looks the other way as discreetly as these two, however. When Coral goes shopping at Burgess's request for "four pair of White or Off-White, and Navy Blue Silk" pajamas, "quite plain and only those two colours," she encounters a significant roadblock (249). The Manager at first merely says, "I'm afraid this gentleman no longer has an account with us, madam." When pressed by Coral to open it again, he politely refuses on the grounds that "the gentleman is a traitor, madam." Bennett then writes Coral another speech of outrage at the hypocrisy of the English, who didn't mind looking the other way when Burgess was only a notorious drunkard and homosexual. Her righteous indignation falls flat when, after her climactic line, "I tell you, it's pricks like you that make me understand why he went. Thank Christ I'm not English," the Manager quietly informs her that this firm isn't English either; it's Hungarian (250–1). The memories of the ruthless Soviet invasion of Hungary in 1956, two years before the action of the play, check Coral's increasingly blind partisanship for Burgess. The implications of his siding with a brutal regime, even if he himself did none of the actual killing, cannot be brushed aside.[5]

The tailor's and the hatter's more tolerant attitudes toward Burgess also raise complex moral questions. The tailor's conjunction of the center of Soviet power and a genteel English town on the Thames ("Moscow or Maidenhead, mum is always the word") suggests a degree of similarity between the closed secret society built by the Soviets and the protected world of the upper-class English, whose rank seems to absolve them from any censure that could be deemed "vulgar." The misreading of the phrase "a real gent" as "a real agent" (249) in one of Burgess's letters at the end of the play brings home in a pun the connection between the secret worlds of the spy and the English gentleman that Bennett first essayed in *The Old Country*. The hatter's identification of Burgess with the nation underscores the many ways in which Burgess, traitor or not, is irretrievably English. Like Hilary and Bron in *The Old Country*, Burgess relishes the signifiers of English life. For them, the comforting props were crossword puzzles, Lyons tea shops, the novels of Anthony Powell, and recordings of the choir of King's College, Cambridge. Burgess also carries the popular culture of England with him, though his tastes are more theatrical. Coral follows the sound of his voice reciting Tennyson's "The Lady of Shalott," when she is trying to find the door of his flat. She has to endure listening to Jack Buchanan singing "Who Stole My Heart Away" over and over again at lunch (it is his only record). And Burgess and his Russian boyfriend, Tolya, play Gilbert and Sullivan's "Take a Pair of Sparkling Eyes" from *The Gondoliers* on the accordion and harmonium (in the stage version it's a balalaika and pianola). In the TV play, the final image is of Burgess resplendent in his new outfit from his London tailor walking across a Moscow (actually Glasgow) footbridge in a snow shower while the sound-track swells with the chorus of "For He Is an Englishman" from *HMS Pinafore*.

Burgess, like Hilary before him, is aware of the paradox at the heart of the matter. He has betrayed his country, given its secrets to its enemy, but he has not severed his attachment to England. As he tries to explain to Coral after finishing an Elgar piece on the piano, "So little, England. Little music. Little art. Timid, tasteful, nice. But one loves it. Loves it. You see I can say I love London. I can say that I love England. I can't say that I love my country. I don't know what that means" (244). Perhaps this paradox is situated in the vaunted English disdain for abstractions, their preference for the empirical over the theoretical. Perhaps it's an expression of Forster's preference for the personal over the political, the greater courage lying in supporting one's friend rather than one's country. Perhaps it's Bennett assertion that culture is stronger than ideology, that what's bred in the bone cannot be removed by geographical dislocation or intellectual conversion.

There doesn't seem to be any single or simple answer to Burgess. He is Churchill's formula for the Soviet Union: "a riddle wrapped in a mystery inside an enigma." He has spent his life presenting himself to the world as he chooses, but because his world is steeped in the expectations of class role and class behavior, he has been invisible in plain sight of everyone. He corrects Coral Browne's comparison of him to Oscar Wilde—both homosexuals, both exiled for crimes against the society that once pampered them. "No, no," he insists. It's too easy an identification, too sentimental. "Though he was a performer. And I was a performer. (*He is looking at himself in the glass.*) Both vain. But I never pretended. If I wore a mask, it was to be exactly what I seemed" (243). Wilde denied his sexual behavior in all three of his court trials; he tried to "pass" until that was no longer an option. Burgess, by contrast, claims he never hid any of his antiestablishment views. His "analysis of situations, the precis I had to submit to the Foreign Office, were always Marxist." His saving grace was that he was a gentleman, and he cleverly followed the rule that "If you don't wish to conform in one thing, you should conform in all the others" (244). His colleagues remarked indulgently, as if speaking about a normally unexceptional child who shows a tiny streak of temperament: "'It's only Guy.' 'Dear old Guy.' . . . 'How can he be a spy? He goes to my tailor'" (244). Clothes make the man, as this play demonstrates so concretely. They also make the actor, because if we correctly interpret his statement "if I wore a mask, it was to be exactly what I seemed," Burgess is claiming that the performer's mask is ubiquitous, even when he attempts to be most himself.

The role of Guy Burgess is of course being played by Guy Burgess. As a political prize kept under wraps by the Soviets, he does much to please his audience. One of Bennett's stage directions reads, "The camera should be on Burgess at this point. There is the same sense that one had earlier, that inside the drunken buffoon is somebody watchful" (242). He carefully manages the impression he gives off. He makes Coral promise that she won't tell anyone about her mission to his tailor because "my people here wouldn't like that" (242). In a line that appears in the TV version but not in the printed script or the stage version, Burgess's farewell to Coral tries to correct any errors in the impression he might give to the old country, "I do like it here. Don't tell anyone I don't." Normally, Burgess doesn't have to narrate his meaning to Coral; he simply performs. His loud recitation of "The Lady of Shalott," for instance, a poem which tells of another unhappy prisoner, is no accident. Its very Englishness draws Coral to the right door, the right prisoner. In some ways, it is Burgess's performance of his Englishness that is his major enigma and triumph. As any actor will testify, once he learns his lines and knows his part in a long-running show, he plays it night after night almost by reflex. He could play it in his sleep, or, with a few minor adjustments, in another country, before speakers of another language. Being an English gentleman is just such a part for Burgess. His costume has become tatty and ragged (here's where Coral in the role of glorified wardrobe mistress enters), and the audience is not as responsive as he might hope (these out-of-town tryouts can be murder), but he doesn't have to worry too much because he has the part down cold.

A Question of Attribution (1988)

In 1997, Bennett was asked by the Sainsbury's Pictures for Schools foundation to choose four paintings currently hanging in British museums to be reproduced and distributed "with an information pack to schools local to Sainsbury's stores." Bennett was chosen for this annual effort to improve arts education because of his position as a trustee of the National Gallery and because of his fund of knowledge about painting. In an essay in the *London Review of Books* Bennett explained his four choices (Gossaert's *The Adoration of the Kings*, 1510; George Stubbs's *Hambletonian, Rubbing Down*, 1800; John Millais's *Lorenzo and Isabelle*, 1849; and Stanley Spencer's *Southwold 1937*) with his customary mixture of lightly worn erudition and cryptic autobiographical reference: "Looking at the four paintings I ended up choosing I can see that three of them have to do with my childhood, most obviously the Stanley Spencer with its echoes of prewar summers I was too young to remember."[6] Despite his elaborate and cogent readings of these four paintings, Bennett backs off at the end of the essay from claiming that his analysis of these works is the final one. "Sometimes," he confesses, putting himself in the role of his detested journalistic snoopers, "it's as if paintings were being doorstepped, art historians crowding in on them like reporters from the *Mirror* or the *Mail*. . . . And maybe, hearing what is said about them, some paintings might shrug, saying, 'Well, if you say so.' The Mona Lisa's smile is the smile of art" (10).

The enigmatic nature of art and of human behavior, and their resistance to definitive interpretations, are the twin themes of *A Question of Attribution*, the final part of Bennett's Traitor Trilogy. For years, there had been speculation that Burgess, Maclean, and Philby had had a fourth and perhaps a fifth accomplice. The central figure of the play is Sir Anthony Blunt, eminent art historian, director of the

Courtauld Institute, and Keeper of the Queen's Pictures, before he was publicly unmasked as the "fourth man" among the Cambridge spies. Set in the late '60s, the play is structurally triangulated among three overlapping investigations. First, there is Blunt demonstrating the scholarly detective work he performed in discovering a fourth and possibly a fifth figure hidden in *Triple Portrait*, a painting formerly attributed to Titian. Then, there is Blunt's own interrogation by Chubb, an investigator from British intelligence, MI5, who wants Blunt to name the names of other spies. And finally, there is a chance encounter at Buckingham Palace with the Queen herself, who quizzes Blunt on the nature of fakes, forgeries, and misattributed paintings. Each segment of the triangle resonates ironically with the other two in a tour de force demonstration of Bennett's powers of comic construction and witty yet sympathetic characterization.

Bennett's three main characters—Blunt, Chubb, and HMQ (Her Majesty the Queen)—are exceedingly sly and crafty players, all the more sly and crafty for appearing so artless. Blunt, the aristocratic aesthete who rubs elbows with the highest figures in the British social hierarchy and whose interests seem intimately tied up with maintaining the status quo, once spied for the Soviet Union, whose aim was to level all such hierarchies. If this kind of anomaly were not a sufficient disguise, Blunt throws up additional protective covering by "work[ing] rather hard at being a cold fish." Perhaps he thinks that playing the role of the remote scholar and snob will dissuade anyone from getting close enough to discover his secret political treachery (P2, 316). Chubb, the middle-class autodidact, exhibits deference to Blunt's social connections and professes to be in awe of his knowledge of art history. Chubb sees a direct link between social status and aesthetic taste. He envies Blunt's ease with both. "An art gallery," he confesses, makes him feel odd. "I always come out feeling restless and dissatisfied. Troubled. . . . What am I supposed to think? What am I supposed to feel? . . . I suppose for you an art gallery is home from home" (317–8). Yet Chubb's self-definition as an outsider who looks to the expert in the elite arts for instruction is useful in lulling Blunt into a false sense of superiority. Chubb is no naif. He is highly adept at subtle verbal coercion, feigning hurt in the best passive-aggressive manner—"I'm upset that you find our talks wearisome" (316)—in order to keep Blunt at the task of betraying his old acquaintances. Whenever Blunt resists identifying old photos of Cambridge friends, Chubb reminds him that he can always choose an unspecified "alternative," which to judge from Blunt's quick falling back into line must be public exposure and disgrace. And HMQ, in an exchange in which they discuss the provenance of paintings in her art collection, reveals a capacity for metaphor and suggestion that is as unnerving to Blunt as it is surprising to us. In some ways, she has created the persona most difficult of the three to penetrate. From birth HMQ has been schooled in impression management. The cool and gracious person we see in her public appearances is the product of years of training. It's no accident that Chubb asks Blunt, "What is she really like?" (316). The answer is that no one knows, perhaps not even HMQ herself. When Blunt comments to her that none of her official portraits quite captures her, she answers, "I hope not. I don't think one wants to be captured, does one? Not entirely, anyway" (338). In their shared abilities to conceal some essential aspect of their actions or motivations, Blunt, Chubb, and HMQ are, in a sense, all secret agents, at least in the performative aspects of espionage.

The scenes between Blunt (who was played by Alan Bennett in the original National Theatre production) and HMQ (played by Prunella Scales) were something of a cause celebre; this was the first time a living monarch had been portrayed as a character on the English stage. Bennett treats HMQ with respect and flatters her with a wit and an intelligence few have attributed to her. Despite her complaint that "whenever I meet anybody they're always on their best behaviour. And when one is on one's best behaviour one isn't always at one's best" (335), Bennett presents HMQ both at her best and on her best behavior. The topic she and Blunt discuss is the question of attribution, how to assign a painting its true provenance, which includes the identity of the artist who painted it as well as the meaning he intended in painting it. Their surface remarks conceal an unacknowledged subtext, which occasionally peeks through. In a linguistic cat and mouse game, where everything they say is weighted with implications beyond the literal matter at hand, Blunt attempts to deflect HMQ's use of the terms "forgery" and "fake" into a less judgmental channel:

HMQ: I suppose that is part of your function, Sir Anthony, to prove that my pictures are fakes?

Blunt: Because something is not what it is said to be, Ma'am, does not mean it is a fake. It may just have been wrongly attributed. . . . A painting is a document, Ma'am. It has to be read in the context of art history. (333)

Blunt of course is hoping that he will be judged in a similar contextual framework. In the economic depression of the 1930s, to be a communist was "the right thing to do at the time" (313), so he is not a fake, or traitor, but merely mislabeled according to the prevailing but limited knowledge of the present day. When HMQ later uses the word *forgery* and asks "Have I many forgeries?" Blunt is quick to correct her: "Paintings of this date are seldom forgeries, Ma'am. They are sometimes not what we think they are, but that's different. . . . Paintings make no claims, Ma'am. They do not purport to be anything other than paintings. It is we, the beholders, who make claims for them, attribute a picture to this artist or that" (342–3). As in Burgess's claim that "If I wore a mask it was to be exactly what I seemed," Blunt wants to place all the interpretive responsibility on the audience. But HMQ won't buy that argument. Sometimes the deception is active. "With respect, Sir Anthony," she replies, "rubbish. What if a painting is signed and the signature is a forgery?" (343). There are cases in modern art (and politics, for which art is the clear analogy) where claims have been made by artists with deliberate intent to deceive. These are not the mistakes of art historians working with insufficient information, but the efforts of con men. In her closest, though still oblique, approach to Blunt's case, she succinctly turns the tables on Blunt by appropriating his insistence on context and showing how one kind of context, a pedigree, can be used to conceal, not reveal, the real nature of a reputed masterpiece, and, by extension, an upper-class traitor:

> I suppose too the context of a painting matters. Its history and provenance (is that the word?) confer on it a certain respectability. This can't be a forgery, it's in such and such a collection, its background and pedigree are impeccable—besides, it has been vetted by the experts. Isn't that how the argument goes? So if one comes across a painting with the right background and pedigree, Sir Anthony, then it must be hard, I imagine, even inconceivable—to think that it is not what it claims to be. And even supposing someone in such circumstances did have suspicions, they would be chary about voicing them. Easier to leave things as they are in every department. Stick to the official attribution rather than let the cat out of the bag and say, "Here we have a fake." (344)

Like Chubb, HMQ disarms Blunt with her amateur's views on art. The questions, parenthetical and otherwise, present the appearance of deference to the expert, but they disguise her command of the present situation and her reading of Blunt's own. His credentials resemble those of paintings whose provenance almost defies exposure. We also can tell from her concluding comment about keeping the cat in the bag that HMQ will not be the one to expose him. Her parting remarks reveal, however, that she enjoys letting him know that she is in on his secret. "Be careful how you go up the ladder, Sir Anthony," she solicitously reminds him. "One could have a nasty fall" (345). Blunt had asked Chubb earlier in the play whether anyone else knew about his double identity. Chubb's matter-of-fact reply, "Somebody had to be told. You were promised immunity, not anonymity" (327), must ring in Blunt's ears at this point. To the question from one of his assistants about the nature of his conversation with HMQ, Blunt testily replies, "I was talking about art. I'm not sure that she was."[7]

Getting the label right (Titian, Botticelli, patriot, spy, traitor) is not the whole story, however. There is also the question of understanding what you have labeled. In addition to the falsely attributed *Triple Portrait*, Blunt discusses a painting correctly attributed to Titian, his *Allegory of Prudence*, "an emblematic painting, a puzzle picture. A visual paraphrase of the *Three Ages of Man*, obviously, but something else besides" (325). "Something else" is what Bennett is getting at in this play, or, more precisely, what this play or anyone else cannot get at: how exactly to read the signs in front of us. Chubb, at the start of his education in iconography, sees the dog, the lion, and the wolf in the painting, and he assigns them their usual values: fidelity for the dog, gluttony for the wolf. But Blunt has to correct his reading because, placed in the context of the lion, "they are disparate parts of a three-headed beast which from classical times onwards has been a symbol of prudence" (325). Interpretation isn't always a rote exercise in which constant equivalents can be assigned to phenomena, whether icons in art or behavior in people. Understanding their contextual positioning is crucial, as Goffman's "frame analysis" also proposes. When Blunt tells Chubb that "appearances deceive. Art is seldom what it seems" (326), he is simply asking to be allowed the same latitude in the interpretation of his own behavior. He knows how unlikely that will be and ruefully understands that, "as a fake I shall, of course, excite more interest than the genuine article" (350). Chubb is undeterred. He presses to get to the bottom of the spy scandal: "There is someone else. Someone behind you all. All the evidence points to it" (350). But Blunt looks at the *Triple Portrait*, with its layers of figures, some exposed, some hidden, and at *The Allegory of Prudence*, with its meaning only accessible to someone with knowledge of the context of its iconography, and resists offering Chubb an answer: "But who are they all? I don't know that it matters," replies Blunt. "Behind them lurk other presences, other hands. A whole gallery of possibilities. The real Titian an Allegory of Prudence. The false one an Allegory of Supposition. It is never-ending" (351). Chubb and Blunt sit staring at one another, at an impasse, until the lights fade and the curtain falls. The Mona Lisa's smile is the smile of Bennett's art too.

Kafka's Dick (1986)

If it's true that "Englishness is really Bennett's only subject,"[8] and that "Alan Bennett country" consists of that "grey world north of Watford,"[9] then Franz Kafka seems "an unlikely subject for a Bennett play."[10] If we think, however, of the dark absurdist elements in so many of his TV plays, to say nothing of the tragicomic farcicalities of *Habeas Corpus* and *Enjoy*, Kafka seems a remarkably logical interest: "Kafka's 'fun and pain,' irony, self-deprecation and paradoxes are all qualities of Bennett's writing too."[11] In addition, Kafka and Bennett share a similar, almost constitutional, ambivalence. What Max Brod says in this play about Kafka applies equally well to Bennett: "He was always in two minds," a condition that allows both of them to see the horrors of existence and yet appreciate the absurd comedy inherent in those horrors (*P2*, 97).

In *Kafka's Dick*, Bennett has imagined Kafka turning up in contemporary England to discover that, contrary to his deathbed request, all his unpublished writings have not been burned and that he has become "with Flaubert, Tolstoy, and Dostoevsky" one of the "greatest names in literature" (68). The modern artist's conflicted desires for fame and for privacy, for exposure and for concealment (to use terminology also appropriate to Hilary, Burgess, and Blunt, who sought concealment but were forced to accept exposure), are the central themes of the play. As the rude title of the play indicates, the price of such fame and exposure is as heavy as the price of its opposite—obscurity and oblivion. Kafka learns that in the hands of the critics his writings are not imaginative creations but psychological templates, or quarries from which "facts" about his personal character and experiences can be extracted. Among the indignities Kafka suffers is the knowledge that nothing about his private life, even his penis size, has escaped the scrutiny and speculation of critics and biographers.[12] In an era increasingly obsessed with celebrity, and with gossip about celebrities, Bennett shrewdly foresees in the mid-1980s how biography will become the valorized art form of the late twentieth century and the critic/biographer its dominant literary figure.

According to Bennett, the general public, with no real literary interests or sensitivity, has digested these tidbits of biographical information dispensed by the critics as if they were all one needed to know about literature and its creators. For instance, Linda, the unschooled wife of yet another would-be biographer of Kafka, prides herself on her command of the salient gossip about major literary figures. "I know that Auden never wore underpants and Mr Right for E. M. Forster was an Egyptian tramdriver," she says. "Only some day I'll learn the bits in between," she reassures herself (111). But, as Bennett knows, it's the prurient detail that sticks forever in the mind. Those "bits in between," which are nothing less than the writer's works themselves, have nearly become irrelevant. As her husband, Sydney, has to remind her, "Oh Linda. There's no need [to learn the 'bits in between']. This is England. In England facts like that pass for culture. Gossip is the acceptable face of intellect" (111–2). Bennett's feelings about gossip are always ambivalent, but when it comes to biographical writing, which he sees as a license to print gossip, his distaste is unmistakable. In addition to having a character call biographers "academic blow flies" (41), Bennett has himself equated them with assassins. Speaking of Sydney, he comments, "As he works on his piece Sydney comes to resent his subject, as biographers must often do. Biographers are only fans after all, and fans have been known to shoot their idols" (21).

This kind of hyperbole suits the farcical tone of *Kafka's Dick*, which borrows several of the more familiar motifs of Kafka's works, including metamorphosis, oedipal conflicts, and the terrors of bureaucratic power, and turns them into jokes. Bennett recognizes the danger in the "temptation to English Kafka and joke him down to size" by passing him through the English Channel's "slipper bath of irony" (3). But he can't resist and doesn't care to.[13] "There is something that *is* English about Kafka," Bennett explains, "and it is not only his self-deprecation. A vegetarian and fond of the sun, he seems a familiar crank. . . . He is the young man in a Shaw play who strolls past the garden fence in too large shorts to be accosted by some brisk Shavian young woman who, perceiving his charm, takes him in hand, puts paid to his morbid thoughts and makes him pull his socks up" (3). Bennett's Kafka is not everyone's Kafka, that is certain. In some ways, his version of Kafka may say more about Bennett himself than it says about the historical Kafka. (As we'll see, the Kafka of *Kafka's Dick* isn't even the Kafka of Bennett's TV play *The Insurance Man*.) Looked at from a performative perspective, Kafka in *Kafka's Dick* takes on an entirely different character—not so much the Shavian callow youth but more the straight man in a vaudeville routine, always exasperated by the unpredictable antics of his zany partner.

The play begins in 1919, with Kafka on his deathbed, although he will live another five years—one of Bennett's subtler jokes. As he struggles to ask his friend

Max Brod to burn all his writings after his death, we detect something of a performance under way. Max is obtuse and consistently reacts in inappropriate ways. At first, he frustrates Kafka with his slow grasp of his meaning; then he alarms him with his eagerness to carry it out.

Kafka: Where are you going?
Brod: To buy paraffin.
Kafka: Max. Stay a minute. After all, my writings are worthless. They wouldn't survive anyway. They don't deserve to survive.
    Pause
    Don't you think so?
Brod: You're the one who's dying. I'm Max, your faithful friend. You say burn them, I burn them. (*Going again*) Maybe I'll get petrol instead.
Kafka: Max! (*Pause.*) If you want to read them first, feel free . . . just to remind you. (29)

If Kafka is hoping for some resistance from Brod, he's mistaken. Brod is not going to flatter Kafka's vanity by insisting that his work be spared for posterity. He's just a friend, who'll do whatever his friend wants. Kafka's tormented wavering between his desire for oblivion and his hunger for immortality is intensified when Brod anachronistically tells Kafka that the Nazis will burn the books of the great writers Freud, Proust, Rilke, Joyce, and Gide. "Burn books?" Kafka responds, "Who in his right mind would want to burn books? They must be sick" (31). But his work won't be among them. Max rubs it in.

Brod: People will look at the credits and say: They burnt Proust. They burnt Brecht. They burnt Joyce. Where is Kafka? Not worth burning, maybe.
Kafka: God. I was depressed before. Now I'm suicidal.
Brod: Maybe I can fix it.
Kafka: You think?
Brod: I can see it now: a shot of flames licking round a book jacket, the name Kafka prominently placed.
Kafka: Dreadful.
Brod: Sure, but burn one and you sell ten thousand. Believe me, if the Nazis hadn't thought of it the publishers would.
Kafka: Max, I'm still not sure. Do I want to survive? (31–2)

It's only when Max refers to the bug in *Metamorphosis* as a cockroach that Kafka realizes that he can't allow his words to be left to the mercy of posterity. It's not a cockroach but a beetle, he insists. "That's the trouble with words. You write one thing, the reader makes it into another" (32). End of ambivalence. Burn them all, he demands.

The rest of Act I is set in contemporary England, in the home of Sydney and

Linda. Bennett's instructions about the set establish the oddness of the situation: "I am not sure how representational the room should be. Since some of the happenings that take place in it are downright unreal perhaps the room should look unreal also, but the reverse could be more convincingly argued. An over-scrupulous naturalism would be out of place, though the reality of the bookcase is crucial" (33–4). "Downright unreal" is an understatement. Downright absurd would be more like it. Max Brod, long dead, rings the doorbell to apologize for urinating on the family tortoise. When Linda rinses the tortoise under the tap and kisses it (offstage), it metamorphoses into the even longer dead Franz Kafka. These oddities bother Linda a little but Sydney not at all. He's simply starstruck to be in the presence of his idol and his idol's closest friend. Sydney and Brod conspire to prevent Kafka's discovery that Brod has broken his promise to burn all his work. Being a person and being a famous person are not the same, as Brod explains to Sydney: "He knows he's Kafka. He doesn't know he's *Kafka*" (55). Bennett cranks up the farce engine to keep Kafka just a step behind Brod and Sydney's efforts to clear away all evidence of books by and about Kafka from the overloaded bookcase. But of course the slapstick machinery—the frantic hiding of books, the insistence that Kafka is misreading titles on the shelf (not *Kafka's Novels*, but *Tarzan's Navel*)—eventually runs down, and Brod must admit that he's made him "into one of the biggest names in twentieth-century literature" (68). The only consolation Kafka can find in his despair is the wish that he could witness his father's reaction to his fame. "Pride," suggests Linda. "Disgust," replies Kafka.

The father-son relationship is a rare theme in Bennett's work. If he ever examines parent-child relationships, it's usually between mother and son.[14] In dealing with Kafka, however, Bennett has one of the most famously antagonistic father-son relationships in modern literary history to work with, and he ties that conflict in to the theme of modern literary celebrity. Bennett's treatment of oedipal conflict is wide ranging. In addition to the Kafkas, it also includes the light comedy of Sydney and his father, who is repeatedly reassured by his son that he's not going to be sent to a rest home even as Sydney and Linda wait for the social services people to come and take him away. Although Father is given lines that paraphrase Joseph K's in *The Trial*—"Someone's been telling lies about me" (401)— and, like Joseph K, he must deal with a faceless bureaucracy that can arbitrarily condemn him to an institution, Father is never pitiable in his bewilderment. He is the *senex* of Roman comedy, and Bennett exploits parallels with *The Trial* for laughs. For example, Father keeps prepping to pass the standard mental acuity test (the name of the prime minister, today's date), which he believes will save him from the rest home. But always entering the scene a minute or two late, behind his walker frame, and overhearing conversations that have no bearing on him, he becomes increasingly alarmed that the information he is expected to know has escalated from the prime minister's name to the name of famous Czech authors, from today's date to the true nature of Kafka's relationship with his father. In short, he imagines that he has to be up on all the latest permutations in Kafka Studies. Academic trends and fads being what they are, Father cannot keep up with the dizzying changes and admits defeat. "I give up," he says. "Put me away. My limited studies of Kafka have convinced me that being a vegetable is not without its attractions" (109).

Hermann Kafka, however, is not a father who easily concedes defeat. He demands pity for what he sees as a son's betrayal. The analogy he chooses to define his son's line of work—"A book is a coffin and in it is your father's body" (86)— is, of course, *chutzpah* of the highest order, coming from the bullying father whose choice of epithets for his son include "you teetering column of urine," "you two-faced pisspot," and "you soiled bandage" (88, 89, 92). Bennett presents Hermann K., who enters the play as a policeman, as every inch the monster his son described in "Letter to His Father." He is overbearing, crude, lewd, and castrating. And oddly shrewd about impression management. When he decides that he's tired of the heavy's role in which posterity has cast him and wants to revise his reputation into something more warmly paternal, he blackmails his son into cooperation by threatening to reveal that Franz's penis doesn't measure up to his own. But in the world of literary biography where gossip and conjecture, according to Bennett, often pass for scholarship, the size of Kafka's dick is already old news.

Hermann K:	Putting it bluntly: his old man doesn't compare with his old man's old man. His. Mine. (*He makes an unequivocal gesture.*)
Sydney:	But I know that. Everyone knows that.
Linda:	Even I know that.
Kafka:	You? How?
Sydney:	(*finding the book*) Dreams, Life and Literature. A study of Kafka by Hall and Lind, University Press, North Carolina.
Linda:	So you see, your private parts have long been public property. (107)

When Hermann, ever resilient, realizes that it's only the bad fathers who make it into the public record, and that if he had been the model father perhaps Kafka would never have needed to write, and he, Hermann, would mean nothing to posterity, he is happy to revert to his role as villain. Fame is everything, after all, regardless of its source. It's only because the Kafkas, *pere et fils*, and Max Brod are famous that they can reappear after their deaths in a middle-class English living room. In the twentieth century, fame, not moral virtue, is the guarantor of an after-life, as Hermann now knows. "Bad fathers are never forgotten. They jump out of the wardrobe. They hide under the bed. They come on as policemen. Sons never get rid of them. So long as my son's famous, I'm famous. I figure in all the biographies, I get invited to all the parties. I'm a bad father, so I'm in the text" (108). As Bennett himself remarks in his Introduction to the play,

Hermann Kafka has had such a consistently bad press that it's hard not to feel a sneaking sympathy for him as for all the Parents of Art. They never get it right. They bring up a child badly and he turns out a writer, posterity never forgives them—though without that unfortunate upbringing the writer might never have written a word. They bring up a child well and he never does write a word. Do it right and posterity never hears about the parents; do it wrong and posterity never hears about anything else.

Quoting Philip Larkin's notorious lines, "They fuck you up your Mum and Dad," Bennett continues, "and if you're planning on writing that's probably a good thing. But if you are planning on writing and they haven't fucked you up, well, you've got nothing to go on, so then they've fucked you up good and proper" (7).

When Kafka congratulates himself that at least he has escaped the thankless role of father, Brod reminds him, "You don't need to have children in order to be a father. You were so dedicated to writing, so set on expressing yourself even if it killed you, which it eventually did, that, like the best and worst of fathers you have been an example and a reproach to writers ever since" (109). According to Bennett, Kafka in his role as the "last, authentic, modern saint" (42), whose Hunger Artist "always wanted you to admire [his] suffering," has in his own way set a standard for artistic endeavor that has intimidated succeeding generations of writers and molded their perceptions of the artist's role in society. Kafka, famously anxious himself, has been responsible for inducing the Bloomian "anxiety of influence" in future generations of writers. One of the reasons there are fifteen thousand entries in the Kafka critical library is that his life seems to exemplify what Bennett has Sydney call "the myth of the artist's life": "art is not a gift, it is a transaction, and somewhere the account has to be settled." We like biography in this vein because "we like to be told, you see, that you can't win" (112), and so the writer's life becomes a cautionary tale. The artist pays for his or her gift, either in madness, poverty, or early death. It's a romantic myth that Bennett has no patience with. Kafka is the Father of All Suffering Artists, and *Kafka's Dick* is, in one sense, Bennett's own oedipal quarrel, one literary son's debunking of the model literary parent.

The final scene is a metamorphosis and an apotheosis, set in a jokey Heaven where Max Brod is the Recording Angel, Sydney is Leonard Woolf, Linda is Nurse Cavell, Sydney's father is Bertrand Russell, and Hermann Kafka is God the Father. Kafka takes one look and decides that "Heaven is going to be Hell," not just because he's stuck with his father in charge but because in this Heaven there are only celebrities (Nurse Cavell puts on Carmen Miranda's headgear to dance with God), only famous people being famous at a cocktail party. When Kafka asks if God/Hermann has finally read his books, the Father rebukes his son (his only begotten?), "Are you still on about that? No, of course not. No fiction here any-way. No writing. No literature. No art. No need. After all what were they? Echoes, imitations. This is the real thing" (115). This real thing is Heaven invented by a gos-sip columnist for a celebrity-saturated age. You make it into this pantheon on the weight of being a name that people remember, not according to the quality of your life's work. How many people, after all, have actually read Bertrand Russell or Leonard Woolf? Most of us know of them as pacifists or patient husbands, not thinkers or writers. At the end of the first act, Kafka asserts his right to a life after death when he says, "I'm famous. I exist" (71), the implied *ergo* between the two statements making fame the modern substitute for Cartesian ratiocination. By the end of the play, however, Kafka has learned that the implications of the equation of fame with eternal life are much more sinister than he had originally imagined.

As a writer whose insistence on his own privacy is well known, Bennett is understandably disdainful of academics who pry into a writer's private life and call the results of that activity literary criticism. Yet Bennett's characteristic irony shows up even here. He has appropriated Kafka's life and dragged into full view embarrassing speculations about his private anatomy to show, explicitly, how artists' lives are exploited by critics without their permission. Struck by this inconsistency, Daphne Turner has argued that "logically, Bennett ought not to be writing the play at all" (126), because "desiring not to be invaded or written on, he himself is writing about Kafka not wanting to be invaded or written about" (125). It needs hardly to be stressed, however, that consistency and even logic are not necessarily the artist's defining marks. *Kafka's Dick*, as Michael Billington noted in his review of the original production, "is a play in which formal perfection is often sacrificed to exuberant theatricality and in which there are almost too many ideas; but it is held together by Bennett's overriding, humane belief that our joy and delight in artistic creation has been replaced by nit-picking analysis and prurient fact-gathering."[15] Bennett's ability to be, like Kafka, "always in two minds" (97) about almost everything is one of the paradoxical delights of this work.

The Insurance Man (1986)

Shown on BBC2 seven months before *Kafka's Dick* was staged at the Royal Court, *The Insurance Man* is Bennett's other play about Kafka. This TV play presents a darker and more philosophical exploration of the search for justice and the persistence of betrayal in human experience than does *Kafka's Dick*, with its mostly comic treatment of a contemporary culture that prefers gossip to aesthetic understanding. Bennett's presentation of the varieties of injustice and treason committed every day—some personal, some institutional, some inadvertent, some deliberate—places *The Insurance Man* closer to the ambiguities of spirit and tone in the Traitor Trilogy than to its lighthearted apparent companion piece.

In this play, Kafka is not the central character. That part is taken by a young man named Franz who applies for compensation to the Workers Accident Insurance Institute in Prague in 1910 for a skin condition he claims has been caused by his employment in a dyeworks. The only sympathetic bureaucrat he comes across in his search for a hearing is Kafka in his role as an insurance executive, the Kafka his contemporaries knew, not Kafka the writer, whom later generations would come to know.[16] Instead of compensation, he offers the young man a position in his brother-in-law's asbestos factory. Franz's skin clears up, but in his escape from the dyeworks to the asbestos factory he exchanges one doom for another, as the prologue and epilogue set in 1945 Prague point out. With the Russians on the outskirts of the city in the last days of World War II—another liberation that will prove an enslavement—Franz makes his way to a doctor's office past a body hanging on a lamppost with the sign "Traitor" on its chest. The doctor can't put a name to Franz's lung problems (his chest too has betrayed him), but he recognizes the probable implications of Franz's time in the asbestos factory. "You breathed in the wrong place," is all he will venture. He is more forthcoming about the body hanging outside his office: "I heard him battering at some door last night, begging to be let in. Somebody was after him. Then the door was opened and he thought he was safe. But they were there first. Take care" (P2, 192). *The Insurance Man* is structured on this parable and this paradox.

Bennett, with the visual assistance of the director, Richard Eyre, has created a world of absurd and dark ironies, where the gravest danger often lurks in the apparent haven. The film has a washed out, monochromatic look to it, almost as if it were shot in black and white. The camera peers up and down long spiralling staircases and elevator shafts to give a feeling of dislocation or vertiginous entrapment in spiralling webs. The interiors of the Workers Accident Insurance Institute, filmed at the cathedral-like St. George's Hall, Liverpool, are often overexposed to give a blanched unreality to the setting. Orson Welles's visual style for his 1960 film of *The Trial*—backlighting, dramatic applications of chiaroscuro—was an important influence on Eyre's lighting choices, though not on his use of space. Welles's familiar "vast hangar in which hundreds of clerks toil at identical desks to an identical routine" has no place here. Bennett insists that Welles missed out on the essentially hermetic nature of Kafka's world and invokes instead the warrens and burrows of *Alice in Wonderland* and the urban garrets of Dickens as the appropriate analogues for Kafka's topography (12). A great deal of the power of this TV play derives from the dreamlike qualities Eyre evokes through the expressionistic use of light and shadow, and of confined, cramped, sunless interiors. His direction serves Bennett's script beautifully.

Kafka, played by Daniel Day-Lewis as slightly hunch-shouldered and given to gnomic utterances in a high sing-song voice, refers to the Workers Accident Insurance Institute as "this kingdom of the absurd where it does not pay to be well, where loss determines gain, limbs become commodities and to be given a clean bill of health is to be sent away empty-handed" (184). But for all his acuteness, Kafka is surprised when Franz tells him, "this is a terrible place." "Is it?" he replies, "I always forget that. I find it . . . almost cosy" (188). The paradoxes run to greater depths of absurdity than Kafka the insurance man realizes (though Kafka the writer did), depths that only a petitioner can see. Ostensibly established to serve its claimants and compensate them for their injuries, the Institute in practice exists to frustrate and deny all claims, either by wearing the claimants down through bureaucratic hoop-jumping and delay or by turning the tables on the claimants and questioning their entitlement to relief. One bureaucrat reminds a claimant, "Just because you are the injured party, it doesn't mean you're not the guilty party" (148). The staff seems to enjoy humiliating those they are supposed to aid and serve. These are Goffmanian teams in a perverse social universe who unite to display open contempt and disrespect for their audience, thereby betraying the most basic laws of social interaction. Unlike the Gatekeeper in Kafka's "Before the Law," they are real obstacles, not the mental constructs of the claimants. Speaking about a maimed client, one amused functionary tells another, "So, having fed himself into his machine, we now feed him into ours. Ha!" (155).

Paradoxically, the claimants never stop coming; driven by a hopeless yearning for satisfaction, they storm the citadel of the unattainable love object like smitten suitors. The ruder the staff is, the closer the claimants bond to them, betraying their own dignity and sometimes sacrificing their sanity, as seen in the character of Lily, a crazed claimant reminiscent of Miss Flite in Dickens's *Bleak House*, a Kafkaesque view of bureaucratic excess three-quarters of a century before Kafka. Even the rare successful petitioner seems to be driven mad by the sudden shock of his success. "I've got it. I've got my claim," a man shouts as he runs deliriously up a grand staircase. "I've got it. I've got my claim. I've got it. I've got it. I've got it . . . My claim . . . I've got it, I've got it, I've got it. I've got my claim. I've got it" (163).

The Insurance Man raises again some of the oldest questions about the human condition, such as how to find justice in a world where fairness is not recognized as a charter right and where some would deny any remedy for misfortune, regardless of who is at fault. It should come as no surprise that Bennett looks at the question from several angles. Just as he despises the staff of the Insurance Institute for the contempt they inflict on their customers, he also shows the corrupting influence of relying on the notion of compensation. In their search for reasons, cures, and monetary rewards for the injuries that life and their occupations have dealt them, the claimants undergo a curious change. They become their injuries: Man Without Ear, One-Legged Man, Maimed Woman. Their lives are now consumed by the quest for a favorable ruling from the Tribunal, admittance before which is reserved for those who have earned it through long perseverance, for instance the One-Legged Man—"it's taken me six months to get this far"—or the Bald Man—"it's taken me a year" (166). Some even take pride in their disfigurements as marks of distinction, which earn them compliments from surgeons, people they would never otherwise mix with. The One-Legged Man enjoys the doctor's compliment on the neatness of the amputation: "'You got that fast in the loom? . . . Well, you're lucky . . . If I'd had to take it off in the theatre I couldn't have done it cleaner than that.'" The One-Legged Man even admits that he's adapted fairly well to the loss. "It's a bit unsightly," he says, "but I'm not incommoded. In some respects the reverse. More room in the bed; more scope for manoeuvre. I haven't noticed the wife complaining" (165).

Lily is of course the most egregious example of the damage that can result from an obsession with compensation. Her injury is not visible on the body, but festers in the mind and in the spirit. When she appears before a theater of medical students as a case study, the Lecturer outlines her story:

A box fell on her head. She took a few days off and she felt none the worse. But then she heard that in this enlightened age there is compensation for those that suffer injury at work. 'Is she entitled to this?' she wonders. And the wondering turns to worrying as she begins to lie awake at night suffering from headaches. She is increasingly unhappy. And so begins her quest for compensation but for what? Not the injury, for she has scarcely suffered one. And she is not malingering for the headaches are real. And to those of you who say there is no injury therefore there can be no compensation she can say, 'But I was not like this before my accident. I had no quest. Looking for what is wrong with me is what is wrong with me! (181–2)

More than once we hear someone in authority urge the injured to "try and lead a normal life" (152, 168), which rather than settling a course of action for the claimant raises new questions about the constitution of normality. Injury without complaint? Resignation to imperfection? One of the doctors on the Tribunal, the Angry Doctor, gives the most cogent expression of the traditional Christian view of the postlapsarian human condition. In high dudgeon he shouts, "We cannot compensate people for being cast out of Paradise." If they have learned from their injuries that they once existed in a happier state, "they have achieved wisdom. And a degree of self-knowledge. They should be paying us, not we them" (172). Not constrained by the Christian tradition, Kafka takes the opposite position. He responds to his secretary's sarcastic remark, "People will be wanting compensation for being alive next," with an expression that Bennett in his stage directions suggests "looks as if this might not be a bad idea" (188).

It is of course ironic that insurance should be Kafka's profession, Kafka who demonstrated in his writings that nothing in this world could be safeguarded—in Joseph K's case, not even the memory of his own actions. In this play, Bennett's Kafka is obviously smarter than his colleagues, and it's not just his doctorate and intellectual refinement that set him above their uniformly petty jealousies and crude gropings of the female staff. He's also more conscious of the performative requirements of his role as the insurance man. As one of only two Jews among a staff of four hundred, he knows that diplomacy is necessary if he is to coexist successfully in a hostile environment. For example, by asking a more senior coworker for a "pointer or two" on how to deliver the farewell address to the Head of Department, Kafka defuses his jealousy at not being chosen. Bennett's stage directions call this "an exercise in pure charm" (163). His farewell speech is also perfectly pitched to its audience. It mixes in some crowd-pleasing office humor at the expense of the claimants with a more subversive call for "a scrupulous and vigilant humanity" that will banish "blindness to genuine need, deafness to proper appeal and hardness of heart" (184). It is a masterful performance that wins general approval. And we see the same result in his dealings with Franz. Even though "Kafka ignores him with a smile" (155) the first time Franz sees him, when Franz finally gets his appointment, he tells Kafka, "I've been told you are kind. I've been told you are the one to see. They say you are a human being." Kafka turns the compliment aside to acknowledge the performative heart of social interaction: "No. I do a very good imitation of a human being" (186).

The Insurance Man depicts a world of claustrophobic shadow and artificial light, a world in which the one real human being is by his own admission only a simulacrum, a false god, whose attempt at a good deed condemns the recipient to a fate worse than the one he was rescued from. It's not, however, as if Kafka didn't have an inkling of this irony. He warns Franz, "You are asking for a justice that doesn't exist in the world. And not only you. More people. More people every year" (186). Where people once put their hopes in the afterlife, in a heaven that would compensate them for this proverbial vale of tears, nowadays a secular age looks to the state for an immediate remedy for suffering. Like the "human being" that Kafka is supposed to represent, the state too, or the corporations that are rapidly replacing it, are false idols that demand worship but return nothing. It's significant that no one in the play thinks of turning to God for relief, or even of blaming him for their troubles. His absence is total. Even the Angry Doctor, who invokes the expulsion from Eden as the root cause of the claimants' troubles, takes no comfort in a theological perspective. "It's a wicked, wicked world," he cries. "I've lost my faith" (173). According to Bennett, our need to believe that in the here and now there is redress for life's unfairness, that suffering leads to an earthly reward, and that decay and mortality can somehow be avoided or reversed, constitutes a new kind of groundless faith that will one day disillusion us. Like the Angry Doctor we will run amok in our despair and misanthropy. Like the corpse swinging on the lamppost, like Franz in the asbestos factory, we will be betrayed where we thought we were safe.

102 Boulevard Haussmann (1991)

One of the recurring jokes in *Kafka's Dick* is Kafka's jealous reaction every time Proust's name is mentioned. He's never heard of him before, but the possibility that Proust might be, as Sydney asserts, "the greatest writer of the twentieth century" (58) is more than even fame-shunning Kafka can bear. Brod tries to comfort him by allowing that with "a bit more get up and go . . . you'd have run rings round him," which leads Kafka to invoke his health: "I was ill. I had a bad chest" (57). Sydney's response, that "Proust had a worse chest than you," arouses competitive juices in Kafka he never imagined he had. He won't hear of the asthma or the cork-lined room: "Oh shut up. Max. My room was noisy. It was next door to my parents. When I was trying to write I had to listen to them having sexual intercourse. I'm the one who needed the cork-lined room. And he's the greatest writer of the twentieth century. Oh God" (59).

In *102 Boulevard Haussmann* (Proust's Paris residence between 1907 and 1919), Bennett attacks from a different angle the "myth of the artist" he constructed in *Kafka's Dick*. Bennett's Proust is not a pitiful figure whose physical ailments add luster to his literary achievements. He is a version of the familiar *monstre sacre*. Instead of being the fated genius who must "pay" for his gift, Bennett's

Proust makes everyone else around him pay for the privilege of being acquainted with him and his gift.[17] Proust could not devote all his attentions to his art, with his idiosyncratic working hours (midnight to dawn) and his insistence on his creature comforts (dinner collected from the Ritz every evening) without the devotion of a staff that puts itself at his complete disposal. The doctor who is summoned to the house in the middle of the night more than once has his doubts—"I hope he is a great man: making fools of us otherwise"—but Celeste, the housemaid, apparently has none. In some ways this story is as much about her as it is about Proust.

The TV play begins and ends with Celeste (played by Janet McTeer) sitting motionless and alone in the kitchen in three-quarter profile looking downward, servant and watchdog, listening for the master's bell to ring. A country girl whose husband, Odilon, (Proust's chauffeur) has been called up by the French army during World War I, she has the same kind of concentrated and silent love for her master as Flaubert's Felicité had in *A Simple Heart*. It was a happy day for Proust when Odilon married Celeste and brought her into service with him, although perhaps Odilon's happiness suffered as a result. The primary relationship in the household is between Proust and Celeste. If a chauffeur can take a backseat, that's where Odilon winds up. When he returns on a twenty-four hour leave from the front, Proust immediately presses him into service; it never occurs to him that perhaps the couple might prefer to spend this brief interlude alone. Odilon's sexual frustration is almost palpable as he waits on his master's whims; it is exacerbated by the knowledge that Celeste clearly puts the master's needs first. Late that night, Proust roams the house restlessly and hears discreet noises coming from Celeste and Odilon's room. He rings the bell to summon her to his bed to rearrange the pillows; she obediently and uncomplainingly complies. Bennett does not show Odilon's reaction to this interruption; he doesn't have to. Whether Proust's motives lie in the exercise of power, a voyeuristic perversity, or simple narcissism is not clear. What is clear is that Celeste is there without complaint when he summons her.

The main action of the play, in which Celeste plays an ancillary but key role, turns on Proust's obsession with a young viola player, Amable Massis, whom he has heard playing Cesar Francke's Quartet in D Major at the Concert Rouge in November 1916.[18] At midnight, Proust goes out in his car, with Odilon as driver, to rouse the four string players from their beds to play for him. Despite the hour, the promise of good pay persuades them to comply with this odd request. Proust lies on his chaise longue in the cork-lined bedroom, where the sound of artillery shells falling outside Paris cannot penetrate, while the four men surround him, playing the Francke Quartet. Once they finish, he commands them to "do it again," but when one player demurs he agrees to feed them first. Supper for five from the Ritz is followed by the Francke Quartet one more time, as Odilon stands at attention outside the bedroom door.

Proust's repeated listenings to the Francke piece helped him create the Vinteuil Septet in *A la recherche du temps perdu*, music whose presence is felt throughout the novel, most notably as "the central feature of the soiree at which the Verdurins break with Charlus."[19] Bennett, however, is more interested in the immediate moment and connects the playing of the Francke piece with a form of erotic courtship, the repetition of which is an indication of the lover's unsatisfied appetite, in this case for the "food of love." Amable Massis, who is on leave from the army while he recovers from a wound, is intrigued by Proust. He asks Celeste, "What's the matter with him? Is he ill?" Her reply, "He's a gentleman. He's delicate," sums up succinctly the way Celeste accepts class privilege as a congenital right, perhaps even a handicap.

Proust, half in love with the violist, wants to prevent Massis from being sent back to the war and prevails on his doctor to write a letter excusing him for health reasons. The doctor reluctantly agrees, but he and Celeste conspire to keep Massis and Proust apart. The doctor instructs Massis not to thank Proust for sponsoring the letter, knowing full well that Proust will long to know that Massis is grateful and considers himself in debt to Proust for his salvation. Celeste explicitly states that she wants to protect her master from "young men" who "take advantage" of his good nature. Proust pines for a while, but news that Massis has gone to convalesce in the country with his fiancée pushes him to bury himself deeper in his writing, to turn sexual longing into art, to make his own music, so to speak. When Massis returns to Paris several weeks later and comes to pay his long overdue visit to thank Proust, he is greeted at the door by Celeste, who refuses him entrance. She deliberately holds the door open wide enough for him to see an open viola case on the hall table and to hear the sounds of a viola playing in Proust's bedroom. Massis is the rejected muse/musician; another has taken his place.

Bennett's portrait of the artist as ruthless, charming monster owes part of its appeal to Alan Bates's performance as Proust. Perhaps beefier than one usually imagines an asthmatic and neurasthenic invalid, Bates brings a pale seediness to the unshaven, bedridden writer and a dapper sophistication to the public socialite that constitutes Proust's two identities. Memories of Bates's performance as Guy Burgess in *An Englishman Abroad* enrich his Proust. Like Burgess, Proust has "bags of charm," but he uses charm as a weapon to bend others to his will. Proust demands and wins the devotion of everyone, all in the name of and in service to his genius. He is protected from the consequences of his self-absorption by his social position, by his own assertion of his genius, and by the people who revere him, for whatever misguided reasons. Bennett seems to have taken his view of the difference between a great artist and a great man from Proust's own distinction between art and its creator: "A book is a product of a different self from the one we manifest in our habits, our social life, and our vices."[20]

Like Burgess, Proust is both appealing and appalling, the outsider who bends the rest of the world, represented in these plays by Coral Browne and Celeste, to his will. As both spies and artists they are privy to the darkest secrets of their nations, their cultures, and the human heart. They make their marks and leave their names through the transmission of these secrets, sometimes for fame, sometimes for infamy. While neither can be said to have paid in exactly the way Kafka supposedly did, each is nonetheless left to live in a claustrophobia of his own choosing—the corklined room for Proust, the Soviet state for Burgess.

NOTES

1. "Alan Bennett: He makes it easy for you," *Independent*, Nov. 14, 1999, 6.

2. Since irony is Bennett's favorite "element" the link between Bennett the ironical writer and Hilary the ironical spy is difficult to dismiss as coincidence. Ben Brantly, "Swimming in Irony," *New York Times Book Review* (Oct. 1, 1995): 13.

3. This speech is repeated almost verbatim by Susan, the vicar's wife, in *Bed among the Lentils*, in the first series of *Talking Heads* monologues ten years later. Bennett's recycling of the "wonderful woman" ideal suggests not just his usual economy, but the centrality of that kind of role for a certain type of upper-middle-class English woman.

4. The script of the original television version of *An Englishman Abroad* is found in this edition. The shorter and slightly different stage version can be found in *Plays Two*.

5. Bennett reports that John Schlesinger, the director of the television version, persuaded him (much to his later regret) that the audience wouldn't get the connection between Burgess in 1958 and the 1956 Hungarian Uprising and downplayed that line into a joke that Coral Browne brushes aside. When Bennett adapted the television version for the National Theatre production, he made sure the line had bite by having Coral add, "Oh, I said, and thinking of the tanks going into Budapest a year or two before, wished I hadn't made such a fuss" (*P2*, 298–99).

6. Bennett, "Alan Bennett Chooses Four Paintings for Schools," *London Review of Books*, Apr. 2, 1998, 10.

7. One of the pleasures of this play is the sly ambiguity Bennett has embedded in the remarks of HMQ. It is possible to interpret HMQ's remarks as innocent of any subtext, in which case it is Blunt's guilty conscience that lends them their disturbing appropriateness. But I prefer the more symmetrical arrangement of three secret sharers.

8. Alastair Macauley, *Financial Times* (London), June 7, 1996.

9. Nicholas de Jongh, *Evening Standard* (London), June 11, 1996.

10. Wu, 27.

11. Turner, 126.

12. Bennett estimates that more than 15,000 books and essays have been written about Kafka in the last seventy years (*P2*, 3).

13. Mark Harman's new translation of *The Castle*, Kafka's last novel, "shows a more comic Kafka," according to a recent *New York Times* report ("Kafkaesque, As in Comic and Playful," Mar. 18, 1998), suggesting that Bennett's fears about overironizing Kafka may have been exaggerated.

14. One of the rare exceptions, as we have seen, is the 1982 television play *Intensive Care*.

15. Michael Billington, *The Guardian*, Sept. 25, 1986.

16. Daphne Turner offers an interesting reading of Franz and Kafka as "in some way doubles, opposite halves of a shared identity" (112).

17. As of this writing, there is no published text of *102 Boulevard Haussmann*.

This discussion is based on a viewing of the videotape archived at the British Film Institute.

18. Bennett has based this play on an actual episode in Proust's life. See George Painter's *Marcel Proust: A Biography* (London: Chatto and Windus, 1989), 243–47. Bennett may have read Painter's description; many of the details Bennett uses in the play are also found in Painter.

19. Painter, 245.

20. Edmund White, *Marcel Proust* (New York: Viking, 1999), 97.

CHAPTER FIVE

The Presentation of Self in Everyday Life: *Talking Heads*

A Woman of No Importance (1982)
A Chip in the Sugar (1988)
A Lady of Letters (1988)
Bed among the Lentils (1988)
Soldiering On (1988)
Her Big Chance (1988)
A Cream Cracker under the Settee (1988)

Talking Heads, which was an enormous critical and popular success when it was televised in 1988, has become perhaps the one work that Bennett is most identified with and admired for in Britain.[1] Among theater professionals, Bennett's exalted stature can be measured by the names of the actors he was able to cast in these challenging roles, where one actor carries the entire burden of performance: Patricia Routledge, Maggie Smith, Julie Walters, Stephanie Cole, and Thora Hird. Bennett's ability to attract actors of this prominence to his work may be because "Alan writes so beautifully for women," as Eileen Atkins, another leading English actor, believes. But without denying Bennett's particular interest and skill in creating roles for mature women, it should be pointed out that from the very beginning of his career he has worked with some of the most accomplished actors in Britain. *Forty Years On* featured John Gielgud, one of the greatest stage actors of the twentieth century, in the lead role while Alec Guinness, both a major film star and a fine stage actor, played the lead in *Habeas Corpus* and *The Old Country*. The early TV plays featured mostly veteran character actors, not the big marquee names who appeared in the early stage plays but, beginning in the 1980s, as Bennett's work expanded beyond its northern boundaries, his TV plays featured established and rising stars such as Alan Bates and Daniel Day-Lewis. By the late 1980s,

1980s, Bennett was able to choose from among the most impressive talents of the day for *Talking Heads*.

Bennett's appeal to actors of both sexes probably owes something to his early and continuing experience as a performer. When Bennett writes a part he seems to understand how the lines will sound when spoken aloud. His vaunted ear for over-heard dialogue usually gets the credit for this, as if he were only an eavesdropper, a popular misconception that underestimates the craft that Bennett brings to the creation of his language. Sir Peter Hall, who directed the revival of *Kafka's Dick* in 1998, is convinced that there is a direct connection between Bennett's success with language and the skills he learned on the stage:

> Alan is, as we know, a wonderful actor and comedian and he understands how comedy works. So the timing in his writing is superb. You can imme-diately see the rhythm he intends from the words on the page. It's very speak-able and actors love that. They'll treat bad writing with no respect at all. But with Alan's you don't want to change a word.[2]

Bennett also knows that most actors like to play both sharply defined characters and characters they can empathize with. The most successful characters in these monologues offer the actors precisely the combination of oddness and familiarity that challenges but doesn't intimidate them. The appeal of these monologues also lies in Bennett's old fashioned need to structure them around a riveting narrative. As he puts it, "A story is always being told, and often an eventful one, and that's the oldest theatrical device in the world."[3] With or without narrative hooks, mono-logues that last three-quarters of an hour require actors who can take command of the audience's attention and engage their imagination using only the words Bennett gives them to speak. These parts are star turns that have become defining roles in the actors' careers. Few people remember the title of the play or the character's name, referring instead to "the Maggie Smith monologue about the vicar's wife" or "the Patricia Routledge monologue about the snoop." With such rewards awaiting them, it's little wonder that so many celebrated actors have assumed the challenges that Bennett has offered them in *Talking Heads*, and, ten years later, in *Talking Heads 2*.

The characters these glorious actors portray are actors too, although they would probably not admit it. The most interesting aspects of their performances reside in their presentations of themselves to their audience. When Bennett wrote the intro-duction to the published texts of the *Talking Heads* monologues in 1988, he was quick to point out that the narrators of these dramas are all "artless." He fore-grounded the dramatic irony inherent in these narrators' renditions of their stories: "They don't quite know what they are saying and are telling a story to the mean-ing of which they are not entirely privy" (*TH*, 7). In the process of talking they unwittingly expose some aspect of themselves—homosexual leanings, moral obtuseness, dependence on alcohol—they think remains invisible. Yet artlessness does not adequately sum up these complex characters. In some ways, these speakers resemble benign versions of the unreliable narrators in the Victorian dramatic monologue—Browning's murderous duke or his worldly Renaissance bishop. Through the implications of their language, Browning and Bennett challenge the reader to discover the real persons beneath the mask of their surface appearance. In other ways, Bennett's monologuists remind us of the apparently self-sufficient protagonists of Beckett's monologues—Winnie, Krapp, the Mouth in *Not I*—who do not know why they speak, only that they must.

Erving Goffman's reminder that the layers of everyday performance go deeper than we normally recognize, in particular his assertion that "we all act better than we know how,"[4] offers additional insight into Bennett's take on the performance of everyday identity. Goffman chose the middle-class American girl who allows her boyfriend to think she is less capable and less intelligent than he is, as the social script of the 1950s demanded, as his example of how deeply performance can reach into a person's identity. What interested Goffman more than this young woman's dumbing herself down was the unacknowledged aspect, even to herself, of her identity performance:

> But like herself and her boyfriend, we accept as an unperformed fact that this performer is a young American middle-class girl. But surely here we neglect the greater part of the performance. . . . To be a given kind of person, then, is not merely to possess the required attributes, but also to sustain the standards of conduct and appearance that one's social grouping attaches thereto. The unthinking ease with which performers consistently carry off such standard-maintaining routines does not deny that a performance has occurred, merely that the participants have been aware of it. (81)

Like the middle-class American girl, Bennett's monologuists "sustain the standards of conduct and appearance" appropriate to their "social grouping" with "unthinking ease." The faces they present to us are skillful creations. The wasp-tongued vicar's wife unmasking the hypocrisies around her, the serious actress honing her craft, the widow proud of her independence, the spinster lady guarding public morals—this is how these characters want to be perceived. However, Goffman's familiar warnings, that "the impression of reality fostered by a performance is a delicate, fragile thing that can be shattered by very minor mishaps" (63) and that "everyday performances are subject to disruption" (72), carry extra significance here. The dramatic irony in *Talking Heads* arises out of the Goffmanian irony of failed performances. In this series of six monologues, Bennett dramatizes the ubiquity of everyday performance, its deep-rooted structure at the very core of human personality, and its instability. He steps beyond Goffman into Beckett's territory when these presentations of self collapse to reveal the existential terror at their heart.

A Woman of No Importance (first broadcast November 19, 1982)

Before *Talking Heads*, however, there was *A Woman of No Importance*. Bennett
reports that he devised this first monologue as a directorial exercise for himself. He
felt that one actress, one set, and at most only two cameras would not overwhelm
him in his directorial debut, so he wrote this piece for Patricia Routledge (*OA*, 34).
As it turned out, he did not direct it (Giles Foster did), but instead discovered a form
that would prove especially congenial to his talents.

    A Woman of No Importance, whose title Bennett has appropriated without
comment from Oscar Wilde's play, gives us one Margaret (Peggy) Schofield, an
unmarried, middle-aged office worker whose life spirals downward in six scenes
from apparent good health to death from cancer. Peggy looks directly at the camera and speaks in a confidential tone to us, although she carefully screens and
selects her revelations. She never admits the seriousness of her condition or its
cause. She chatters on instead, like a Yorkshire version of Winnie in *Happy Days*,
determined to keep up a facade of cheerful self-importance.

    The dominant word in the play is "laugh." Peggy says it in one form or anoth-
er thirty times (mostly as "we laughed," but also "she laughed" and "he laughed").
Interestingly enough, Peggy never actually laughs in the course of her monologue.
Instead, she reports this laughter as evidence that she lives in a warm, convivial
atmosphere both at work and in the hospital and that she is herself a congenial person to whom everyone responds warmly. The audience gets a different picture,
however, a picture of a lonely, "boring"—Bennett's own word for her (34)—woman
trying to create a reality that bears little relation to her actual circumstance by performing an identity for us that isn't in full sync with her nature.

    The opening scene of the television film shows her seated on a white chair in a
sterile white hall, a black purse on her lap and a slip of white paper in her hand.
She makes no reference to this medical setting, but launches into a minute description of her "little routine" at the office, especially her daily struggles to get to the
lunchroom at half past twelve to link up with her "happy family" of co-workers,
her special set of four unmarried women and two gay men with whom she invariably lunches, unless she catches them avoiding her by trying to sneak into another
lunch group. Luckily for them, she tells us, she "rescue[s] them in the nick of time"
(37) from these other groupings. "I don't talk about myself" (36), she tells us, a
claim that may be technically correct, since we learn very little about her real feelings. This reticence is counterbalanced, however, by her weakness for knowing
everything about everyone else's life and making judgments thinly disguised as concern: "Her acne's heaps better"; "She's black but I take people as they come"; "She
shouldn't wear trousers"; "your wife's in and out of mental hospital" (37–8). Peggy
is so short of real content in her life that she elevates the most mundane decisions
into major philosophical positions. It's not enough to say "no, thank you" to the
offer of pepper. She must instead give some autobiographical background: "I'm not
a big pepper fan" (38). It's a safe bet that she thinks no one with any sense should
be.

The second scene finds her in her living room sitting in a chair with a tea mug in her hand. She recounts with an oddly inappropriate lightheartedness her visit to her doctor because of an "upset tummy" caused, she implies, by her violating her sacred rule to eat only salad at lunch. She has tried the hot dish—steak pieces—only to discover it's "mainly gristle." Her patronizing feelings of liberal tolerance toward the black woman who served her the gristle are sustained by the observation, "I don't suppose they distinguish in Jamaica" (38). Dr. Copeland examines her with the assistance of a grim-faced medical student who persists in questioning her psychological frame of mind, which elicits a surprising outburst against her aged father, now in a nursing home, for his many years of philandering with a "blondified piece from the cosmetics counter" of a local pharmacy and "a shoe cream demonstrator" from a department store (40). Dr. Copeland refers her to a specialist, which pleases rather than alarms her because this particular doctor's wife is a socially prominent supporter of the Music Festival. Peggy is a snob, one of Bennett's many status-conscious genteel ladies from an undistinguished background.

Peggy is lying in a hospital bed in the third scene, looking pale against the white sheets. She fills us in on the details of the specialist's posh home, but barely mentions his diagnosis: "one of those big double-fronted houses in Park Square"; "lovely fireplace"; "a beautiful carpet" (41). She apparently accepts at face value the specialist's assurance that "there's nothing to get worked up about but we ought to have a look" and sees nothing amiss in his question: "Have you got something special on in the next couple of weeks? . . . Because ideally what I would like to do is take you in, run a few tests and then go on from there" (42). Whether Peggy is really taken in by the doctor's bonhomie is questionable, even if she is susceptible to the good manners of her social betters. Still, she doesn't let on otherwise and chooses instead to tell us that her departure for the hospital "caused chaos at work" (41). Peggy's self-esteem receives another boost when the woman who shampoos and sets her hair in the hospital compliments her on having the kind of hair that Italians prize for wigs.

In the fourth scene Peggy is seated next to the hospital bed dressed in a fawn bathrobe with a copy of the *Daily Mail* in her hand, a sign of her middle-class female refinement. We see the notice "Nil By Mouth" over the bed, an ironic reminder that Peggy, like the voice in Beckett's *Not I* who refuses to admit that the disastrous life she describes is her own, speaks unceasingly to deflect attention from her dire situation. As she awaits her "op" the next morning she tells us of her indispensable role in the running of the ward. She helps the nurses with their duties by reminding them of things they might have forgotten. Nurse Gillis's sarcastic thanks, "I don't know how we managed before you came, Miss Schofield, I honestly don't," is reported without comment (43). Perhaps Peggy is immune to sarcasm, or perhaps she doesn't want to let on to us that she isn't. Nonetheless, she says, "I get on like a house on fire with the nurses. We do laugh. Nurse Trickett says I'm their star patient. She's little and a bit funny-looking but so goodhearted" (43). This is the same Peggy Schofield we recognize from the office: she starts with a cliché, claims camaraderie, asserts the centrality of her position, and ends with a backhanded compliment. Nonetheless, we also see beneath the facade of smug cheerfulness as she starts to pick nervously at the name tag on her wrist. There are four get-well cards on the table, not many for someone who claims to have been the center of the universe at work. Only one of her coworkers has been to visit. As the scene ends she sounds weaker and her face contorts with an emotion that she doesn't verbalize.

She returns from her operation in the fifth scene and is found sitting in a chair looking out the hospital window. She looks wan and tired, but brightens up when she tells us that her supervisor at work, Mr. Skidmore, has popped in for a visit. She had always regarded him more highly than her other coworkers, and probably not just because his social skills are more refined than theirs. Even when he lets slip that he is "killing two birds with one stone" because his mother-in-law is receiving treatment in the psychiatric ward, she accepts his apology for his poor choice of words: "We laughed. He does look young when he laughs" (45). And just as she had earlier taken great pride in knowing that several years ago Princess Alexandra had stopped by the bed she now occupies, she basks in recounting the doctor's claim that "he's never seen a scar heal as quickly as mine" and proudly informs us that the specialist's students "stop longer at my bed than with anybody" (46).

The laughter stops in the final scene. Peggy is clearly declining; her head rests motionless on her pillow as her speech becomes more labored. Her pleasure in constructing her specialness weakens. She responds to the priest's remark that suffering is God's way of marking out special people by telling herself she could "do without being special this lot." When she is complimented for drawing up the most phlegm of anyone in the ward, she makes perhaps her only truly witty remark in the play. "Was there a prize?" she asks (47), which is Bennett's transposition of Kafka's joke on his own deathbed.[5] She lets down her guard even further when she mutters, "I wish they wouldn't laugh . . . there shouldn't be laughing" (48). Laughter has become the enemy. It's no longer the social glue that bridges all those awkward moments, that covers over the difficult truths that everyone would rather avoid. But just as Peggy recognizes its falsity in the face of her imminent demise, she retreats into her performed identity almost immediately. She notices a solitary fly buzzing around her head. "Must like me. . . . Here's my friend. This fly . . . I said to Nurse Gillis, 'It's singled me out.' She laughed" (48). Those are Peggy's last words to us, as the camera moves in for an extreme close-up of her face. The final shot is of an empty hospital bed.

Peggy Schofield is not of course the only performer in this monologue. Everyone plays the role he or she has been assigned and hardly anyone lets the mask slip. Her fellow workers assure Peggy that she's a "lynch-pin" in the reorganization of their operations, even though it's likely that her absence has finally allowed them to revamp more efficiently. She was always an obstacle to efficiency; it's ironic that in her illness she is now its cause. The doctors and nurses likewise never mention cancer, though the nurses seem to treat her more kindly as she declines; nor does the visiting vicar mention death or prepare her for it. Peggy at no time admits what we ourselves can see, that in appearance and health she is rapidly deteriorating. These physical changes are meticulously presented to us, but Peggy never alludes to them. The denial of her ill health is as important to her as the denial of her ultimate unimportance and aloneness; she is dying with only a fly as her companion and "friend." Bennett's allusion to Emily Dickinson's poem "I heard a Fly buzz—when I died" works ironically too, because, unlike Dickinson's speaker, Peggy can discern nothing in the fly that transcends herself. She assigns it the role of companion to and verifier of her own egocentricity. To the end, Peggy remains true to the image she wants to present to us.

A Chip in the Sugar (first broadcast April 19, 1988)

This play inaugurated the series of six monologues gathered under the umbrella of *Talking Heads*. It starred Alan Bennett in the role of Graham Whittaker, a middle-aged bachelor of somewhat precarious mental health, who narrates his reaction to his seventy-two-year-old mother's rediscovery of a boyfriend from fifty years before. Graham's close relationship with his mother—strangers sometimes mistake them for a married couple—offers him a stability that strikes the audience as odd. He speaks of her bodily functions in familiar terms that sound both parental and spousal: "Give me your teeth. I'll swill them"; "Come along, mother. We don't want piles"; "What about your pelvis?" (*TH*, 16–7) The arrival of her old beau, Frank Turnbull, on the scene unsettles this tidy domestic relationship and makes the audience realize there are topics and feelings that Graham cannot speak of as frankly as he speaks about his mother's physical debilities, although, when threatened enough, he seems willing to reveal what many people in his circumstances prefer to keep quiet.

Graham wants the audience to side with him in his attempt to disillusion his mother about this old suitor, who, we later learn, cannot deliver on his offer of marriage and a honeymoon in Tenerife because he already has a wife. In part, Graham's distaste for Frank is based on rivalry and jealousy, because Frank endangers his "marriage" to his mother; Frank also undermines the role of liberal intellectual that Graham has assumed with his mother. In the course of the monologue we learn that Graham is willing to reveal some of his deeply held secrets in order to hold on to these central identities.

Graham tells us early on that he is an enlightened liberal in the midst of lower-middle-class reactionaries. Just as Peggy Schofield defines her refinement by reading the *Daily Mail*, Graham establishes his credentials as a left-wing thinker by reading *The Guardian*. Graham condescendingly reports that he has trained his mother to his point of view:

> The thing about Mam is that though she's never had a proper education, she's picked up enough from me to be able to hold her own in discussions about up-to-the-minute issues like the environment and the colour problem, and for

a woman of her age and background she has a very liberal slant. She'll look
at my *Guardian* and she actually thinks for herself. (16)

This isn't actually so, as we soon see when she comes in contact with Frank's considerably less liberal outlook, and she begins to parrot his beliefs that "it's the
blacks" (22) and not the Thatcher government that's to blame for the country's
problems. Whether with her son or her old beau, Vera Whittaker is one of those
old-fashioned women who are content to let the men in their lives shape their opinions about the world.

Another way in which Graham has set himself above his surroundings is in his
sense of taste. He flatters himself that he has more discernment than anyone else.
That's why when Frank suggests they all go for coffee, Graham expects that they'll
follow his lead. "Now the cafe we generally patronise is just that bit different," he
tells us, offering details that identify these differences as restaurant clichés from the
seventies. "It's plain but it's classy, no cloths on the tables, the menu comes on a little slate and the waitresses wear their own clothes and look as if they're doing it
just for the fun of it" (18). Frank has other ideas, however, and introduces them to
a new place "done out in red." As Graham disapprovingly confides to us, "if there's
one thing Mother and me are agreed upon it's that red is a common colour"(18)—
"common" being one of those devastating putdowns favored by Bennett's own status-conscious mother (10). Graham's mother, however, takes to this new place
immediately and even agrees to experiment by ordering a cheeseburger. It's here
that Graham sees the offending "chip in the sugar," a fat, soft, northern version of
the American french fry lying in the sugar bowl. To him it sums up the untidy disorder that such vulgar places represent; to Frank it's "a detail" that shouldn't
detract from this adventure.

As Graham reports to us their conversation at the cafe, he begins to undermine
some of his most prized pretensions to distinction. As a salesman of men's clothing,
Frank has firm opinions on men's fashion. He shows us Graham in ways that
Graham himself would not be able to. When his mother asserts that "Graham's
quite refined," Frank retorts, "Well, he could do with smartening up a bit. . . .
Plastic mac. He wants some of those quilted jobs. . . . And flares are anathema even
in Bradford." His mother's defense, that "Graham doesn't care. . . . He reads a lot,"
offers Frank the chance to couch his assault on Graham's awkward sense of style
in terms of gallantry toward his mother: "If I were squiring a young lady like this
around town I wouldn't do it in grey socks and sandals" (19). Plastic raincoat,
flared trousers, and open sandals paint a picture of Graham more as an outdated
eccentric than a sophisticate. His contempt for Frank becomes so great that he simply refuses to rise to the bait. "I didn't say anything," which is repeated six times
in the course of the monologue, becomes his way of dismissing Frank's opinions as
unworthy of a reply, as well as his mother's opinions when they mimic Frank's.
Silence is his assertion of power, however passive, and not merely a withdrawal
"from confrontations and his own jealous feelings,"[6] as Daphne Turner suggests.

In order to dislodge Frank from his mother's life, Graham is willing to use, and thus disclose to the audience, his history of mental illness. As a ploy for sympathy he reminds his mother, "Dr. Chaudhury says I should have a stable environment. This isn't a stable environment with your fancy man popping in every five minutes." His mother's advice is always the same: "Have one of your tablets" (22–3). He tells us about his paranoid delusions of being watched, which had originally driven him to seek professional help, and now he fears they are returning. In truth, his sense that someone is watching the house is no delusion. It turns out to be Frank's daughter, who is eager to break up another of her father's bigamous schemes with elderly widows. Graham's relief and pleasure at this turn of events is palpable. Frank's daughter reproaches him: "I don't know what there is to look so suited [pleased] about" (25).

In the final scene, Graham, who has been telling us this story with his hands tightly folded in his lap, begins to relax a little and even places his hands on the arms of the easy chair he sits in. It's a small gesture, but a telling one, especially since it doesn't last long. He has to tell us one more "truth" about himself. In her grief and disappointment at the news, which Graham has broken to her almost triumphantly, his mother lashes out, "You don't understand. How can you understand, you, you're not normal?" The audience assumes that she is referring to his mental troubles, but she's digging deeper than that, at another secret. "You think you've got it over me, Graham Whittaker. Well, you haven't. I've got it over you. . . . I know the kind of magazines you read." When he counters that they're chess magazines, she scoffs, "They never are chess. Chess with no clothes on. Chess in their birthday suits. That kind of chess. Chess men." He mildly replies, "Go to bed. And turn your blanket off" (26). Earlier references to his buying his "reading matter" after he parks his mother at her usual spot near the war memorial, and the sight of him placing a magazine high on top of the wardrobe of his bedroom just as the final scene begins, are the clues that Bennett uses to signal Graham's homoerotic interests.

In an earlier television play, *Marks,* in 1982, Bennett had drawn a similar connection between homosexuality and an unusually intimate domestic relationship between a young boy and his mother. Here, Graham might be that young man grown old, now all but married to his mother. Graham's disclosure of these two social taboos in working-class England—mental illness and homosexuality—works, he hopes, as a distraction from the central truth of his life: his desperate need to hold on to his mother and to preserve his persona as the advanced thinker who is superior to his philistine environment. We might think that his triumph over Frank Turnbull would leave Graham with nothing to desire. But Bennett's ending leaves us with another thought. In the final lines of the monologue we see that his position both as the arbiter of what's tasteful and appropriate and as the man of the house has been completely restored. Having forgotten the anger of the previous evening, his mother asks him, "What's on the agenda for today, then?" He suggests a "little ride to Ripon," and she replies "Oh, yes, Ripon. That's nice. We could go to the cathedral. We like old buildings, don't we, you and me?" (27). The look on Graham's face as he speaks the final words, "She put her arm through mine," tells us that this victory has not been without cost. She is once again "his echo,"[7] and his "wife." Graham's tight-lipped expression reveals his mixed emotions about this restoration of the status quo, its stability also an entrapment.

A Lady of Letters (first broadcast April 26, 1988)

At first glance, this mordant comedy appears to be Bennett's presentation of the maiden lady as a small-town espionage agent, heir to the mantle of Hilary, Blunt, and Burgess. But readers of Goffman will recognize that at heart Irene Ruddick is a critic of performance. Miss Ruddick presents herself to us as a conscientious citizen, a guardian of the public good, whose task in life is to watch for and correct any lapses in other people's behavior. Whether it's a broken step, the length of the Archbishop of Canterbury's hair, dog dirt in front of Buckingham Palace, or a suspected case of child abuse, Miss Ruddick picks up her pen ("a real friend," she tells us), and fires off a letter (*TH*, 45). She appears to be a busybody who has to know everybody's business on the street, peering out at them from her window, assuming the worst in their actions, and then writing letters to the authorities reporting them for their alleged crimes. Self-righteous and judgmental, she seems to possess the deepest cynicism about the sinfulness of human nature. She sits in judgment of her neighbors the way a reviewer might assess the actors in a local theater production, then file a critique in the paper. Instead of writing a review, Miss Ruddick pens letters of complaint to the authorities.

The first case she brings to our attention is the letter she has written to the local mortuary complaining about the hearse drivers, who smoke in view of the bereaved party. She is moved not by her own sense of violated grief—she admits she barely knew the deceased and went along to the service because she had nothing better to do on a Wednesday afternoon—but by a sense of outraged decorum. Smoking at a crematorium doesn't fit her idea of what's appropriately reverent, although Bennett enjoys the irony in her complaint. She is delighted by the apologetic reply from the director of operations, replete with cliché-ridden promises of severe punishment against the perpetrators: "jump on the culprits with both feet"; "come down on the offenders like a ton of bricks" (44). Judging by the hyperbolic and trite nature of his reply, it's doubtful that the director will take any action, which probably doesn't matter much to Miss Ruddick. Her satisfaction derives from the attention she has received. After all, what really bothers any critic is being ignored.

The second case she tells us about involves the new couple who have just moved in across the street from her: "[They] don't look very promising. The kiddy looks filthy" (45). They fulfill her worst expectations. The husband seems to spend most of his time repairing the car; they turn their transistor radio up loud; the wife doesn't use a table cloth for the evening meal, and the child looks thin and underfed. She thinks to herself, "Well, you've got a car, you've got a transistor, it's about time you invested in some curtains" (45–6). Curtains, however, would seriously interfere with Miss Ruddick's public duties. She keeps her eye on them in the belief that she's fulfilling a traditional role in a changing world:

> My mother knew everybody in this street. She could reel off the occupants of every single house. Everybody could, once upon a time. Now, they come and they go. That's why these tragedies happen. Nobody watching. If they knew they were being watched they might behave. (47)

Here in a nutshell is the nightmare collision of a traditional, close-knit community with Orwell's vision of Big Brother, sinister surveillance confused with benign caring in the mind of Miss Ruddick. The tragedy that she suspects across the street is child abuse. She has noticed a bruise on the child's arm, and after a long spell of sitting "in the front room in the dark watching the house" (48), seeing the parents go out every evening without the child, apparently leaving him alone without a sitter, she writes a letter to the police charging the parents with neglect, or worse. When two police come to her door with the news that the child has died of leukemia in a hospital in Bradford, we see that all her suspicions have been founded on false assumptions. The child was not alone in the house because he was in the hospital, and that's where the parents were going every evening, not to the pub, as she suspected. Miss Ruddick does not admit her mistake to us, but Patricia Routledge, playing another woman of invented importance, registers confusion with a sideways bob of her head as if reeling from a blow, and her voice cracks as she reports to us what they said.

Having previously accused the pharmacist's wife of being a prostitute and the school crossing guard of molesting the children he is assigned to watch, Miss Ruddick is a known quantity to the police. For this latest false accusation, she is given a suspended sentence on the condition that she write no more letters. But her need to critique others' performances is stronger than her fear of the consequences. She decides that, under the guise of "community policing," the local policeman spends too much time "watching" No. 56. "In there an hour at a stretch. Timed it the other day and when eventually he comes out she's at the door in just a little shorty housecoat thing. . . . He wants reporting" (51). This is the final straw and she finds herself in prison.

Prison transforms Irene Ruddick. For one thing, she now allows herself to be called Irene, a name she hasn't answered to since her mother died, insisting instead on Miss Ruddick. More importantly, she has moved, in Goffman's terms, from the front, where you give your performance—in Irene's case "The Scourge of Other People's Bad Performances"—to the back region, where she can relax from her act and let down her guard with other performers. Miss Ruddick's audience has not been an appreciative one, and the role she has played has not been particularly rewarding for her, but backstage, in prison, all this changes. Her teammates are real offenders, like herself, not imagined ones. Her cellmate, she tells us, is "Bridget from Glasgow. She's been a prostitute on and off and did away with her kiddy, accidentally, when she was drunk and upset. Bonny little face, you'd never think" (51). This off-handed acceptance of murder is matched by her equally breezy acceptance of Shirley, who "sets fire to places." Because they are now her "friends," she doesn't give them their performative labels of "child murderer" and "arsonist." "The human want for social contact and for companionship,"[8] which Graham Whittaker sacrifices to maintain the status quo with his mother, is now within Irene's reach.

Patricia Routledge, who has presented Miss Ruddick to us as humorless, disapproving, almost shrill when she details her suspicions about her neighbors, and genteelly smug when she reflects on the good her vigilance has done for her community, now plays Irene in prison as manically animated and effusive. She trills, "They laugh at me, I know, but it's all in good part. Lucille says, 'You're funny you, Irene. You don't mind being in prison.' I said, 'Prison!' I said, 'Lucille. This is the first taste of freedom I've had in years'" (52). The freedom she feels comes from dropping the pose of stern moral guardian and accepting the fallibility of her fellows. One of Bennett's richest ironies in this play full of ironies is that the performance of righteous guardian of public morality may be the loneliest of all, and the most entrapping.

In the final scene, Irene sits in a darkened cell looking at the bed across the room, watching with a benign purpose now. She tells us in a quiet, gentle tone, "Sometimes Bridget will wake up in the middle of the night shouting, dreaming about the kiddy she killed, and I go over and sit by the bed and hold her hand till she's gone off again" (53). Miss Ruddick, who predicted that she would never be happy in this life, has found happiness in prison, away from the middle-class proprieties she was trying so hard to force on others by her surveillance. Her enthusiasm about learning from Bridget "the rudiments" of sex, in case she should ever find herself in bed with a man, as well as how to smoke and how to swear, strike us as comic, but endearingly so. We fully believe Irene's last line, when she looks directly at us in close-up and says, "And I'm so *happy*" (53). Patricia Routledge pauses several seconds before she says the word "happy," underlining Irene's surprise and delight that this is the only appropriate word to describe her condition.

Bed among the Lentils (first broadcast May 3, 1988)

This monologue is probably the most celebrated and familiar of the six, owing largely to Maggie Smith's performance as Susan, the vicar's alcoholic wife, a part she recreated in 1994 for a stage adaptation. This monologue also contains the darkest and wittiest writing in the series. Bennett has said that the idea for this monologue originated with his discovery of the words *Get lost, Jesus* written in "tiny, timid letters" in a hymnbook at his school.[9] And from the opening line, "Geoffrey's bad enough but I'm glad I wasn't married to Jesus," we know we're in the presence of a similarly blasphemous voice, a barbed and sarcastic wit belonging, to our surprise, to that stalwart pillar of the Church of England—the priest's wife (*TH*, 30). Of course once we discover that she's a secret alcoholic, it's tempting to excuse or dismiss her scorn for religion. Alcohol only fuels Susan's bitterness, however. The real source of her despair is that blasphemous or reverent, drunk or sober, she finds herself trapped into performing a self she despises, whether it's for her husband, his congregation, her AA group, or even us.

Unlike Irene, in *A Lady of Letters*, who begins in front of an audience and finds release only when she enters the back region, Susan begins backstage, in the kitchen of the vicarage, where she should be able to relax and reveal the shams that constitute her performance as supportive church lady and her husband's as vicar. Her scorn for her husband, for his small but devoted congregation, and for her own role as his wife is couched in the language of the stage. She calls the congregation Geoffrey's "fan club." She wonders why, if an actor's wife doesn't have to view his every performance, a vicar's wife is supposed to go to every church service. She describes her husband's physical appearance in the language of celebrity: "what 'Who's Who in the Diocese of Ripon' calls his 'schoolboy good looks.'" She reserves her juiciest sarcasm for Geoffrey's false modesty, which she terms "his 'underneath this cassock I am but a man like anybody else' act," an act she knows the women of the congregation lap up like cream (30–1). Perhaps her sharpest and bitterest insight, which comes later in the monologue, is that these women think "they love God when they just love Geoffrey" (38).

Susan is violating the audience's initial expectations of what a vicar's wife should say and feel, but in Goffman's analysis of performance she is merely indulging in what he terms the "ritual profanation of the front region," a process he first observed in the kitchen of the Shetland hotel, where the staff would mock the guests behind their backs.[10] What's unusual about Susan's backstage behavior is that she isn't communing with teammates, as Irene did in the previous monologue. But she's still performing—for us. She is working hard to maintain the impression of someone smarter than the people around her with their foolish superstitions and bad faith. She wants us to agree that she is in fact victimized by their tedious adherence to these beliefs. Yet her own language gives away how deeply imprinted she herself is with this brand of Anglicanism. Left alone on a Sunday she muses, falling unselfconsciously into the language of the Book of Common Prayer:

> Roads busy. Sunday afternoon. Families having a run out. Wheeling the pram, walking the dog. Living. Almighty God unto whom all hearts be open, and from whom no secrets are hid, cleanse the thoughts of our hearts by the inspiration of thy holy spirit that we may perfectly love thee and worthily magnify thy glorious name and not spend our Sunday afternoons parked in a lay-by on the Ring Road wondering what happened to our life. (31)

The broadcast version of the first scene ends with Susan absently running her fingers along the rim of an empty glass as she wonders aloud why the woman at the off-license from whom she buys her sherry doesn't seem to approve of her. Bennett, who directed this monologue, introduces the rather obvious device of the glass to make clear to the viewer that Susan's puzzlement is disingenuous, and that her merciless puncturing of Geoffrey's performance and that of his "fan club," as well as her apparently no-holds-barred revelation of her own crisis of faith, don't offer a completely frank picture of her situation. She is still performing a version of herself that she hopes will win not only our approval, but her own as well.

The kind of woman Susan once hoped to be is the same all-purpose "wonderful woman" that Bron described so nostalgically in *The Old Country*, the "wise, witty" paragon who dies as "peacefully, continently and without fuss" as she has lived (33). Along the way to this canonization Susan would have proved her mettle by learning a few essential skills, in other words, "all [the] weapons in the armoury of any upstanding Anglican lady": "how to produce jam which, after reaching a good, rolling boil, successfully coats the spoon; how to whip up a Victoria sponge that just gives to the fingertips; how to plan, execute and carry through a successful garden fete" (34). The comedy of this genteel portrait is upstaged, however, by the more acerbic reality of Anglican womanhood in Geoffrey's parish. Susan sums it up pithily with one comparison: "If you think squash is a competitive activity try flower arrangement" (34). Susan's power struggle with Mrs. Shrubsole over whose turn it is to decorate the main altar, a battle Susan cannot win in the face of Mrs. Shrubsole's "Forest Murmurs" floral creation, drives her into the vestry "to calm my shattered nerves," which ultimately results in an inebriated roll down the altar stairs and a collision with the communion rail. Susan reports this to us as an innocent accident, without admitting that drinking the communion wine has played a central part in her slapstick humiliation in front of Geoffrey's "fan club."

Susan's need to escape the prying eyes of the parish leads her to an all-purpose newsagent's in Leeds owned and operated by Mr. Ramesh, handsome and twenty-six years old, where she can buy sherry and find sympathetic company. Mr. Ramesh introduces Susan to the Hindu gods and their more casual attitude toward sex. They don't demand, as Geoffrey says the Christian deity does, that sexual behavior be offered up for their approval, which leads Susan to pity the Christian God, who is the recipient of "the rare and desiccated conjunctions that take place between Geoffrey and me" (30). She decides that these busy and polymorphic gods look "a bit more fun than Jesus anyway" (33). One evening, Mr. Ramesh closes the shop early, visits her in the back room where she has gone to sleep off her drinking, and asks her to take off her clothes. She willingly complies. In time, he makes her a bed in the storeroom upstairs, where "I can put my hand out and feel the lentils running through my fingers" (38). Her discovery of sexual pleasure with Mr. Ramesh is interpreted in the only context she knows: "I ask him if they offer their sex to God. He isn't very interested in the point but with them, so far as I can gather, sex is all part of God anyway. I can see why too. It's the first time I really understand what all the fuss is about. There among the lentils on the second Sunday after Trinity" (38). Mr. Ramesh is more than Susan's exotic seducer, the dark other whose sexual heat melts her English frigidity. He is also Susan's savior, the one who asks her point-blank the question her own husband can't verbalize: "if intoxication was a prerequisite for sexual intercourse. . . . Because if not he would like to float the suggestion that sober might be even nicer. So the credit for the Road to

Damascus goes to Mr. Ramesh" (40).

The final scene presents an entirely different picture of Susan. Instead of the lank-haired, dark-cardiganed, stooped figure who rarely looks directly at the camera, we see a well-coiffed woman wearing makeup and light clothing with a tasteful brooch at the collar. She looks at us directly and announces that she is an alcoholic. This is the "new woman" she has become. But while it's undeniable that "her posture is upright, with some dignity and assertion" in her person, it simply isn't true that "she now has more self-respect."[11] The condition in which Susan finds herself now is actually no better, and perhaps even worse, than the one in which she began. And this bitter irony arises from the fact that Susan has moved into the drawing room of the vicarage, the Goffmanian front region, where she is performing her new role as the redeemed wife of the devoted vicar, who explains his wife's conversion from alcohol abuse with the slogan, "we met it with love." Susan acerbically remarks, "as if love were some all-purpose antibiotic, which to Geoffrey it probably is" (40).

Susan is now trapped as an accomplice in Geoffrey's ambitions to rise in the church hierarchy. At a "diocesan Jamboree," she is trotted out as an example of his successful ability to bring a stray lamb back into the fold. He exploits her most embarrassing drunken episodes, such as the flower-arranging debacle, for audience applause, making his compassion and tolerance the focal point, not Susan's suffering. As she notes with understandable sarcasm, the other priests seem to be envious of Geoffrey, wishing they had been "smart enough to marry an alcoholic or better still a drug addict, problem wives whom they could do a nice redemption job on, right there on their own doorstep" (40). Geoffrey's career is now made. "Looks certain to be rural dean and that's only the beginning" (41). He thinks that all this has brought them closer together, and Susan doesn't correct him.

Susan performs also at AA, which she attends "religiously," crediting Geoffrey with getting her there, never letting on about Mr. Ramesh, certain that they would assume her affair with him was a symptom of her hitting bottom rather than a sign of her liberation. And now that Mr. Ramesh has gone back to India to collect his young wife and has closed his shop in Leeds in anticipation of opening another in Preston, Susan has no outlet for expressing her real desires. Trapped in both AA and the Anglican services, she concludes her monologue in anger and despair, "I never liked going to one church so I end up going to two. Geoffrey would call that the wonderful mystery of God. I call it bad taste. And I wouldn't do it to a dog. But that's the thing nobody ever says about God . . . he has no taste" (41). On one level we are hearing the frustrations of an Anglican lady who has retreated into disapproval of bad conduct and chides lapses in decorum; God has acted in bad taste toward her. On a deeper level Susan's final remarks allude to the Anglican hymn "O taste and see," which invites Christians to partake in the rich sensual pleasures of God's world. Susan is telling us, however, that her God, unlike those polymorphic gods of Mr. Ramesh, has nothing savory to offer, only an intermittent sequence of "desiccated conjunctions."

If Susan's previous act was transparent—everyone in the parish knew she was an alcoholic—this new act is frighteningly impenetrable. She has become the wonderful woman of Anglican myth. It's a marvel of impression management. Its very success condemns Susan to misery. If Peggy Schofield in *A Woman of No Importance* resembles Winnie in Beckett's *Happy Days* by virtue of her cheerful avoidance of the truth of her appalling condition, then Susan, the vicar's wife who has no last name, resembles Winnie in her progressive paralysis. Figuratively buried from the waist down when she was a social embarrassment, as a paragon she is now buried up to her neck. Bennett, like Beckett, allows us to enjoy the dark wit he brings to this dilemma—an almost perverse bravado of comic language—while also offering us sufficient space for horror and pity.

Soldiering On (first broadcast May 10, 1988)

Only a week separated the initial broadcasts of *Bed among the Lentils* and *Soldiering On*, but the contrast in tone and character places them in very different universes. Muriel Carpenter, recently widowed, belongs to the upper middle classes who inhabit the suburban home counties surrounding London. Her accent is posh, her manner that of a hostess trained to be a successful husband's gracious helpmate. Her monologue reveals to us, however, a severely dysfunctional family. The black sheep daughter suffers from mental problems, the beloved son is a financial swindler, and her adored husband's overfondness for his daughter may have been the cause of her troubles. Unlike Susan, who has a razor-sharp understanding of her predicament, Muriel refuses to face the implications of what she tells us. Even as she slides down the social ladder, slowly divested of the material signs of her former prosperity, Muriel keeps up her cheery demeanor. Late in the monologue, she repeats what a Hare Krishna has said to her about the purpose of this life: "His view is that life is some kind of prep. Trial run. Thinks we're being buffed up for a better role next time" (*TH*, 78). She doesn't disagree with that view, but she doesn't seize the insight either—that she has been playing a "role" and it's only one of a multitude of possibilities.

We first see Muriel seated in an elegant room: period furniture, tastefully framed pictures on the wall. We think she's reminiscing about a case of hostess jitters because she tells us about the difficulties of entertaining a houseful of people she barely knows, with all the attendant problems of choosing a menu, facilitating a social mix, and avoiding awkward silences. It slowly becomes obvious that she is describing the postfuneral reception she has held for her deceased husband's colleagues and friends, many of whom she did not know. Her greatest triumph has been not to "blub," slang in her social circle for crying. In fact, grief is never allowed to enter into this public performance of the perfect hostess; it's only back in the kitchen, out of sight of the guests, that she can shed a tear or two with Mabel the cook. Their lapse is temporary, and, before anyone can notice, they are adjusting their makeup and heading back on stage, or, as Muriel prefers to put it, "powdering our noses and hurling ourselves back into the fray" (71).

One of Muriel's more idiosyncratic traits is her fondness for hyperbolic and surprisingly violent clichés. She can't serve afternoon tea at the reception because "we'd have had a mutiny on our hands" led by the hungry guests who have "trekked" all the way from Wolverhampton. Mabel "holds the fort" while her son takes her to lunch, where he "cracks the whip and gets me to sign lots of papers." When her son consigns his sister to a state mental institution, Muriel confesses that if only they had more liquidity "one would have fought tooth and nail to keep her in the private sector." Nonetheless, she is determined to get the best possible treatment for her daughter, and so she decides to approach the hospital secretary, whom in her language she "beard[s] . . . in his den" (70–75). She undoubtedly wants us to read these exaggerated and trite expressions as signs of a lively and happily engaged person, but they strike us more as symptoms of an underlying and not clearly targeted hostility, a mask worn by a woman so dissociated from her true feelings of resentment that even when she attempts to throw up a smokescreen of bright and peppy language she cannot completely disguise her anger.

And there's a great deal in Muriel's life to be angry about, but it wouldn't do for a woman of her class and breeding to admit it. All she really wants is coaching on how she should behave and feel in her new role as a widow. Her role as perfect wife has concluded; what part should she play now? Everyone tells her the same thing, "not to take any big decisions" (72). These wait-and-see urgings, which suit her tendency toward passivity anyway, actually serve her advisers' interests better than hers, allowing them to peck slowly away at her as if they were vultures and she, not her husband, the corpse. In fact, her monologue is composed of a series of increasing divestments—of property, of status, of space. It begins comically with requests from charities for her husband's personal effects. Cystic Fibrosis and Muscular Dystrophy squabble over his suits, ties, and shoes. The local library would like her to hand over his books, and the Health Centre puts in a bid for his spectacles. When her son removes "three or four of the best pictures, the two carriage clocks and a couple of other choice items" to thwart the estate duty assessors, or so he claims, Muriel admits to feeling "a tiny bit shifty," but even then she has nearly qualified her uneasiness out of existence (73).

By the third scene we hear her allude to some problems with her son's handling of her money, although she is happy to accept his assurance that "it's nothing to worry about, although we may have to pull our horns in a bit further" (75). Experienced viewers of *Talking Heads* know by now what to expect in the next scene, and we are not disappointed. We see Muriel seated amid the packing cases in her once-elegant room, now stripped bare. Her son's financial dealings have bankrupted her and forced her to sell all she has. She of course looks on the bright side. Perhaps a little less materialism in her life will make her a better person. In her search for ready-made wisdom she can borrow, Muriel quotes a familiar piece of Scripture and manages to make it sound like an advertising slogan: it's a "lay not up for yourselves treasures on earth type of thing. The lilies of the field syndrome" (76).

Muriel is not of course the only one brought down in this crash. Hundreds of other investors have also lost their life savings, everyone except her son, who has engineered this disaster. Still, she doesn't budge from her position as his defender: "I suppose Giles has been a scamp. But I don't think he's been wicked. Just not very bright that's all" (77). Muriel is pleased to report that his house in Sloane Street was put in his wife's name.

Our final glimpse of Muriel finds her in a tiny rented "flatlet" in some seaside town, looking rather ordinary. The beauty parlor coif has been replaced with what looks like an amateurish home permanent; the baby blue twinset with pearls has been superseded by a plaid skirt, blue blouse, white cardigan, and sensible shoes. Her son doesn't visit because "it upsets him" to see her in such a state, but her daughter, whom she has probably unconsciously resented and always undervalued ("she was Daddy's little girl"), and who has begun to recover once the family has disintegrated, comes to take her to lunch "like a normal girl" (78–9). Still, we don't suppose Muriel will ever shift her allegiance from son to daughter. She saves her sympathy for her husband when the daughter tells her about her relationship with him ("Sorry for him, I suppose"), which, to judge by the reticence of Muriel's reporting ("Talked about Ralph, etc."), must have been sexually exploitative (78). She has invested too much emotional capital in that shaky male fund to divest herself of it even now.

She says her farewell to us by reaching for a Walkman and headphones, and, before she loses herself completely in the music, she tells us with a smile, "I wouldn't want you to think this was a tragic story. . . . I'm not a tragic woman. . . . I'm not that type" (79). Of course, tragedy requires a self-consciousness and a willingness to self-examination that Muriel refuses. The headphones perfectly insulate her from disturbing thoughts and doubts. The music she hears may be Johann Strauss's, according to the stage directions, depicting the gentility and order of a rose-colored world, the one Muriel once inhabited uncritically and performed in very successfully. It remains the one she prefers to construct for herself even in her reduced circumstances. Because Muriel's entrapment in her performance is self-willed, we don't feel the pity for her that we feel for Susan. Perhaps our patience with stiff-upper-lip routines is limited; perhaps we prefer the bracing freshness of Susan's anger to the repressed ambiguities of Muriel's clichés.

Her Big Chance (first broadcast May 17, 1988)

Because Bennett has created here a character who lacks even the pathos of self-consciousness, it's tempting to dismiss this monologue as lightweight.[12] Unlike Muriel, who represses the truth of her situation, Lesley is too dense to understand her own predicament. As played with subtle vulgarity by Julie Walters, Lesley is an aspiring actress whose only talent is her ability to fool herself that she is a serious performer. She is the classic ingenue as airhead, who can rationalize performing in the nude as the artistic expression of her psyche, and who views her own sexual promiscuity as a form of scientific inquiry: "My hobby is people. I collect people" (*TH*, 57). We can tell early on that her claims to intellectual and artistic depth are imaginary. So we laugh at her as the butt of a joke that everyone gets except her.

If Lesley's performance is too easy to read, too transparent to challenge our critical faculties, this would-be actress is still fascinating to watch, especially as she tries to negotiate the slippery boundaries between professional performance and everyday performance. It should come as no surprise to the viewer that Lesley barely notices the difference. From the pabulum in self-actualization books she has developed the philosophy that any skill or information she acquires in the course of her life can be pressed into the service of making her a better actress. Whether it's chess or waterskiing, "spoken Italian, selling valuable oil paintings [or] canoeing," Lesley believes that "the more you have to offer as a person the better you are as an actress" (67). In other words, all life is a props department of skills and attitudes to use at the next audition.

The monologue opens with an upside-down view of Lesley lying on her bed under a sunlamp reflected in a mirrored ceiling. Add to that her portentous opening lines, "I shot a man last week. In the back. I miss it now, it was really interesting," and we have a capsule summary of a woman whose confusion of the real and the performed is central to her character (56). The sunlamp, the mirrored ceiling, and the bed offer the visual cues about her immersion in the illusory games of the physical and sensual, and the upside-down camera angle offers a visual shorthand for her skewed perception. Her words, we soon discover, have no reference to real life. She is reminiscing about a part she has played in a video "for the West German market." She misses it, because the part of "Travis" offered her a rare opportunity to indulge her fantasy that she is a serious artist who can create a character, although her choice of "interesting" to describe the experience (she repeats that word more than a dozen times in the course of the monologue) exposes the actual limitations of her expressive imagination.

"Professional" is also one of Lesley's favorite words. She repeats it almost as a mantra—"I am professional to my fingertips"(56)—without a hint that she understands it as an ironic double entendre. The high point of her professional career so far has been playing an extra in Roman Polanski's *Tess.* As the touchstone experience of her working life, it represents the beau ideal she returns to nostalgically whenever the slipshod arrangements of her current enterprise become too obvious. Insinuating an intimacy of first names, she remembers especially fondly Roman's superior manners, the glories of the croissants offered by the catering service, and the immaculate conditions of the toilet facilities. We have already gathered that she has been cast in the part of Travis because she has a thirty-eight-inch bust and looks good in her bra and panties, as the acerbic wardrobe-makeup-propman Scott remarks, and not because in her audition she has impressed the casting director with her insights into the character. If anything, Lesley's interview reveals additional layers of self-assured ignorance. For example, to the question of whether she can play chess, she responds:

"Chess, Simon. Do you mean the musical?" He said, "No, the game." I said, "As a matter of fact, Simon, I don't. Is that a problem?" He said, "Not if you waterski. Travis is fundamentally an outdoor girl, but we thought it might be fun to make her an intellectual on the side." I said, "Well, Simon, I'm very happy to learn both chess and water-skiing, but could I make a suggestion? Reading generally indicates a studious temperament and I'm a very convincing reader," I said, "because it's something I frequently do in real life." I could tell he was impressed. (58)

These ludicrous suggestions do not, of course, exhaust Lesley's ability to imagine and create a character. As she is being pushed out the door she comes up with the idea of Travis in a bikini with a briefcase—"the best of every possible world" in her opinion—and returns to the office a minute later to clarify that she didn't mean an old-fashioned briefcase but the type that opens up into a small writing desk. As she pops open the door to Simon's office to say, "She could be sitting in a wet bikini with the briefcase open on her knee," she overhears him saying on the phone, "You won't believe this," but the sarcasm is lost on her (60).

Lesley's dedication to her art becomes increasingly annoying to the film crew of what is obviously a soft porn video. When the director asks her to take off her bikini top, Lesley demurs, as if she were playing Chekhov. "Would Travis do that?" she asks. "We know that Travis plays chess. She also reads. Is Travis the type to go topless?" (63–4). In time, the director's assistant learns that he can talk Lesley into taking off not only her bikini top but also her bottom by appropriating the jargon of Stanislavskian character motivation: "The real Travis wouldn't [take off her bottom]. But by displaying herself naked before her boyfriend's business associate she is showing her contempt for his whole way of life." Lesley is ecstatic: "At last Gunther is giving me something I can relate to" (64). Lesley happily reports to us how she sat there on the yacht stark naked, applying suntan lotion in a deeply serious attempt to get to the core of her character.

The crew must not only overcome Lesley's pretensions, but circumvent her lack of acting ability as well. They scrap the rudimentary dialogue she's been assigned— "I can't help it, Alfredo, I have a headache"—and replace it with Alfredo's exposition, "You and your headaches." Most actors would note the diminution of the part, but Lesley is fooled by Gunther's bow to Stanislavskian realism: "Gunther then thought it would be more convincing if my headache was so bad that I couldn't actually speak." She eagerly contributes the observation that if it were a migraine Travis was suffering from, she almost certainly wouldn't be able to speak. Gunther's resigned, "Whatever you say," sends her off into another rhapsody: "It's wonderful, that moment, when you feel a director first begin to trust you and you can really start to build" (65).

Alongside Lesley's complete incompetence we see a sexual promiscuity that seems to belie her insistence that she is committed only to nurturing her craft.[13] At the end of nearly every scene she ends up in the bed of some man connected with the film, whether it's Spud, the electrician; Terry, the camera assistant; Kenny, the animal handler (this section was excised from the television film but appears in the published script); or, finally, Gunther, the director. Her references to being a "professional" and to giving a "performance" acquire an added resonance, in this light. We don't, however, dislike Lesley for these one-night stands. She isn't motivated by lust. Sex offers her the best chance to be close to those who run the business. A kind of loopy dedication to the whole project of acting drives her into their beds. If it takes lying down on a casting couch to get a part, then Lesley sees it as part of the job, part of being a professional.

Her final words are "Acting is really just giving" (67). While the viewer appreciates the obvious innuendo, Lesley doesn't. She really has persuaded herself that she is a serious thinker, actor, and person, and not what we see: a disposable plaything with only the meagerest resources at her disposal. At the very least, Lesley confuses appearance with substance. If she can mouth deep thoughts, she must be a thinker; if she can get a part in a film, she must be an actress; if many men in the film business sleep with her, she must be making valuable contacts. Lesley plays at playing all the time. All of experience and thought, whether waterskiing or reading, canoeing or learning Italian, are useful equally. But only as they contribute to her ability to play additional roles. Her parting remark to Scott as the filming wraps up, "Now it's back to real life," is parried by his reminder, "Some of us never left it" (67).

A Cream Cracker under the Settee (first broadcast May 24, 1988)

Ten years before he created the character of Doris for this monologue, Bennett reminisced in his diary about his mother's obsession with dirt and the astonishing number of rituals and tools that helped her control it. "My mother maintained an intricate hierarchy of cloths, buckets and dusters, to the Byzantine differentiations of which she alone was privy. Some cloths were dish cloths but not sink cloths; some were for the sink but not for the floor. There were dirty buckets and clean buckets, brushes for indoors, brushes for the flags" (*WH*, 278). As the wife of a Yorkshire tradesman, whose home was her only sphere of influence, Bennett's mother believed that cleanliness was one of the ways the lower middle class could distinguish itself from those on the next lower rung of the social ladder.

In Doris we see a woman who has spent a lifetime trying to sweep away the dust and dirt she associates with the lower orders only to collapse in defeat at the end. It's a literal collapse, in that she falls and breaks her hip as she attempts to dust the top of a tall buffet, but it's also an emotional surrender to the inevitability of decay and death. Bennett has said that of all the six characters in *Talking Heads*, only Doris "knows the score . . . but though she can see it's her determination to dust that's brought about her downfall, what she doesn't see is that it's the same obsession that tidied her husband into the grave" (8). Of course it's not only her husband who has been tidied into the grave. Doris's insistence on maintaining this front of hyper-cleanliness as a badge of her class standing ultimately sterilizes her whole existence.

Dust to dust, ashes to ashes. The dominant note in the opening scene is that of frustration. Doris is sitting in a chair, unable to move because her leg has gone numb after her fall. Dust is what she wanted to do, dust is what she faults the home help, Zulema, for not doing, and dust is what she fears most, next to being assigned to Stafford House, a home for the elderly who can no longer care for themselves. As she massages her leg, she rehearses her grievances against the untidy world she has grown old in: a gate that bangs in the wind because Zulema didn't secure it properly; neighbors' trees whose leaves fall into her yard, exposing her to criticism for not keeping her property tidy; strangers who come into her garden "and behave like animals. I find the evidence in a morning" (*TH*, 85).

Doris is the most recent embodiment of Bennett's fiercely independent northern woman, a line that stretches all the way back to *Sunset Across the Bay*. In some ways, she is Mam in *Say Something Happened*, ten years down the road, now a widow and faced with the unpalatable choices of either putting the HELP sign in the window or trying to survive on her own resources. The cream cracker of the title suggests how depleted Doris's resources are at this point in her life. In the second scene, when Doris has moved onto the floor in an attempt to reach the window, she can see the cracker lying under the settee, additional proof of Zulema's slipshod housekeeping, another reason to believe that "you're better off doing it yourself" (82). The cream cracker is the perfect image of the meager nourishment Doris has subsisted on by "doing it for yourself." It's not food enough to sustain, just food enough to leave annoying crumbs, as she soon discovers when she brushes it off and eats it.

Doris wonders how things might have been different. Perhaps if she'd had a child there would be grandchildren now, and she "wouldn't have been in this fix" (88). But her only pregnancy ended in a stillbirth, a fetus the midwife thought fit only to be wrapped in newspaper, placed in a shoebox, and taken away for disposal. You might think that the tidiness of the act would have appealed to her, but she still protests half a century later—"Wrapping him in newspaper as if he was dirty. He wasn't dirty, little thing" (88). Her husband's suggestion that they get a dog didn't lead anywhere either. By the time she had relaxed her objections to cleaning up after its "little hairs," he had lost interest. They had one another, but since she doesn't reminisce about happy times with him, only the frustration she felt with his inability to carry out his projects, it doesn't seem to have been a particularly intimate relationship. They apparently had few friends, and all the old neighbors have either died or moved away. "We were always on our own, me and Wilfred. We weren't gregarious. We just weren't the gregarious type. He thought he was, but he wasn't" (89).

In the course of the monologue, help seems at hand, but each time she fails to secure it. The first possibility is a small boy she sees enter her garden. She shoos him away, however, when he begins to urinate. Force of habit overwhelms her present need, and her reflex revulsion against all kinds of uncleanness trumps every other consideration. Her reaction to the boy is not a fluke. She has already told us, with strenuous disapproval, of the evangelical Christians who once shouted "Good News!" through her letterbox. She refused to admit them because they had left her gate open. We suspect that the Christians would be greeted with the same cold response if they returned now and hadn't learned better manners. "Love God and close all gates," she tells us, a piece of advice that seems oxymoronic (86).

In the final scene, a policeman comes to the door and asks if she needs help, because he has noticed that her lights are off. She turns him away by assuring him that she's fine and has merely dozed off. This refusal of help does not arise from force of habit or reflex. It's a conscious decision born of an afternoon spent assessing her life. Doris seems resigned to dying there on the floor of her own house rather than face almost certain assignment to an institution like Stafford House, "stuck with a lot of old lasses," all "smelling of pee" (89). Rather than live in a world where young boys urinate in your garden, and you're unable to keep your own place as clean as you'd like it, dependent on the likes of Zulema, who talks a good clean but barely musters any effort at it, Doris accepts that "it's done with now"(91). Her time has passed.

Goffman's reminder that we sometimes overlook the performative aspects of people's class and age is pertinent here. Doris—not just Thora Hird, the actress, who received the British Academy Award for best television actress in this role— has been performing for us the role of a lower-middle-class elderly woman born and raised in Yorkshire. She defines herself for us by her insistence on cleanliness, her disapproval of her new neighbors—"I don't think they're married, half of them"(85)—and her refusal to "mix" with other people after a life of self-suffi-ciency. She wants us to believe that a time and a place existed "when people were clean and the streets were clean and it was all clean" (89). She also wants us to approve of her standards since her identity depends on them. It's a consistent per-formance, consistent unto death, where, ironically, dust is everywhere and every-thing. Bennett sees this kind of person with some degree of sympathy, doomed to unhappiness in an imperfect world, but he also recognizes, as his remark that Doris tidied her husband into his grave indicates, the flaws in her performance of herself that lead to her inability to live in a changed world.

The profoundest irony of this final scene is that this is the only occasion in the six monologues when a second person appears. Every one of the six monologuists is desperately alone, but none in a more literally life-threatening way than Doris. And she turns away the other person, the person she had earlier called "Salvation" (85). Bennett allows us to read this refusal not only as a stubborn inability to accept change and difference but as an act of enormous existential courage. Doris is will-ing to look into the darkness that has been slowly descending during the mono-logue. She knows precisely what turning away from help means. "You've done it now, Doris," she tells herself. "Done it now, Wilfred," she tells her dead husband. She harbors no illusions about salvation—social or religious. She will die, most probably of hypothermia. She will not wait for Godot, she will not accept the increasing immobility that Winnie adapted herself to, she will not deny, as Krapp does, the unhappiness that has dogged all her days. Doris's monologue is Bennett at his most Beckettian. So far.

NOTES

1. The success of *Talking Heads* has led to what might be seen as the ultimate compliment—its adoption as a set text for advanced-level high school students, who must study *Talking Heads* alongside more traditional canonical plays like *Death of a Salesman* and *A Streetcar Named Desire*. Bennett doesn't seem to appreciate the honor much. He reports that he's been "plagued by students wanting to know what the monologues meant" ("Talking Shop," *Radio Times,* Oct. 10–16, 1998, 32).

2. "Alan Bennett: 'He makes it easy for you,'"*Independent*, Nov. 14, 1999.

3. Bennett, "Talking Shop," 34.

4. Goffman, *Presentation of Self*, 80.

5. Kafka reportedly joked as he was dying of tuberculosis and spitting up a great deal of phlegm, "I think I deserve the Nobel Prize for sputum." Quoted by Bennett in his Introduction to *Two Kafka Plays*, xi.

6. Turner, 60.

7. Turner, 64,

8. Goffman, *Presentation of Self*, 201.

9. Turner, 57.

10. Goffman, *Presentation of Self*, 169–70.

11. Turner, 62.

12. Daphne Turner rates *Her Big Chance* as "less substantial" and the "least satisfactory" of the monologues (59, 61).

13. Lesley's promiscuity bothers Turner, who writes, "The trouble with the piece is that there is no clear connection between what interests Bennett in the character and the casual promiscuity, emphasized by the way he shapes the monologue" (61). Viewed from a performance perspective, however, the connection between the character and her promiscuity is less puzzling.

CHAPTER SIX

Millennium Approaches: *Talking Heads 2*

The Hand of God (1998)
Miss Fozzard Finds Her Feet (1998)
Playing Sandwiches (1998)
The Outside Dog (1998)
Nights in the Gardens of Spain (1998)
Waiting for the Telegram (1998)

Nearly ten years after the broadcast of the first *Talking Heads*, Bennett presented a follow-up series in the fall of 1998 on BBC2. In preparation for many years, these six monologues were slow to see the light of day; Bennett says he consigned them to a desk drawer as "too gloomy to visit on the public." He has tried to account for their darkness, but can find no better reason than "it is just the way they turned out. . . . It's simply that though I may sit down with the intention of writing something funny, it seldom comes out that way any more" (*TH2*, 8). The absence of comedy is not, however, the distinguishing mark of this series. True, none of the plays is particularly funny, with the possible exception of *Miss Fozzard*, but then Bennett's plays have always had a dark side. As he has admitted, "*joie de vivre* has never been my strong point."[1] What is different here is that Bennett's tidy sitting rooms have been flung open onto the wider ugliness of a weary society at the edge of the millennium, where many of the characters find themselves in terrifyingly life-altering situations. With characteristic understatement, Bennett calls this shift in tone "some acknowledgement of the often uncomfortable world we nowadays inhabit."[2] Where once his characters' secrets consisted of private vices like alcoholism or obsessive-compulsive behavior, now they consist of spousal abuse, the sexual molestation of children, and complicity in murder. Violence that was once emotional is now physical, and the performance of normality that each character tries to present has become more unstable. Dramatic irony still plays a role, but the characters are much more self-conscious of the performances they are giving. Unlike Muriel, Graham, and Leslie in the first series, several of Bennett's new characters come to a shattering awareness that their situation is desperate, an awareness they cannot long disguise from the audience. It's highly unlikely that Bennett could claim, as he did in the first series, that any of these new talking heads is "artless."

Once again, five of the six monologuists are women, but they are not merely lonely women yearning for some human connection. Three of the five women— Marjory, Rosemary, and Miss Fozzard—are caught up in dangerous or unorthodox sexual situations that they seem powerless to control. And the one male monologuist—Wilfred—is caught in the grip of an even more powerful force, his compulsive attraction to young girls. It's as if the grim tide of despair in *Bed Among the Lentils* and of death in *A Cream Cracker Under the Settee* has washed over into this series and colored all its stories. Or nearly all, for as always Bennett is compassionate in handling his characters' predicaments, softening some of the worst horrors they as performers, and we in the audience, face. For instance, before Wilfred's secret failing is revealed, Bennett allows him to gain a measure of acceptance from the audience, even though for most of them the sexual abuse of children is the basest of crimes. In the same way, Bennett complicates and deepens our understanding of the dangerous territory Marjory and Rosemary occupy in their marriages by presenting these women not as victims of male violence but as complicit witnesses to it. Bennett's sympathies still lie with the outsider, but where the first series featured marginal figures whose stories would hardly make the local news, "nearly all these [new] monologues could be seen as stories behind the headlines, and behind the tabloid headlines in particular."[3] Bennett has gone from telling the stories of private people, a process Daphne Turner characterizes as "speaking for the unheard,"[4] to imagining the stories of people thrust into the public eye by some sensational event. These are people whose stories the journalists inevitably distort, people who are not so much unheard as misrepresented.

The Hand of God (first broadcast October 13, 1998)

Although broadcast second in the series, this play opens the published collection of *Talking Heads 2*. In some ways it is the monologue closest in tone and impact to those of the first series, with the speaker's public presentation of herself undermined by nearly everything she says. Awash in the speaker's stream of unconscious ironies, we find ourselves judging her self-deception to be as pitiable as Leslie's in *Her Big Chance*, her self-righteous concern as hypocritical as Irene's in *A Lady of Letters*. Described by Eileen Atkins, who portrays her, as "a snob who's worked hard at covering her northern roots,"[5] Celia is not a sympathetic character, which may explain why her monologue was not broadcast first. Perhaps BBC2 feared that, though readers of the published scripts could pass quickly on to the next play if they didn't like the opener, viewers who disliked the first offering might decide to skip the whole series.

Celia is an antiques dealer with acid opinions about the declining standards in her business. The young men at Christie's and Sotheby's may look like gentlemen, but she dismisses them as no better than "barrow boys," curbside merchants. She reserves special scorn for those antique shops that are "eking the job out with jam and pots of chutney." As she tells an inquiring customer, "I shall start doing chutney, madam, when Tesco [a supermarket chain] start doing gateleg tables." She also takes great pride in her own shrewdness. The first words out of her mouth establish her imperious confidence and set her up for a fall: "I won't touch pictures. I make it a rule. I've seen too many fingers burned" (*TH2*, 24). Since her story will turn on her failing to recognize a Michelangelo drawing—a sketch for the hand of God on the Sistine Chapel ceiling—the frontloaded ironies begin to pile up immediately and almost too heavily, although it probably would take a second reading or viewing to notice them all. What is unmistakable is that Celia's snobbish self-assurance makes her ripe for humbling. She doesn't stand a chance of surviving this monologue with her pretensions intact.

The monologue opens with Celia seated alone in her shop, which is filled with heavy darkwood tables, chests, and clocks, but empty of customers. The atmosphere is austere. Customers are intruders here unless they spend great sums of money. She calls her shop "a goldfish bowl" where she is always on display, which underscores the theatrical nature of her public image. She sees herself as a woman of taste and refinement who is just gracious enough to allow the hoi polloi to gawk at the beautiful objects that are beyond their understanding. She doesn't see herself as cold and forbidding and even tries to suggest that she cares for a local maiden lady, old Miss Ventriss, because she "took two Crown Derby plates off her once, just as a favour, one of them chipped." But seeing Miss Ventriss looking into the window of the shop, Celia's concerned observation that she is "looking a bit frail" is immediately followed by her mercantile assessment of the "lovely cameo brooch" she is wearing (25). Over and over again, Celia's rapid-fire appraisals of Miss Ventriss's belongings undermine her human concern for the old woman's declining health. "Thin little hand. Like dried leaves. Tragic," she says, only to move her eye quickly to the "lovely bedside table with piecrust molding" (26). The home help's description of Miss Ventriss's precarious condition, "you've only to look at her under that nightdress and there's nothing there," leads Celia to ask, "Yes. Where did that nightdress come from?" (27). The ultimate expression of her rapacity comes when she lifts up the mattress on which Miss Ventriss is sleeping to examine the 1830 bed. Celia reports, "I'm just tucking the sheet back when I see her little eyes are open and she's watching me. I think she said, 'Happy?' . . . Of course when she said 'Happy?,' what she probably meant was that *she* was happy" (28). It's an improbable reading, which Celia is too smart to really believe, but it suits her needs. She claims that the other dealers in town are "the sharks," whose greed is "so transparent" (27–8), while her concern and caring extend equally to the beautiful objects in the house and to their owner.

Oscar Wilde's definition of the cynic as the person who knows the price of everything and the value of nothing fits Celia well. She can identify the provenance of nearly every object she sees, down to the decade of its manufacture, but she cannot see beyond that to its emotional value. A minor example is her "appreciation" of the embroidered cloth that the priest uses to cover the chalice when he comes to anoint Miss Ventriss. "Arts and Crafts by the look of it and a beautiful thing. Pity it can't be used for something," she concludes, presumably meaning something that will allow it to enter the open market and return a profit (28). Her indifference to the long marriage of art and religion reaches its absurd zenith when she is offered a small gift by Miss Ventriss's niece, a box of odds and ends that includes "a rather smudgy drawing of a finger," which isn't of much interest to her, although "the frame is very distinctive. Quite small but with little doors that open so it looks a bit like an altar, nineteenth century probably" (29).

Earlier in the monologue, Celia had talked about the "oldest dodge in the world": a customer feigns interest in something other than the real object of his attention and then casually asks, "Oh . . . incidentally, how much is this little thing?" "And they expect you to be taken in by it," she exclaims in disbelief (25). Of course, in keeping with the simple ironies of this piece, Celia is taken in by just such a dodge. When a well-dressed and well-spoken customer comes into the shop in search of a refectory table she notices that his attention is taken by the framed drawing, although he puts it aside to measure the table. Just as he is about to leave, promising to telephone her once he checks the dimensions of his dining room, he inquires about the frame and says he doesn't care much for the drawing, but turns down her offer to remove it from the frame. Celia had originally thought she might get as much as thirty pounds for the frame, especially if she removed the drawing and replaced it with a flower print, but she takes a chance, guessing from his "educated voice" that he has the money, and asks for one hundred pounds. When he puts the frame down, signaling that the price is too high, she lowers the price to ninety pounds. He hastily writes out a check and leaves. Celia feels pretty smug about this transaction, especially since, as she notes with additional satisfaction, "I'd come down to ninety pounds but he was in such a rush he'd still made it out for one hundred pounds" (30).

Six months later, the newspapers report on this young man's extraordinary find. He is of course one of those "barrow boys" Celia has such contempt for, a "young blood from Christie's" (31). Estimates are that the drawing will fetch anywhere from £5 million to £10 million at auction, since it is a unique study for the hand of God, Michelangelo having wittily placed the ring of his patron, Pope Julius II, on God's finger. It doesn't surprise us when Celia says "I don't see the joke" (31). Eileen Atkins plays the final scene with a stiff upper lip, proclaiming, "No, I wasn't the sort of person who is resentful," but we can see a slight quiver in her chin as she speaks, and we know that she is deeply shaken, though she will hardly admit it (30). Once the man from Christie's has revealed where he found the drawing— "Says in the paper he picked it up in a junk shop. Junk shop," she repeats, deeply affronted (31)—she becomes even more the goldfish in the bowl, as her shop becomes a stop for curiosity seekers. The last thing we see is a pyramid display of tomato chutney on the unsold refectory table. Celia looks at it, somewhat sheepishly, and then averts her eyes downward, unable to face the scrutiny of the camera and her audience.

We might feel sympathy for Celia's humiliation if it weren't for one thing she tells us just before the end. She thinks of Miss Ventriss's niece, who gave her the framed sketch without knowing what it was, and who, living in Canada, might not have heard the news. So she writes to inform her, not in commiseration as a fellow sufferer, but to "wipe the smile off her face" (31). Malice isn't pretty, especially when it comes from someone who has recently proclaimed that she isn't the resentful type.

Celia's monologue doesn't describe a life-altering experience, though the next four in this series will. The worst that can be said is that she has suffered a professional loss of face, damage to her reputation and her ego. She has been, so to speak, poked in the eye by the finger of God, but she will survive this setback, although she won't have learned much from it. We end up regarding Celia differently from such similarly self-deluded characters as Leslie and Irene in the first series. Leslie, in *Her Big Chance*, is too dim to learn anything, so we don't expect her to get the meaning of her own story. Irene, in *A Lady of Letters*, moves beyond her self-righteousness into something approaching an understanding of human weakness, so we relax our judgment of her frailties. Celia, however, is smarter than Leslie and less capable of change than Irene. We are happy to leave her stuck with, and in, her own superiority.

Miss Fozzard Finds Her Feet (first broadcast October 6, 1998)

Patricia Routledge holds a special pride of place in Alan Bennett's repertory company. His first dramatic monologue, *A Woman of No Importance*, was especially created for her, and *Miss Fozzard* is the fourth of his TV plays she has appeared in. Routledge's particular gift is her ability to convey smug self-satisfaction without sacrificing the audience's sympathy. Here, as earlier, her character is a chatterbox, eager to share her point of view, which she sees not as a personal perspective but as the only one decent people would have. She's innately conservative, with a smallish mind (the *-ish* construction being a discriminating locution her characters would approve of) and limited experience, although these deficiencies never inhibit her self-assurance. She is usually well-spoken, with a cultivated accent that suggests a bit of social ambition, and is invariably a spinster lady of middle age. Though they are bastions of northern English middle-class female propriety, Patricia Routledge invests her characters with an individual humanity that transcends the type. Her one-note performances as Hyacinth Bucket in the TV series *Keeping Up Appearances* only helps us to appreciate the infinitely subtler work she has done with Bennett's characters.

As Miss Fozzard, Routledge signals the uncharted depths of her character by performing the other voices in the story she tells, not merely reporting their speech. When she shifts back and forth from her chirpy female voice to a gruffer or heartier male voice, we get the impression that this woman has a great deal more gusto and life than her circumstances have so far allowed her to express. Miss Fozzard is full of voices, of performative selves heretofore untapped, and Routledge prepares us for this journey of self-discovery with her own subtle and rich insights into the character.

Miss Fozzard (this is the only time one of the talking heads has not been given a first name) is a woman who must cope with two vexing problems: the rehabilitation of her brother, Bernard, who has had a stroke, which interrupts her career as a department head at a store in Leeds, and the loss of her chiropodist of many years, which necessitates her finding a substitute. In her mind, finding a competent home attendant for Bernard and a suitable chiropodist for herself are of at least equal importance, although we suspect she cares more about her feet than she does about her brother's mobility and speech. In the British idiom, "to find your feet" means to establish your independence and to achieve it under your own power, a process recommended to fledglings. Miss Fozzard is no fledgling in age, but her knowledge of the world beyond her prim spinsterish boundaries is in its infancy. In finding Bernard a therapist—Miss Mallory Molloy from Hobart, Tasmania—and in finding herself a new chiropodist—Mr. Dunderdale of Lawnswood, a most respectable suburb of Leeds—Miss Fozzard breaks through to a new sympathy for the irregularities of life. "I never thought I had a life," she tells us, until she discovers that sexual desire takes many unusual forms and that a woman's feet may be the way to a man's heart (*TH2*, 44).

Our first view of Miss Fozzard, with her humorless chatter, her neat dress ("peppy but classic," in her words) and her helmetlike coiffeur, reminds us of Bennett's earlier thick-skinned obsessives. She takes an unexamined, literal view of the world, at least at the start. She wouldn't recognize irony unless it walked up and introduced itself. Even then, she might decline further acquaintance because irony would complicate her comfortable view of the world. A proud career woman, she doesn't see the paradox in her rejecting Cindy Bickerton as her new chiropodist. "Cindy?" she says with disdain. "That doesn't inspire confidence. She sounds as if she should be painting nails not cutting them" (34). In the same vein, she follows to the letter Bernard's doctor's advice that "the more language one can throw at him the better," by tediously repeating her whole day's activities to him each evening (35). When the first word he finally speaks is "Cow," she doesn't take it personally, as she should, considering the longstanding antipathy between them. She actually believes the doctor when he tells her, "it doesn't matter what you say so long as it's language: language is balls coming at you from every angle" (37). Perhaps that is why, when Mr. Dunderdale asks her what her brother did for a living, she can say, without the slightest hint of irony, "Not to put too fine a point on it, Mr. Dunderdale, he was a murderer. . . . Well, he was a tobacconist which comes to the same thing. Sweets and tobacco, a little kiosk in Headingley" (38–9). Language indeed becomes "balls," if the word "murderer" can blithely be applied to Bernard's profession. In her narrow moralism, Miss Fozzard has no difficulty in embracing Bernard's stroke as his punishment for smoking, being overweight, liking his drink, and presumably ushering half the population of Leeds down the road to their own strokes. In other words, "he's paying for it." But she cannot understand why she should be caught up in a punishment that's rightly his. "Only what seems unfair is that I'm paying for it too," she complains (39).

In the course of her monologue Miss Fozzard discovers that the link she shares with Bernard goes well beyond her imaginary martyrdom for his excesses. Bernard's relationship with the strapping Miss Molloy evolves quickly into his paying her "for services rendered," until she decamps for the Maldive Islands and he is left with an empty bank account (43). For perhaps the first time in her life, Miss Fozzard doesn't climb the pulpit to lecture Bernard, because she has found herself in an equally compromising position with Mr. Dunderdale. "Pillar of the community" and a widower in his seventies with a full head of hair, Mr. Dunderdale has an interest in ladies' feet that goes well beyond the professional. He recognizes a fellow obsessive in Miss Fozzard, and visit by visit he flatters her into modeling his collection of ladies' footwear, which includes the exotically named "fur-lined Gibson bruised look" bootee in "Bengal bronze" (40). Her once-a-month appointment is upped to once a week, at no extra charge. Miss Fozzard is pleased with Mr. Dunderdale's attentions, and she is more than happy to comply with his request that she alleviate his chronic pain by trampling on his back wearing the bootees. She betrays to us only the slightest disquietude as she describes leaving him lying face down on the hearthrug, too blissful to accompany her to the front door.

Even though the weekly sessions of back trampling crowd out her foot treatments, Miss Fozzard keeps coming back for more, until Bernard's second stroke curtails her visits. She can't afford both a new attendant and a chiropodist. At this point Mr. Dunderdale proposes a new scheme: "Why don't we reverse the arrangement. . . . I pay you." He counters her objection that "it's very unusual" with smooth flattery: "'You're a very unusual woman. . . . Because you're a free spirit, Miss Fozzard. You make your own rules.' I said, 'Well, I like to think so.' He said, 'I'm the same. We're two of a kind, you and I, Miss Fozzard. Mavericks'" (44). Mr. Dunderdale may have seen something in Miss Fozzard that we would never suspect. More likely, he knows that language—words such as *unusual, free spirit, two of a kind, mavericks*—can be a seductive tool for defining reality and behavior in ways that make unorthodox actions palatable to orthodox sensibilities. Miss Fozzard, that "free spirit," assures us, "It's all very decorous," even as he assures her, "We are just enthusiasts, Miss Fozzard, you and I and there's not enough enthusiasm in the world these days." Bennett cannot resist reminding us just what that enthusiasm is for, as Mr. Dunderdale adds, "Now if those Wellingtons are comfy I just want you in your own time and as slowly as you like very gently to mark time on my bottom" (45). Miss Fozzard ends her monologue by saying, "I suppose there's a word for what I'm doing but . . . I skirt round it" (45). Patricia Routledge looks at the camera somewhat quizzically, as if still surprised by herself.

Miss Fozzard has learned in the course of her monologue that she is not immune to life's messiness, and that being caught up in life itself inevitably forces you down from your moral pedestal. "People don't like to think you have a proper life, that's what I've decided. Or any more of a life than they know about," she remarks. "Then when they find out they think it's shocking. Else funny. I never thought I had a life. It was always Bernard who had the life" (44). Most poignantly of all, she learns that words do matter. They're not just balls to be batted around haphazardly. Sometimes it's better to "skirt round" the word, rather than give it the judgmental concreteness that society so often demands of unconventional or unorthodox behavior. Miss Fozzard finds herself a secret outlaw, just the sort of person she was once quick to condemn or categorize as, say, a "murderer." Now the shoe is on the other foot. Some might see Miss Fozzard's reluctance to put a name to what she is doing with Mr. Dunderdale as a form of denial, a refusal to admit how much she has compromised herself. But perhaps this silence is a kind of liberation instead, a new sensitivity to the power of language, a new respect for privacy. Miss Fozzard has joined the human race, not all of whose messy desires and habits can be labeled simply, especially when those labels serve to diminish behavior understood best by those who participate in it. In a way, rather than yield up her secrets, as most of the talking heads do, Miss Fozzard keeps hers, and we like her the better for it.

Playing Sandwiches (first broadcast October 20, 1998)

The first few lines of Wilfred's monologue set a pattern. We see how he wishes us to perceive him; in time we'll also see how circumstances tend to disrupt this self-presentation:

> I was in the paper shop this dinnertime getting some licorice allsorts. Man serving me said, "I wish I was like you." Shouted out to the woman, "I wish I was him. Always buying sweets, never gets fat." I said, "Yes, I'm lucky. Only I cycle." She said, "Yes, I've seen you. You work for the Parks Department." He said, "Weren't you a lollipop man once?" I said, "No." He said, "I thought I'd seen you, stood at the crossing." Racks and racks of magazines. Always men in there, looking. (*TH2*, 48)

This anecdote, in which Wilfred presents himself as a public servant who elicits unsolicited admiration from strangers, is told in an affable, smiling manner by David Haig. However, if the shopkeeper knew Wilfred's full story, he would undoubtedly not wish to be him. As we discover in the course of the monologue, none of Wilfred's statements and observations can be taken at face value. To start with, he doesn't buy the candy for himself, and the only "cycle" in his life is that of recovery and fall. He has been a "lollipop man," the English term for a school crossing guard, but he has a good reason for denying it. Moreover, his disapproval of pornographic magazines is rooted in a complex sexuality that is alternately prudish and tormented. Wilfred is, it turns out, a convicted pedophile, whose story is one of the riskiest Bennett has undertaken. Part of the risk, as Bennett sees it, is that according to the moral standards set by the tabloid press, "murder and grievous bodily harm are thought of as respectable crimes and sexual offences are not . . . the press hysteria over paedophilia, and in particular offences that occurred long in the past, has reached dangerous proportions . . . But such is the atmosphere surrounding the subject that one thinks twice before setting out any opinions one might have on the matter" (*TH2*, 16–17).

Bennett may have had second thoughts, but he forged ahead anyway to create a portrait of Wilfred that is remarkable for its sympathy and psychological insight. In many ways an ordinary man with limited prospects, Wilfred might have been a happy breadwinner with a large family. He has an impeccable work ethic and a strong sense of responsibility. His Parks Department job is, ironically, to clean up the messes that other people leave behind. He is forever clearing away used condoms, discarded tampons, dog excrement, and human vomit, to say nothing of the usual litter of beer cans and fast-food containers. The opening camera shot looks down at Wilfred as he diligently sweeps piles of leaves that never seem to diminish in size, a Sisyphean endeavor that suggests the intractable nature of his problem. He is, in a less comic way, the male version of one of Bennett's classic types—the hygiene-obsessed housewife. Except, in Wilfred's case, we sense that he is trying to clean the Augean stables of a filthy society awash in its own waste, all the while denying his own complicity in the mess. As a native of Leeds he remembers a time when order reigned in public places and antisocial displays such as obscene graffiti were unimaginable. "When I was a boy," he reminisces, "the fountain went. The band played. People kept off the grass. It was lovely" (53). A lonely figure in a changing landscape, he prefers things the way they used to be and idealizes a long-gone past.

An irony Bennett embeds in this character is that the language he uses to express his apparently genuine concern for the welfare of children reveals him to be as much of a moralist as those who condemn him. His distaste for people who use the park for sex at night rests largely on the way they impinge on the children who play there: "They do it in the playground too, laid down over one end of the slide where the kiddies slide along with their bottoms, then just chuck the evidence down anywhere" (48). He also mentally chastises his brother-in-law for allowing his German shepherd to roughhouse with the children: "That's irresponsible in my view, a dog that size when there are kiddies about. One snap and they're scarred for life" (49). Similarly, when he expresses disapproval of a woman for having her daughter's ears and nose pierced, he says, "I wonder the law let them do it, because that's interference in my view, ornamenting your kiddies, hanging stuff on them as if they were Christmas trees" (52). His worries about their "bottoms" being soiled, or their being "scarred for life," or the lax state of the "law," which allows "interference" with their bodies, reveal a subversive manipulation of the language that has been used to define his own offenses against children. Wilfred seems to imply that children are regularly violated by ordinary life, with no one taking much notice, so perhaps what he does with them is really no worse. Like the catcher in the rye, Wilfred has appointed himself the savior of children. He insists that his relationships with children are superior to those of most adults: "I didn't foist them off like grownups do. I looked at them. I listened to them" (57). He beams with pleasure as he describes various scenes of children at play. It's a self-serving argument, of course, but it serves to unsettle, if only for a moment, our demonizing of the sexualization of children above all other abuses.

Considering his paradoxical self-image as a moral guardian, it's not surprising that the custodial task Wilfred takes the most pride in is his removal of the used condoms that clog up the drains and flood the bandstand. The publicly discarded condom is his symbol of a particularly brutish and nasty sexuality between adults. Proud of clearing away the evidence of such grossness, Wilfred fails to accept that his own sexual behavior is just as destructive. His tortured rationalizations reveal what he cannot admit openly to us. When he recounts being left alone with a seven-year-old girl, a circumstance he has obviously been trying to avoid, he shifts the blame for his acts onto the weather, telling us, "it was the rain that did it because I'd given the bandstand a wide berth all week" (54). Likewise, when he and the girl play a game she calls "sandwiches" ("I put my hand on my knee and she put hers on top of it, then I put mine on it and she topped it off with her hand"), he interprets her giggling pleasure as sexual knowingness. He decides that her insistence on wriggling the piece of licorice out of his closed fist meant "she knew what she was doing. She must have known what she was doing. . . . So I took her in the bushes" (56). The ambiguity of that statement (he led her to the bushes? he sexually forced himself on her in the bushes?) does not disguise its brutal finality.

Despite a pleasing manner, a record of hard work, and a fairly incisive awareness of the ills of modern society, Wilfred's self-presentation collapses at this point. No audience can accept his rationalization of why he has done this, although we may be unsettled by his remark that "It's the one bit of my life that feels right and it's that bit that's wrong" (57). We are certainly disturbed, in the final scene, by the sight of Wilfred with one eye bruised shut, his arm bandaged and in a sling, thanks to the "treatment" pedophiles are subjected to by the morally outraged murderers and swindlers in prison. As the lights in the prison block go out one by one and leave Wilfred in darkness, the script specifies one final sound—"and in the black a long drawn-out howl" (57). The film offers instead a close-up of Wilfred crying into his bandaged hands, his body trembling with anguish, fear, and, undoubtedly, shame.

One of Wilfred's appealing traits is his relaxed attitude toward his Indian coworker at the park, Mr. Kumar. He doesn't seem to share in the overt racism of his family and acquaintances, although he shares in some stereotyping, telling us that Mr. Kumar is "from Bombay so he takes all this filth in his stride. Born a street sweeper, apparently, what they call an untouchable, though he's very neat, you'd never think it" (48). At the end of the monologue the only person to visit him in prison is Mr. Kumar, who pats his hand and says, "I miss you Mr. Paterson. I miss our walks with our barrows and brushes. You are the untouchable now" (57).

Perhaps it takes one outsider to sympathize with another, although we know how seldom that actually occurs, especially when the offense is pedophilia. A measure of Bennett's success in this monologue is not that Mr. Kumar feels a solidarity with Wilfred, but that the viewing audience is moved a few, perhaps grudging, steps closer to recognizing a flawed human—not a monster—behind the tabloid headlines. After the first airing of this monologue, the television critic of *The Times* testified to the power of Bennett's project: "By making him an affable, smiling and hardworking man, with an endearing twinkle in his eye, Bennett manages to leave his audience in a far more uncomfortable position than if he had painted Paterson as an unalloyed ogre."[6]

Yet Bennett is attempting something much more ambiguous than showing that pedophiles don't have fangs. He doesn't want us to forget that Wilfred's self-presentation is also a performance, a method of impression management. Despite or because of his charms, Wilfred cannot be completely trusted. In *A Chip in the Sugar*, Graham's sexual dysfunction poses a danger only to himself; Wilfred Paterson's sexuality is more problematically antisocial. Bennett's real achievement in this monologue is that he has made us listen to a person we normally don't think deserves to be heard, someone whose story we think we already know. Bennett challenges us to listen to Wilfred's version of himself, weigh it against what we know of human nature from our own experience, and try to reconcile the limitations of both points of view. Any pity the audience feels at the end comes from our empathy with a figure who is brought low by forces neither he nor we can confidently determine the origin of. The untouchable's story has touched us. Whether we would touch him, as Mr. Kumar does, is of course one of the questions Bennett leaves to us in this difficult and complex portrait.

The Outside Dog (first broadcast October 27, 1998)

After the first screening of *The Outside Dog*, Nancy Banks-Smith, a TV critic for *The Guardian*, was moved to remark that Julie Walters "looked as if she was being hauled through Hell by her hair. While keeping her voice down. . . . These monologues are getting blacker by the week," she added. Her dismay barely contained by flippant familiarity, she asked, "Alan, lad, whatever's up?"[7] If the first three monologues in the series had raised doubts about the wholesomeness of Bennett's new subjects, *The Outside Dog* confirmed them. Fans found themselves no longer in the sad but wry Bennett Land they had come to expect. Marjory's desperate situation resembles a hell indeed, where the connections between violence and sexuality are even more explicit and disturbing than they were in *Miss Fozzard* or *Playing Sandwiches*, which had previously established the standard for viewer discomfort. A foot fetishist with a masochistic streak and a pedophile with a winning smile now seem like ordinary chaps alongside Marjory's husband, Stuart, who works in a slaughterhouse by day, "slitting some defenceless creature's throat," according to Marjory, and roams Yorkshire by night, doing that and more to the women he encounters (*TH2*, 61).

Bennett has said that *The Outside Dog* is "another version" of "a recurring dream" he had as a child: "My mother and I were sitting in a spotless house when suddenly the coalman burst through the door and trailed muck throughout the house. . . . Looking back I see that this intrusive coalman was probably my father" (*TH2*, 19). Bennett has used this dream in a slightly altered form in *Intensive Care* to point up the oedipal conflicts of the main male character. In *The Outside Dog*, Bennett identifies the adult male as the violator of order and purity much more literally. Stuart is the Yorkshire Ripper, and Marjory, unlike Bennett's mother, who "took this intrusion quite calmly," learns incrementally that she has much to be alarmed about. Her growing realization of her dangerous predicament propels the story forward.

Like so many of Bennett's monologuists, Marjory at first presents a view of herself and her experiences that is at variance with reality. She wants us to see her as the secure monarch of all she surveys. She has divided her world into two spaces, her home and everything else outside it, a division she believes is in her power to maintain. By applying standards of antisepsis and hygiene any hospital might envy, she tries to seal off her home from the contaminating other. Outside the house lie the realms of dirt and uncleanliness, represented by her husband's profession of slaughterman—he must go through several cleansing rituals before he's allowed back into the house each day—and by his large barking dog, Tina, which she never allows to enter the house (hence the title of the piece). Whereas the women of Bennett's mother's generation relied on the scrub buckets, pails, and mops he describes with such precision in earlier plays, Marjory's weapons of dominion are more modern—the carpet shampooer, the washing machine, and the ubiquitous rubber gloves. But though the weapons change, the war against male and animal uncleanness is ultimately one and the same. And equally futile.

Marjory imagines that her influence over both her husband and his dog is absolute. And if it isn't, she doesn't want to know about it, as long as her home remains inviolate. When her slatternly mother-in-law marvels at how Marjory manages to maintain such a spotless place (which she frankly finds "unnatural"), Marjory smugly replies, "I've got him trained," adding for emphasis later on, "It was me that trained Stuart. Me that trained the dog" (61). Marjory's pride derives partly from her view that order and hygiene are signifiers of her middle-class status, somewhat like Doris in *A Cream Cracker under the Settee*. She scolds her husband for using the washing machine after midnight instead of at a "cultivated hour." And she sneers at her in-laws for leaving a cooking pot on the dinner table, a sign that "they've no culture at all" (60–1). Her misuse of the terms "cultivated" and "cultured," as well as her thick Yorkshire accent, not only undermine her superior pretensions, but suggest a more damaging misapprehension of reality, her odd notion that she has trained man and beast to civilized standards of behavior. Stuart and Tina have a secret life together that Tina in her daily licking of the slaughterhouse blood from Stuart's boots only begins to hint at.

Marjory's unspoken bargain with Stuart, that she will repress all doubts about him as long as he doesn't bring his "filth" into her clean house, is severely tested when he's arrested on suspicion of being a serial killer and the police and newspapers begin to besiege the house. She maintains a steady hostility to police inquiries, which necessitate disruptive searches of her cupboards—"Don't put those sheets back," she tells one officer, "I shall have them all to wash now you've been handling them"—and to the members of the press, who constantly barrage her with requests for interviews and offers of money for her "side of the story." Marjory must yield to the police, but she bars the press from her door, ignoring them as if their presence outside the house meant that they didn't exist at all. "I just sit there in the dark and don't take on," she tells us proudly (65). Only through the letter-box can the outside world gain entry and violate her seclusion, as when packets of excrement from morally outraged citizens land on her floor. Her home is literally her castle, and her performance of indifference to the world outside is the moat that protects her from the invaders. In contemporary terminology, she is a media event that refuses to happen.

The media and the police are not, however, the real dangers, despite their incursions into Marjory's territory. Stuart is. She suspects something is wrong when he begins to return in the middle of the night from hours-long walks with Tina and to force her into increasingly violent and loud sex. At first she suffered these episodes patiently, thinking only about what the neighbors might say if they heard him. "It's a blessing we're detached," she remarks, in one of Bennett's few heavy-handed puns (61). But Marjory's detachment is challenged repeatedly by evidence even she cannot ignore. While the jury is deciding Stuart's fate, she discovers a pair of Stuart's khaki trousers, missing since the night of one of the murders, clogging a drain in Tina's kennel (an emblem of pollution akin to the condoms Wilfred must dislodge), and is almost pushed to act. But just as she is "wondering whether there's anybody I should ring up," the verdict of acquittal is announced by the reporters pounding on her door, and she hides the trousers, later reburying them in the kennel (68).

Stuart has won more than acquittal. His return to her house and her bed signals the triumph of male brutality over female vulnerability. Marjory can no longer pretend that the barriers she has erected can protect her. To make her capitulation total, Stuart demands and wins Tina's admission into the house, not only to the kitchen but more significantly to their bedroom. He asks Tina "if she's taking it all in," as he and Marjory have sex, an act that more resembles rape than love and suggests a reenactment of his murder scenes (69).

Julie Walters's performance as Marjory adds immeasurably to the impact of the story. On the page, the monologue lacks the psychological penetration of some of the others because the "whodunnit" elements sometimes overwhelm the nuances of character exploration. But Walters brings a range of readings to the lines that deepens our appreciation of her character's dilemma. She begins confidently, secure in her hermetically sealed environment, speaking to us in a confidential tone, rolling her eyes with impatience at the vulgarity of everyone else she must put up with. When she begins to put two and two together, her voice cracks as each new piece of evidence mounts up. The mask of blasé control begins to slip. When she confides to us that the cornerstone of the defense's case is based on a lie—that Tina is allowed to run free and could have picked up the blood on her fur without Stuart being present—the panic she is trying to suppress is evident. She covers her face with her hands, breathes deeply, turns her back to the camera, then turns her right profile to us and says, "he's lying, of course" (66). Her discovery of the trousers in the kennel and the news that Stuart has been acquitted leave her breathy and trembling until, in the final scene, as she describes her terror, she sits in darkness, her hair disheveled, hands over her face. But in the end she swallows hard, and we see her face resume its original mask of tight-lipped control.

In an irony reminiscent of *The Insurance Man*, Marjory is trapped in a haven of her own making. The ugliness of the outside world has penetrated her defenses, and no amount of disinfectant will cleanse this home turned kennel. The enemy lies within. Marjory has fallen victim to the fallacy that as long as your own space is safe it doesn't matter what goes on outside it. But if she had gone to the police with her initial suspicions, she would have had to wait her turn. In one of Bennett's mordant jokes about how women view the male potential for brutality, Stuart tells Marjory that "mothers [were] queuing up apparently" to report their sons to the police as prime suspects in the killings (63). Stuart's own mother, whose intelligence Marjory has always disparaged, was one of them.

Nights in the Gardens of Spain (first broadcast November 3, 1998)

We have seen Rosemary's story before in these monologues: a naive middle-aged woman leads a fairly sheltered life until she encounters sexual passion for the first time, or "life," as her sense of decorum denotes it. Susan in *Bed Among the Lentils* first comes to mind, but Rosemary lacks her sardonic bitterness. Rosemary's story shares a kinship to Miss Fozzard's, however, just taken up a step in social status and cranked up a notch in sensationalism. They might be fellow students in a crash course on life's wild surprises, variations on the theme of self-liberation. Miss Fozzard breaks through to a new knowledge of life's possibilities that, while acted on only in private, is still an improvement on her original state. The comic denouement of her story is her discovery that the path to happiness may not be lined with primrose bushes and that to walk it you may need more exotic footwear than tight-fitting court shoes. Rosemary likewise comes to understand the limits of her own experiences and seems to glimpse an alternate way of life, but, unlike Miss Fozzard, she cannot take advantage of her new insight. She ends up with knowledge but no freedom to act.

The dominant metaphor in Rosemary's story is the garden, but the perfumed gardens of Granada and Sevilla that the title evokes are ironically inappropriate. Her suburban English garden is no romantic trysting place, and the garden she is transplanted to in Spain does not lie in de Falla's moonlight, but in the bright glare of the Costa del Sol, where golf courses receive loving attention while home gardens wither in the merciless sunshine. As played by Penelope Wilton, Rosemary is a tidy, quiet, suburban wife, who has probably never worked outside her home in the thirty years of her childless marriage. She appears immune to excitement and emotion, except for the energy and passion of her gardening. Plants and flowers are her surrogate children. Her anger is reserved for people who carelessly break limbs off a magnolia grandiflora tree (she knows and lovingly uses their Latin names), and her aggressions seek an outlet in parental discipline, putting an overgrown patch of borage "in its place," or reading "the riot act" to the ill-mannered alchemilla mollis (*TH2*, 77). So, it is no surprise that her delivery is lowkey when she breaks the news that the woman across the road has murdered her husband and has sought her out for assistance in dealing with the aftermath. "Nobody normally gets killed round here" is her way of introducing this lurid story of a woman driven to murder by years of sexual and physical abuse (72). Rosemary seems eager to establish a pedigree of respectability in front of us and to distance herself from Fran's violence. But she cannot. Fran's act of rebellion against "a saga of protracted and imaginative cruelty," in her lawyer's words, opens a crack in Rosemary's faux-Edenic life (77). Her knowledge of good and evil forces her out of Eden and into exile.

The snake in the garden is once more male sexuality. Fran's husband is the last link in a chain in *Talking Heads 2* that includes the kinky (Mr. Dunderdale), the compulsive (Wilfred), and the bestial (Stuart). Not only did Fran's husband break her bones and burn her with cigarettes, he also forced her to perform sexually while hooded in front of other men. The dog collar, the leash, and a set of handcuffs are the chief instruments of his pleasure. Demonstrating the proposition that in the war between the sexes what a man calls a terrorist a woman calls a freedom fighter, Rosemary's outspoken neighbor, Sheila, acidly comments on the two-year prison sentence that Fran receives: "Worth every minute of it, dear, if you ask me. A couple of years basket weaving and you get the bed to yourself. Cheap at the price. I just wish I had a gun. As it is I'm pinning my hopes on his prostate" (78).

Rosemary doesn't share Sheila's views, at least not at that moment. Her only experience of men has been Henry, and she has long ago decided that he is harmless. She isn't thrilled that he calls her "young lady," that he pats her on the knee in a patronizing manner, that he is so undemanding sexually, but she feels protective of him. She regrets describing Henry to Sheila as "very considerate," because she knows what that euphemism will tell the rest of the world about their marriage. "I saw her smile and she's a nice woman but I know it'll be up and down the road by tomorrow" (77). Rosemary interprets Henry's sexual indifference to her as his unease about sex in general. When she mentions to him that Fran didn't seem to have anything on under her dress on the morning of the murder, and he resists her dwelling on such details, she reads it as embarrassment. "He's such an innocent," she explains to us (73). Similarly, when she notices that during Fran's trial her husband loses a noticeable amount of weight and can't work, she chalks it up to his worry about Fran's fate. "I've misjudged Henry," she says (77). In Bennett's dramatic monologues, comments such as these set off alarm bells, warning us that such assurances will soon be ironically deflated and turned on their head.

Sure enough, Fran reveals to Rosemary that one of the men present at her hooded ordeals used to whistle under his breath throughout the proceedings. Since we've
already heard Rosemary describe Henry's penchant for whistling under his breath,
the connection seems more neat than surprising. After all, as a coworker says insin-
uatingly to Miss Fozzard when news of her secret life starts to get around, "Ooh,
still waters!" It is surprising, however, when Rosemary admits that just as Fran
says, "one of them . . . had a funny habit," Rosemary "knew what she was going
to say the second before she said it." Even though Rosemary adds after a pause that
"Of course, a lot of people do that," she cannot disguise the truth from herself, a
truth that she seems to have been prepared for at some deep level anyway (78). She
tells us, "I look at him a lot now, this once upon a time spectator, or maybe still,
who knows, somewhere. And I think . . . Well, sometimes I just think, 'You dark
horse.' Other times I think about Fran and get upset" (79). Her largely dispassion-
ate contemplation of her husband's involvement in the sexual abuse of another
woman leads her to wonder "whether all these years he'd been wanting to see me
crawl round the room naked on my hands and knees" too. She turns aside that
thought with a mild, self-deprecating joke: "though if I did it nowadays I'd have to
have my knee pads on, which might take the edge off things a bit" (79). Rosemary
has seriously "misjudged Henry," but because she herself seems never to have been
touched by such physical passions, she neither condemns him nor attempts to
understand him. She deflects her uneasiness with a joke at her own expense, except
when she thinks of Fran.

Rosemary's real emotional awakening comes from her friendship with Fran. In
the first place, both are gardeners. Before the murder, they had only spoken to one
another to exchange pleasantries about the magnolia grandiflora in Fran's yard,
and it is the reporters' destruction of part of the tree that provokes Rosemary's only
outburst in the story. While Fran is in custody, and before her house is sold,
Rosemary daily tends her garden for her, opening her up to tired quips from the
neighbors such as "Who do I have to shoot for you to come and do my garden?"
(76). In prison, Fran's green thumb transforms the inmates' garden into a virtual
Sissinghurst *cum* Horn of Plenty, with prize onions and tomatoes testifying to her
earth-mother touch. When Rosemary begins to visit Fran in prison without telling
Henry, the ostensible bond of the garden gives way to a more direct connection.
Fran becomes a confidante, a best friend, someone Rosemary connects with in a
way unique to her experience. As she puts it, "I've never had a best friend, the sort
you can tell everything to. Never had one, never been one, even when I was a girl"
(78). They spend her monthly release afternoons visiting old churches, attending
garage sales, viewing gardens. One day on a visit to Fountains Abbey, a medieval
Cistercian ruin that figures largely in Bennett's first television play, *A Day Out*,
Fran takes Rosemary's hand as they descend the stairs and doesn't relinquish it at
the bottom. "It was just like it was when I was a girl and a boy did it," Rosemary
tells us. "Such a bold step. And so meant." During those stolen afternoons together, Rosemary confesses, "sometimes I think I have never been so happy in my life,"

and she tells Fran, "I know what this is. . . . It's life" (80). The scene ends with Rosemary, in her modern, immaculate kitchen, lovingly holding a large red tomato, presumably from Fran's garden, up to her cheek.

Right after Fran murders her husband, a social worker is brought in to counsel Rosemary, because she had witnessed the aftermath of a violent crime. Rosemary is advised that "it helps to look things in the face right from the start" (75). When she claims that she hasn't been traumatized by viewing the corpse, the social worker warns her that "there is a potential for distress" long after the event (76). We see an unexpected form of distress in the final scene, which moves Rosemary from her kitchen to a veranda in Spain. She tells us that in the interim Fran has died of cancer and that she and Henry have sold their house and moved to Marbella, where Henry plays golf all day, and she must face the challenge of growing a new kind of garden in the sunbaked soil. We see a small cactus plant on the table, a pitiful contrast to the profusion of greenery that filled her home in England.

In part, Rosemary's distress comes from her exile in Spain, a place she has gone to because Henry desired it. Thinking about the collar and leash that Fran had to endure, Rosemary concludes, "that's what my marriage has been like too, being jerked along. I mean what else is Marbella?" (80). She has obediently followed Henry to Spain, even though she knows "I should have packed my bags" when Henry's only remark on Fran's death was, "Best thing that could have happened" (81). Best thing for him, of course. Now, there's no one left to implicate him as a witness to the sadistic games Fran had to endure. Rosemary has no choice now but to "look things in the face," but she doesn't know how to rebel against them. Seeing a large number of exiled English criminals living the good life in Spain, she can't help but be distressed at the injustice, raising the same question Miss Fozzard asked vis-à-vis her brother and herself. "Of course it's just what would happen in a play. Fran shot him so she had to pay. Only this place is crawling with people who haven't paid. Unless you count just being here as paying" (81).

Rosemary is not the woman we met at the start of the monologue, who had to admit that although she volunteered at the hospice twice a week, "they think I'm not really ready to administer the consolation yet" (72). Fran's final days are spent in the same hospice and the consolation Rosemary offers is heartfelt and personal, not the product of a course of training: "I used to hold her hand, kiss it. And she'd kiss mine. We'd talked about a little garden centre" (81). But just as Fran's cancer was diagnosed too late and so was incurable, Rosemary's emotional and intellectual maturity, her ability to look things in the face, have also come too late. At the very end, she sits on the veranda pondering the question of whether some plants prefer shade. They certainly can live in shade, she concedes, but "give them a bit of sun and suddenly they come into their own" (81). It's hard to imagine, however, that the Spanish sun will offer the same kind of gentle encouragement that the milder English sun would have, especially to nonnative transplants like Rosemary. She must instead contend with reality, a "flat, square, stony" garden, one that bears a troubling resemblance to "an exercise yard" in a prison. Her final remarks to us signal the quiet despair of her condition: "I sit here at night, listening to the frogs and the crickets, and Henry, whistling under his breath" (81). It's a more genteel entrapment than Marjory's, but it suggests a paralysis just as terrifying.

Waiting for the Telegram (first broadcast November 11, 1998)

The first five monologues in this series were broadcast on successive Tuesdays on BBC2. This final segment was shifted to a Wednesday to coincide with the eightieth anniversary of the end of World War I, a day the English commemorate as Remembrance Day and the Americans as Veterans Day. The memory of that war, when Violet, played by the veteran actress Thora Hird, was a young woman, looms large in this symmetrically structured final play, as do the less literal wars between past and present, men and women, language and silence, life and death.

Violet, who is in her nineties, speaks to us from her wheelchair. She has had a stroke and lives in a nursing home. Like Bernard in *Miss Fozzard*, she has suffered damage to her language skills. Nearly the first phrase out of her mouth is "what-do-you-call-it" (*TH2*, 84). But we're wrong to think she is struggling to find the right word. Unlike Bernard, she is articulate enough to carry the monologue all by herself. "What-do-you-call-it" is the right word for Violet, because she's describing a fellow rest home inmate exposing himself to her. The nurse insists she use the word "penis," but Violet belongs to another age, when circumlocution about penises was the norm. Stroke or no stroke, "penis" is simply not a word she can bring herself to say. Nevertheless, Violet is not a prude. Her take on the flasher is one of amused indifference. The young nurses who insist she use the proper words are much more shaken. The clinical precision of their language camouflages a wealth of hostility. Nurse Bapty advises Violet, "Penis is its name. All the other names are just trying to make it more acceptable" (84). She also reminds her, "you're a victim and choose how old you are, you're still flying the flag of gender" (85).

Bennett's suspicion of the "caring" professions and their humorless agendas carries through strongly in this play. The counselor Verity (Violet remembers her name by thinking of the brand names of two potentially lethal items—a cricket bat and a gas oven) reacts with anger when Violet compliments her on her breasts by describing them as "them two things with pink ends that men like." She replies, "Things are different now, Violet. Women have control of their own bodies" (86). Men and their intrusive sexuality are the enemy to this generation of women. We remember the ludicrous mixture of sex and sport in the prescription Miss Fozzard is given to help her brother regain his language ("Language is balls coming at you from every angle"), so we shouldn't be surprised to hear Nurse Bapty move the contest off the court and onto the battlefield: "'Language is a weapon, Violet. We're at war.' I said, 'Who with?' She said, 'Men'" (84). Bennett creates a rich interchange between the language of sex and war in this monologue, reminding us that as much as things change they remain the same.

One of the sliest ironies of the play is the place sex still holds in Violet's life, even as she approaches death. Her flirtation with Francis, the nurse who cares for her, is saturated with sensuality, mostly on her part, since Francis is homosexual. Violet tells us that "he's a lovely looking lad" and "he has some grand arms" (86, 85). When another patient throws up on him and he must remove his shirt, it's not only the young women who admire his physique. Violet may not be able to find all the words she wants, but her meaning is unmistakable: "And by, he's a grand-looking lad! Not a mark on him and right big (*She mimes shoulders*) . . . here. It made you want to . . . (*She mimes a kiss*) . . . do that, whatever it's called. Lovely. Devon came in I saw her having a look" (87). Francis's youth and physical beauty help Violet recall another young man she knew more than seventy years earlier, during the First World War. Courtship back then was "a struggle," Violet tells us, a notion Nurse Bapty would not find strange or outdated today. Violet recounts her first love, Edward, who was killed in France.

> He'd manage to get one button undone one night, and another the next. And lasses weren't supposed to do much in them days, just lie back and get ready to draw the line. And because I'd let him get so far one night, he'd know where the front line was, so the next night he'd get there a bit quicker and push on a bit further . . . another button, you know. It was that . . . grudging somehow. But it was the way you felt you had to be then. (89)

The night before Edward leaves for the trenches, he decides to mount an assault on the home front. Violet's mother has cooperated by leaving them alone for the evening, setting out Violet's favorite flowers and lighting a fire in the front room. But the strength of her resistance surprises even Violet herself. Defeated by the byzantine buttoning system of her best frock, Edward takes off his own clothes in frustration, and standing before her in front of the fire ("Oh and he looked a picture . . . Not a mark on him") he tells her, "Take your clothes off now." But Violet cannot: "And I didn't. I didn't. And I wanted him so much. I don't know . . . it was just the way I'd been brought up. And he stands there looking down at me . . . then he just picks his clothes up and goes next door and after a bit I heard the front door bang" (89–90).

Violet's regret at her performance of virtue ("it was the way you felt you had to be then") has lasted all her life. She weeps as she tells this story to Francis, concluding, "Only I should have let him shouldn't I? I've never forgiven myself" (91). Violet gets no second chance. Edward is killed in the war, the news reaching England via telegram, delivered by a uniformed boy on a bicycle. These telegraph boys "brought news of deaths in the trenches so that a single boy in four years of war might tell the fate of thousands," Bennett tells us. "Seeing him go by women would stand at their doors to see which house he stopped at, this pageboy of death" (*TH2*, 21). A letter from the king followed later. This reminds Violet that herself will be receiving a telegram from the queen when she reaches her hundredth birthday, the congratulations inevitably melding into a *memento mori* that ties her fate to Edward's, three-quarters of a century ago, and to Francis's today, because his generation of homosexuals faces its own doom. He reassures Violet that nowadays young men "don't die like that"—in the trenches—but he hides from her the name of the modern spectre of death; his homosexuality and the pneumonia that kills him identify the spectre as AIDS. Bennett apologizes for sanitizing AIDS, "deaths from AIDS seldom [are] so quick or so clean as I have made his departure" (*TH2*, 21). Bennett should perhaps also apologize for choosing so stereotypic a target for AIDS, but to his credit he gives Francis the same sympathetic treatment he gave homosexual characters as far back as 1971 in *Getting On*. His respect humanizes them and makes a place for them as ordinary citizens of the world. As Violet says when she hears of Francis's death, whether it was "lads or lasses" he was drawn to, "he was a love," an incarnation of Edward, an unrequited love lost once again (91).

Violet does most of her speaking seated in a wheelchair. It's unclear how much time elapses between each scene, but, as Bennett has said, "in an old people's home time goes at a trickle anyway, what year it is not of much consequence, least of all to the residents whose own age is often something of a mystery as it certainly is to Violet" (*TH2*, 20). By the final scene Violet is lying in bed, the covers up to her chin. She is clearly weaker. Whether she will reach her hundredth birthday and receive a telegram from the queen we can't say for certain. But the "pageboy of death" will call for her, regardless. Her conversation becomes more disjointed as she sings an old song from childhood and then concludes her monologue with a troubled awareness of the dehumanizing indignities of old age:

> Pets is what you want in this place. Else babies. Summat you can . . . (*She makes a stroking movement*) do this with. Not have to talk to.
> *Pause.*
> It's no game is this.
> *Pause.*
> We're the pets. Fed and cleaned out every day. It's a kennels is this.
> *Pause.*
> Pedigree Chum. Pedigree Chum. (92)

The sudden image of the elderly reduced to captive animals and fed dog food throws the reader or the viewer off balance and is reminiscent of Bennett's double-edged treatment of human physicality in *Habeas Corpus*. At least there we could salvage a positive spin. We must have the body, it said, and we must dance across the minefield of mortality as long as we can. But *Waiting for the Telegram*, with its echoes of *Waiting for Godot* and *Endgame* ("It's no game this"), doesn't allow much room for cheer. We must have the body, but it betrays us if we live long enough. Arthur Wicksteed's bravado declaration at the end of *Habeas Corpus* that "he whose lust lasts, lasts longest" sounds hollow in the rest home. Wicksteed might very well have turned into the flasher Violet tells us about at the start of her monologue—if not merely a nuisance, then a joke. Beauty and sexuality, and the beauty of sexuality, in the persons of Edward and Francis, are killed off. All that remains is a lost and lonely survivor who in her youth was caught in the role of virtue and now in old age is caught in the role of victim. Violet's sudden anger and despair upset our sentimental appreciation of her endurance and her pluck, but Bennett insists on the disturbance.

NOTES

1. Bennett, "Talking Shop," 33.
2. Bennett, "Talking Shop," 34.
3. Bennett, "Talking Shop," 33.
4. "Speaking for the Unheard" is the title of Part Two of Turner's book.
5. Bennett, "Talking Shop," 34.
6. Joe Joseph, *Times* (London), Oct. 21, 1998.
7. Nancy Banks-Smith, *Guardian*, Oct. 28, 1998.

CHAPTER SEVEN

Adapting to Stage and Screen: Joe Orton, Mr. Toad, and George III

Prick Up Your Ears (1987)
The Wind in the Willows (1990)
The Madness of George III (1991)/*The Madness of King George* (1995)

From the beginning of his career as a playwright, Alan Bennett seems to have harbored the ambition of having one of his plays produced at the National Theatre, England's most prestigious venue for drama, the theatrical equivalent of Carnegie Hall. It took more than practice to get there. In the late sixties, when the National was an acting company without a permanent home, under the direction of Laurence Olivier, Bennett submitted an early version of *Forty Years On*, entitled *The Last of England*. It was rejected.[1] Twenty years passed before the National Theatre, now established in its concrete fortress on the South Bank, turned a favoring eye on him and commissioned *Single Spies*. Two years later, the National gave Bennett's adaptation of Kenneth Grahame's *The Wind in the Willows* an elaborate production on the Olivier stage, the largest of its three spaces. Bennett's next effort for the National, his first original full-length play in five years, *The Madness of George III*, must have seemed the reward he had earned by proving himself with these two relatively risk-free adaptations (his own *An Englishman Abroad*, which made up the first act of *Single Spies*, and a popular classic starring Mr. Toad).[2]

It is ironic that Bennett achieved his breakthrough at the National with adaptations of already well-known works, because for Bennett adaptation has never really been safe or come easily. From his first attempt to write a screen version of Joe Orton's life, ten years before the National Theatre plays, he seems to have recognized that the process of adaptation—selecting, editing, and recasting—opens him up to a scrutiny he normally prefers to avoid. The adaptor's choices can be placed alongside the original, revealing psychological preoccupations and artistic quirks.

Bennett has admitted to feeling uneasy even when a point of comparison arises because he has unconsciously repeated himself in some of his own pieces. Looking back over *Talking Heads*, he reports, "I am disturbed as I was with a previous collection of television plays to note so many repetitions and recurrences. There are droves of voluntary workers, umpteen officials from the social services, and should there be a knock on the door it's most likely to be a bearded vicar. Even Emily Bronte turns up twice" (*TH*, 8). The recognition of small economies in his works— the repeated themes, character traits, and even names—makes him a little nervous, as if the unexamined aspects of his creative process were suddenly on public display and subject to unflattering comment. So although he will admit that naming all the dogs in his monologues "Tina" probably betrays "the poverty of my imagination," he steers clear of suggesting to us what all the murders and murderers in *Talking Heads 2* signify about his imagination (*TH2*, 10).

As Bennett approached this high point of his career, as he sought and received the cultural imprimatur of the now grandly renamed Royal National Theatre, and as he achieved more international fame as a writer for the movies, he also began to expose, in a preliminary and tentative way, more of a kinship with his material. In the full-scale adaptations, because Bennett struggled so long with them, he is more ready to accept the autobiographical implications of his choices, although he doesn't offer to interpret much of their significance. Bennett's somewhat coy admission, in his version of *The Wind in the Willows*, that "My additions and alterations . . . are, I am sure, as revealing of me as the original text is of [Kenneth] Grahame" (*WW*, xxiii), can be applied to his other adaptations as well: his Joe Orton screenplay, *Prick Up Your Ears*, and his screen adaptation of his own *Madness of George III*. A disclaimer, also from *The Wind in the Willows*—"I have tried to do a faithful adaptation of the book while, at the same time, not being sure what a faithful adaptation is" (*WW*, xv)—shows Bennett taking an agnostic stance that preempts criticism and, in a not so subtle bow to the force of his own personality, gives him permission to put his own stamp on the material. Still, Bennett leaves the audience to draw its own conclusions about the autobiographical meaning in these adaptations.

Prick Up Your Ears (1987)

Although Bennett has confessed his "ambivalent feelings about gossip and biography, and about Orton himself" (*PUYE*, 10), the prospect of adapting John Lahr's biography of Joe Orton for the movies must have appealed to him, perhaps because the strutting and preening Joe Orton is in many ways the anti-Alan Bennett. What Bennett says he "found hard to take" about Orton "was his self-assurance and conviction (however painfully and necessarily acquired) of the superiority of his talent" (viii), a posture that the self-deprecating Bennett would never assume. Still, he clearly admires Orton's plays, "particularly *Entertaining Mr. Sloane, Loot*, and *The Good and Faithful Servant*" (vii), although, in a significant omission, he doesn't mention Orton's masterpiece, *What the Butler Saw*, from which Bennett seems to have drawn inspiration for the more anarchic sentiments in *Habeas Corpus*.

An inveterate diarist who has for many years published an annual diary in the *London Review of Books,* Bennett must have felt some kinship with Orton for also keeping a diary. Bennett's diaries observe his work, his travels (many visits to churches and art galleries), and the oddities of human speech and behavior that strike him as amusing. He can be brutally rude in attacking politicians and their hypocrisies, but in private matters he is invariably discreet, protecting his own privacy and that of his friends. Orton's diary is something altogether different. Although it too provides social commentary, satirizing England at the beginning of the "Swinging Sixties," its fame, or more accurately, its notoriety, arises from the unrelenting detail it devotes to Orton's sexual activities. He tells us on a daily basis who he has sex with, where, and how, as well as who he'd like to have sex with, where, and how. From the public restrooms on the Holloway Road in London to the vacation villas of Morocco, Orton's diary revels in his promiscuities and is not shy about sharing the details. Although Bennett and Orton both write their diaries for public consumption, of the two, Orton's diary more closely approximates Gwendolyn Fairfax's requirement that diaries should always offer "something sensational to read in the train."[3] Despite these differences in personal style, the one connection between them that Bennett couldn't miss was the similar arc in their careers: Orton too was a northern lad who left the provinces to achieve fame on the London stage. Though he came from Leicester, not Leeds, and was more decidedly working class, he and Bennett were young at the same time and Bennett felt that connection as well.

John Lahr first approached Bennett and the director Stephen Frears in 1978, before the Orton biography was published, and offered them an option on the film rights. Bennett and Frears spent the next ten years trying to find a production company that would neither shrink from the often lurid subject matter (as the tabloids might put it: "Gay Playwright Has Brains Beaten Out With Hammer by Envious Boyfriend") nor commercialize it beyond recognition to attract a wider audience. Early responses were discouraging. A Hollywood producer said he liked everything about the project, with only two reservations. Orton should be American and heterosexual. A British production company let it be known that what it really wanted was an English version of *La Cage aux Folles* (viii).

In addition to the delays caused by moronic producers, Bennett's ambivalent attitude to Orton and to Kenneth Halliwell, Orton's lover, blocked his writing. A line Bennett wrote for Orton's homophobic brother-in-law to speak—"I hope nobody hears about this in Leicester" (74)—mirrored Bennett's own doubts about the project early on. In 1981, on the anniversary of his father's death, Bennett lists in his diary things he'd like to be able to send his father beyond the grave. One that he wouldn't like to send is "the Orton script that I've been struggling with all year" (*WH,* 116) Perhaps it's the untidy state of the script that Bennett wouldn't want his father to see, but perhaps it's also the unapologetic presence of homosexuality that would have embarrassed his father, and by extension Bennett too. Through various drafts Bennett tried to dilute his distaste for Orton and the belief it fostered in him that Halliwell was the aggrieved party in the relationship. Bennett, ever attempting to be fair, realized that "this version didn't work nor was it true to the facts" (viii). He experimented with the structure of the screenplay through several drafts as well, at one point adding both Lahr and himself as characters, authors of the biography and the screenplay. This Pirandellian layering didn't make much sense either, and it was only in 1984, when another producer expressed interest in the project, that Bennett finally hit upon the idea of using Peggy Ramsay, Orton's agent, as the voice-over narrator. Bennett attributes this breakthrough to the inspiration of Joseph Mankiewicz, who successfully used Addison de Witt (George Sanders) in a similar role in *All About Eve*, another story about envy in the theater (ix).

Much more significant than discovering the appropriate structure for the narrative were two other decisions Bennett made. The first was to cast the Orton-Halliwell story as a marriage gone wrong, and the second was to view Orton's cockiness, and Halliwell's insecurity, as examples of a successful performance of identity and a failed one. These decisions offered Bennett familiar footing: the marriage analogy would neutralize some of the more uncomfortable aspects of homosexual couplings, and the performance theme would cast a more acceptable and recognizable light on Orton's arrogance. They would not, however, help him overcome his ambivalence and guilt for prying into a writer's life in ways that he himself would object to, if the searchlight were turned on him.

Marriage, or its facsimile, gets a closer look in Bennett's films than in his stage or TV plays, where the isolated individual is usually the focal point. Joe Orton and Kenneth Halliwell join Joyce and Gilbert Chilvers and, later, George III and Queen Charlotte, as the domestic grounding points of dramas whose ambitions extend to the larger social world (postwar Britain, the Swinging Sixties, the Regency crisis). The intimate relationships of the couples serve as the microcosm for the larger turmoil in society and as a measure of the health of that society as well. Joe and Kenneth's relationship, which is sexually consummated in the film while they are watching Elizabeth II's coronation on television, carries some of that same era-defining weight. The "New Elizabethan Age" may not have recaptured the glory days of empire, but with it came changes that few in England could have anticipated. The hoped-for egalitarianism didn't occur, as Bennett showed in *A Private Function*, but other social changes, equally remarkable, did. Chief among the surprises was the sexual revolution of the sixties and seventies, pulled along by the second wave of women's liberation, the marketing of a reliable method of birth control, and the beginnings of gay liberation.[4]

To tell Joe Orton and Kenneth Halliwell's story as a portrait of a marriage was, on one hand, a bold choice, espousing a remarkably advanced viewpoint for the time, considering how slow the rest of society has been to acknowledge that homosexual relationships can, and sometimes do, model themselves on heterosexual marriages. But at a time when homosexuality in England was a felony offense punishable by imprisonment, it was also a choice that failed to present some important differences between the Orton-Halliwell relationship and a conventional heterosexual marriage. The issue of sexual fidelity is one example of those differences. Orton violently disagreed with Halliwell's insistence that "a home life should have the stability of a loyal relationship," though he didn't object to Halliwell's concession that it was "all right letting off steam on holiday." Orton did not want a conventional marriage, scorning all ties of sexual fidelity as bourgeois repression. "You sound like a heterosexual," he told Halliwell.[5] Nonetheless, Bennett defined their relationship as "a first marriage," with Kenneth as the first wife (ix). Bennett felt fairly sure that Orton, if he had lived, would have left Kenneth for someone who could share his fame and public adulation more congenially. Penelope Gilliatt, who knew both Orton and Halliwell, took a similar view: "Halliwell was the wife who doesn't notice that her husband is coming up in the world and is changing."[6]

Bennett structures his screenplay on parallels between the Orton-Halliwell marriage and that of Anthea and John Lahr, whom Bennett finally decided to leave in the film as the author of Orton's biography and editor of his diaries. Anthea Lahr is cast in the role of helpmate, transcribing Orton's diaries for her husband, preparing his meals, entertaining his literary friends, tagging along after him on his research, bearing his child. Although Anthea's disaffection with being taken for granted is visible, she is mercifully spared hearing Lahr say that wives "cramp our style" in agreement with Peggy Ramsay's remark, "At moments of triumph men can do without their wives" (57). In actuality, Halliwell was not spared hearing the insults of Joe's friends, who called him a "middle-aged nonentity" to his face.[7]

Halliwell began calling himself Orton's "personal assistant" to explain his ubiquity once Orton gained a place in the public eye. Though Bennett clearly sees Halliwell as a homosexual version of Anthea Lahr, Halliwell would never have called himself "wife," because he wanted to be more of an equal than that. But personal assistant is a role that doesn't satisfy Halliwell either and prompts him to more than one exasperated public outburst. The funniest example in the film comes at Halliwell's art opening, where he discovers that no one is interested in his collages, though they're all agog over Joe Orton. When a woman asks him what being personal assistant to Orton entails, he bitterly tells her, "It entails washing his underwear. It entails taking his jumpers to Sketchley's. It entails poaching his fucking eggs and it entails reading his manuscripts and finding every single thing I have ever thought or said has been included." When the woman absently replies, "that must be very rewarding," Halliwell bellows back, "if you are referring, madam, to the occasional bout of mutual masturbation, no, it is not rewarding at all" (13).

A great deal of the film is given over to Orton's initiation of the more timid and reluctant Halliwell into "cottaging," sex in public restrooms, as a substitute for the lack of sex between them. On its release, these scenes gave the film its reputation for daring. But they may have obscured the more complicated realities of Orton and Halliwell's sexual relationship.[8] Despite Halliwell's loud reference to the "occasional bout of mutual masturbation," Bennett never shows any sex between them after the first seduction in 1953. Orton's entry in his diary for May 3, 1967, however, reveals that they had vigorous sex up until a few months before their deaths. Bennett obviously read the diaries before writing the screenplay—some speeches in the screenplay come verbatim from them—so his decision to airbrush out most of the private sexual intimacy between Orton and Halliwell leaves us with a relationship that has outgrown its sexual roots, making Peggy Ramsay's observation "that people shouldn't marry young" (13) carry more weight. Considering the already dizzying unconventionality of their sex lives, Bennett's choice is understandable but misleading.

If a look at "marriage" is a thread that joins this screenplay to his others, the performance theme links the film to most of Bennett's other work for stage and television. Orton and Halliwell were performers who created an identity for themselves the way an actor creates a character in a play. The crucial difference between them was that Joe found a role that suited him, but Kenneth never managed to connect his idea of who he wanted to be with his ability to act that person. Bennett has written a darkly comic final speech for Halliwell, just before he kills Joe, a brief soliloquy that reveals the frustrated core of the man. He stares at himself in the mirror, pondering the mysteries of identity: "I don't understand my life. I was an only child. I lost both my parents. By the time I was twenty I was bald. I'm homosexual. In the way of circumstances and background to transcend I had everything an artist could possibly want. It was practically a blueprint. I was programmed to be a novelist or a playwright. But I'm not. And you are" (70).

When they met as students at the Royal Academy of Dramatic Arts (RADA) in 1951, Halliwell had already developed a persona of the worldly sophisticate who condescended to partake in the class exercises for his amusement, not because they could possibly teach him anything about acting. "Movement. Enunciation. Breath Control," he says to Orton at their first meeting. "It's all so wildly dated. Don't you agree?" (26). Kenneth desperately wants to shine at something artistic, and he tries on new roles as the previous ones fail. He goes from acting to writing novels to creating visual collages. Recognition never comes his way. As he grows older we see him acquiring a toupee, a gift from Orton, and applying makeup before going out in public, neither particularly subtle ways of constructing a public face. Orton, on the other hand, who began as Halliwell's apprentice in the arts, discovers his real gift as a writer while serving a short prison term for defacing library books. It's as if all he needs to create a new identity, one that is his alone, is time away from Halliwell out of his shadow. We see him lifting weights to shape his physique, and we see him manipulating the prison psychiatrist into believing that he's a married man with a child, an impersonation that wins the doctor's sympathy and indulgence. Orton has already learned how to play with authority and to subvert it for his own gain, a technique he would perfect in his plays. Halliwell, on the other hand, tells the truth about his feelings for Orton and is treated with contempt by the prison psychologist.

While Halliwell helped Orton in an editorial capacity, which Orton is always eager to acknowledge in the *Diaries*, the plays come from the core of Orton's anar-

chic personality, a place Halliwell with his middle-class pretensions to sophistication can never reach. Halliwell's joke that "cheap clothes suit you. It's because
you're from the gutter" (29), touches on Orton's ability to use his lower-class identity to achieve a position of strength. Even as a famous playwright he didn't want
to become careful and conservative. He wanted to continue to rage and outrage.
Bennett captures that recklessness most strikingly in the public sex scenes. But also
the control. We see that Orton is both stage manager and director of these encounters. When Kenneth is with him, he sets the scene, coaches him through his lines,
and pushes him into action. When he's on his own he carefully orchestrates the
players, even to the point of adjusting the lighting to a more flattering level
(unscrewing the light bulbs in the lavatory). He always gives a confident performance. Kenneth is always in a panic, always flubs his lines, and never makes a good
impression. What may finally have driven Halliwell to destroy Orton and himself
was not the fear of being cast aside in favor of a trophy wife, but his realization that
he could no longer compete with Orton's performances. The last words Bennett
puts in Halliwell's mouth before he kills Orton are "You do everything better than
me. You even sleep better than me" (70).

The Wind in the Willows (1990)

A rereading of Kenneth Grahame's 1908 fable reminds us of how adaptations earlier than Bennett's, such as A.A. Milne's *Toad of Toad Hall* and Disney's 1949 car-
toon (*Ichabod and Mr. Toad*), have squeezed out a great deal of the mythic and
poetic subtext of the original by cutting out the sections that don't advance the
adventures of the madcap Toad. In the original fable we discover that Mr. Toad's
lack of self-control and his obsessive acquisitiveness are not just charming eccentricities best expressed as a ride at Disneyland. Toad's lust for up-to-date material
possessions threatens the pastoral ways of the River Bank. He is the first shopa-
holic, the consumer from hell. His weakness for new gadgets and new sensations
demonstrates a lack of respect for the traditions that constitute the core myth, the
essential nature, of the English character. What Blake termed "England's green and
pleasant land," what John of Gaunt called "this scepter'd isle" is a sacred trust to
be preserved intact, but to Toad it is no more than his personal playground. His
reckless behavior opens the door for the weasels, the stoats, and the ferrets from the
Wild Wood, Grahame's trope for the dangerous urban underclasses who will rise
up and appropriate the pastoral landscape.

The two sections of Grahame's original fable that are usually excised because
they don't advance the Toad plot are "The Piper at the Gates of Dawn" and
"Wayfarers All." In the first, Mole and Rat join the search for a missing otter child
and in the dawn encounter a Romantic vision of Pan, the God of Nature, who
guards the sleeping infant. With Wordsworthian reverence they worship this mani-
festation of the benevolent power of the natural world. And like Wordsworth's
human child, who comes "trailing clouds of glory" from his heavenly home, Mole
and Rat are gifted with forgetfulness, lest "the awful remembrance should remain

and grow, and overshadow mirth and pleasure, and the great haunting memory should spoil all the afterlives of little animals."[9] In "Wayfarers All," Rat must resist the seductive invitation of a seafaring cousin to go south with him, to "the warm South / Full of the true, the blushful Hippocrene," an eternal summer that may be as dangerous to the English character as the oblivion offered by Keats's nightingale. The swallows are "taking daily a southing tendency" (141) as summer ends, but Rat must resist their siren call and be content with the "quiet water lilies swaying on the surface of an English stream" (146). England may be slow moving and tame, but Rat must accept its steady and wholesome tempo, not abandon it for the warmer and swifter currents of the south. Grahame's view of England is innately conservative and protective. Even more than Rat, Toad must be taught to respect the status quo and see how deep his investment in it really is. And he does. At the end, his great and surprising achievement is that he learns modesty and reticence, familiar virtues in the English pantheon of good behavior.

In 1987, Richard Eyre, the newly appointed artistic director of the Royal National Theatre, supplied the original impetus for Bennett's adaptation. He commissioned Bennett to write a play combining Kenneth Grahame's life with *The Wind in the Willows*. Bennett decided not to take that tack once he discovered the miserable particulars of Grahame's depressing life: orphaned at an early age, forced into a bank career when he dreamed of becoming an academic, married late and unhappily, all this topped by the suicide of his only child, whose tantrums may have inspired the creation of Mr. Toad. Adding Grahame to the characters in *Wind in the Willows* would have cast "a dark shadow over that earthly paradise" (*WW*, xiii), Bennett decided. In 1990, the project was revived as a children's Christmas show that "would be virtually all sunlight and would display to advantage the technical capabilities of the Olivier stage" (xiii). *Virtually* is the important word in that statement because no Bennett work is all sunlight. In his reconstruction of Grahame's fable, Bennett unearthed some of the complex adult realities of social behavior and identity formation that Grahame chose to ignore, making *The Wind in the Willows* "as revealing of me as the original text is of Grahame" (xxiii).

Chief among his alterations, Bennett places Mole in the foreground, as a youngster. Dressed as "an old-fashioned northern schoolboy" (1), perhaps a version of Bennett himself, Mole enters the larger world of the River Bank by suddenly bursting out of his hole and refusing to be limited to his prescribed rounds of duties. He wants "light . . . air . . . *freedom*" (1). Bennett calls the play "Mole's *Bildungsroman*" (xvii), the story of his education into the ways of the world. His mentors are Rat and Badger; Toad, of course, serves as an example of how not to behave. Mole learns more than Rat and Badger, the archconservatives, imagine, because, Bennett tells us, "Mole is the only one of the characters I have allowed to have doubts" (xvii), doubts that this is the best of all possible worlds and that engineering Toad's reform is the *sine qua non* for happiness, his own and theirs. To Rat and Badger's rapturous pleasure that Toad has "learned to behave himself. No more crazes. No more showing off. He's one of us," Mole offers this doubt, "I just thought that now he's more like everybody else, it's got a bit dull" (100). Bennett's characteristic ambivalence, his commitment to an ironic view of human (and animal) desires, reveals itself in this tiny skeptical voice. The social imperative for order that requires the stifling of Toad's anarchic impulses thus takes the edge off the freedom Mole was looking for when he burst from his hole. Rat and Badger insist complacently that conformity brings peace, but Mole has the good sense to wonder about the price.

Bennett also altered the Wild Wood, updating it into the sylvan equivalent of a "provincial bus station on a Saturday night," (27) where the weasels and ferrets are the racist gangs of the damaged inner cities. When Mole loses his way in the Wood, he is greeted with more than the metaphysical terror that Grahame evoked. He is taunted for his difference from the locals: "Go back to where you belong . . . We don't like moles . . . We don't like little black animals . . . Moles are dirty . . . Moles smell . . . Who's a smelly little mole then?" (28) The stoats, ferrets, and weasels then assault him, knocking him to the ground and beating him. It takes the arrival of Rat to disperse the gangs and save Mole. Bennett has made visible and ugly what Grahame thought was too vulgar to do more than hint at.

The Wild Wooders serve double duty in Bennett's adaptation. Once they breach the walls of Toad's mansion and set up their own operations there they become the representatives of "vulgar commercialism . . . the property speculators of the mid-eighties boom," the estate agents and leisure center developers that Mrs. Thatcher's fiscal policies spawned by the thousands.[10] Chairman Weasel's announcement that "our plan is to convert Toad Hall into a nice mix of executive apartments and office accommodation, and shove on a marina, and a cafe or two to fetch in the tourists" (94–5) returns Bennett full circle to his first play and the prophetic words of the retiring headmaster in *Forty Years On*: "Country is park and shore is marina, spare time is leisure and more, year by year. We have become a battery people, a people of underprivileged hearts fed on pap in darkness, bred out of all taste and season to savour the shoddy splendours of the new civility" (95).

There are other changes as well to the original story. Bennett introduces a touch of heterosexuality into the bachelor animals' lives, prompted perhaps by the end of his own bachelorhood when, in his forties, he began to share his Yorkshire residence with the woman he refers to in his diaries as "A".[11] The jailer's daughter kisses Toad, who insists that Rat be kissed and then Mole. Rat's initial reluctance gives way to mild enthusiasm once the deed is done: "Oh. I say. That's not unpleasant. I think my friend Mole might like that." Mole's kiss elicits only the monosyllables "Mmm. Yes." Bennett remarks in his stage directions, "Life, one may imagine, is never going to be quite the same again at least for Rat and Mole." When Mole enquires, "What about Badger?" Rat wisely admits that there's a limit to this late blooming heterosexuality: "I don't think it's Badger's thing at all" (98). When a journalist asked Bennett about the addition of this sexual dimension to the animals' lives, especially the hint he gives of Badger's homosexual orientation, he replied: "If you were to ask whether Badger wants to take Mole to bed, I have to say Badger would rather die than do that. But it's possible, looking at the the play from the out-side to deduce that Badger's problem might be solved if he admitted there was a possibility he might like it if he did. But it's certainly not a play about gay men."[12]

Perhaps the biggest change from the original and, interestingly enough, the one that Bennett insists isn't really a change, is Toad's reform at the end. In Grahame, Toad reforms his anarchic ways rather abruptly, a transformation that satisfies the didactic needs of the story but is implausible psychologically. In Bennett's version, Toad goes through the motions of reform too, but this time with a Goffmanian twist. Toad recognizes that all he's really being asked to do is to disguise his true nature and to perform for his audience the solid selfless virtues that Badger and Rat insist on. Bennett calls this process "keeping it under." It's the "social lie" that all young men learn: "our social acceptability [is] dependent on how much of our Toad we can keep hidden" (xxi). Bennett's point is that difference must be disguised, kept, so to speak, in the closet. He makes it again, when Toad is sentenced to a long term in jail for stealing a motorcar, creating some obvious allusions to the Oscar Wilde trial, even down to having Badger take off his hat as Toad is led away through the jeering mob, just as Robbie Ross did to honor Wilde. But as any per-former knows, what you want from an audience is applause, not pity, and Toad, who is a born actor (his impersonation of the washer woman is one of his best roles), quickly catches on to the benefits of giving the audience what it wants. "Why didn't you tell me before?" he asks Rat, "about not showing off, being humble and shy and nice." "What you didn't say," he chides his friend, "was that this way I get more attention than ever. Everybody loves me! It's wonderful" (100). Maybe Mole shouldn't worry too much that Toad will become impossibly dull, like everyone else. Toad will undoubtedly act very differently backstage than he does when he's on.

Daphne Turner finds that Bennett's *Wind in the Willows* has a much lower "emotional temperature" than the book because Bennett has undercut Grahame's pastoral vision with comedy.[13] That Bennett should leaven the sentiment with com-edy isn't surprising since, going back to *Forty Years On*, he has consistently demon-strated an equivocal attitude toward the prevailing myths of Albion. And it isn't just the comedy in Bennett's adaptation that undercuts the pastoral vision and adds shading to the "virtually" sunlit world he provided the Royal National Theatre. Bennett keeps in check his reverence for tradition and his susceptibility to nostalgia with practical references to the world he really inhabits, a world hemmed in by racist and predatory Wild Wooders and stultified by a conformist ethos where Mole's doubts are met with "I'd try not to think like that if I were you. . . . It does-n't do" (100). Luckily, there is Toad to point the way to the only modus vivendi that allows you some freedom: "keep it under" and do what you want when the audience files out. Seeming *is* being, a lesson that the main character in Bennett's next play, *The Madness of George III*, will also learn, but in a much more painful way.

The Madness of George III (1991)/*The Madness of King George* (1994)

Richard Eyre, who was artistic director of the National Theatre at the time, has said that he was "surprised by the subject matter of *The Madness of George III*" and judges it "the least Bennettian of all his plays."[14] Yet in many ways, both obvious and subtle, this play is quintessential Bennett. It has its roots in Bennett's under-graduate ambitions to carve out a career as an academic historian; it foregrounds his abiding interest in successful and failed performances of public identity; and its exploration of the origins, manifestations, and treatment of madness grows out of Bennett's own experiences of mental illness in his family—his own mother suffered from depression and was institutionalized, which was not widely known until the recent publication of "Untold Stories."

Despite lukewarm reviews—a "slightly sentimental view of royal pluck," "dull-ish, crudish"[15]—*The Madness of George III* was a huge success with its audience, thanks partly to the sly parallels Bennett suggests between the sorry state of the English monarchy at the end of the twentieth century and the crisis of George's reign two hundred years before, and thanks partly to Nigel Hawthorne's extraor-dinary performance as the tormented king. It played for two years in repertory at the National, then toured Britain and five cities in the United States. This popular success led to its transfer to the screen, with Bennett for the first time adapting his own stage play for the cinema and Nicholas Hytner repeating his role as director. The film version received a fair degree of attention as a lavish costume drama; reviews in the American press were largely appreciative.[16] It garnered four Academy Award nominations, including nods to Nigel Hawthorne and Helen Mirren for best actor and actress and to Bennett for best screenplay adaptation. Today, if Americans do recognize Alan Bennett's name, it's as the Oscar-nominated writer of *The Madness of King George*, as the film came to be titled. Fame is funny, as Bennett would be the first to agree.

Bennett's interest in the turbulent life and reign of George III has a long history, dating back to his days at Leeds Modern School, when he was cramming for a scholarship to Cambridge (*MGIII*, 5). As a budding historian, Bennett was drawn to the contradictory views of George promoted by competing historiographic schools. Long dismissed as a tyrant and a boor by Whig historians, in the 1950s George III was being studied by revisionists with greater sympathy; some even cast his "attachment to his people and his vision of the nation over and above the vagaries of politics" (viii) as a harbinger of the modern monarch. George's "mad business," his periodic lapses into and recoveries from what appeared at the time to be lunacy, and the political maneuvering that erupted over the speculation that George might be incapable of ruling, carry a dramatic and tragic interest of their own. The Prince of Wales's faction, the Whigs led by James Fox, advocated the Prince's installation as Regent and locked horns with the Tories, headed by the king's Prime Minister, William Pitt the Younger, who were determined to cling to power regardless of the king's mental condition. Bennett remembers copious and repeated revisions leading to the stage premiere—"I have never worked on a play

where so much reconstruction has been required" (xi)—partly because of the difficulty of meshing the personal tragedy, George's illness, with the details of the political turmoil that the illness occasioned. As time went on, Bennett conceded that he
had to foreground the dramatic and sacrifice some historical accuracy, not an easy
decision for a man who once aspired to an academic career in history.

But the writing of the screenplay brought even more drastic revisions. Bennett
jokingly explained that the title was changed to *The Madness of King George* as a
"marketing decision," so as not to confuse the sequence-saturated American audience, "a survey having apparently shown that there were many moviegoers who
came away from Kenneth Branagh's film of *Henry V* wishing they had seen its four
predecessors" (*MKG*, xiv) The shift in title is more than a joke, however. This decision to appeal to a wider audience signals that Bennett is sticking by a rule he
devised a dozen years earlier when he wrote his first screenplay, *A Private Function*:
"There is no such thing as a good script, only a good film" (*PF*, 9) The liberties with
historical fact that he felt compelled to confess to in the stage play (ix) are now
compounded so heavily that he throws himself on the mercy of the historical court.
He has been "forced into departures from history by the exigencies of the drama,
the insistence of the director and sheer desperation," he pleads in his introduction
to the screenplay (xxi). Actually, it's not just the fudging of the facts that makes this
adaptation seem so different from its predecessor. In his screenplay, Bennett has
given up the struggle to present the political intricacies of the period in their full
complexity, a challenge he hadn't completely abandoned in the stage play. The
emphasis in the film falls squarely on the domestic and personal aspects of the madness crisis.[17]

This shift from the public to the private, this pruning away of some of the historical foliage, has the effect of throwing into higher relief a core truth in Bennett's
work—his belief in the essentially performative nature of human behavior. George
III is deemed mad because he can no longer "perform" his role as monarch. He is
not what he should be. He does not "seem" the king. "Monarchy is a performance," Bennett writes in his introduction to the screenplay. "Part of the King's illness consists in his growing inability to sustain that performance" (xxi).

In the stage play, one of Bennett's sliest jokes conflates politics with acting. Early
on in the action, Edmund Burke, the famed orator, asks Richard Brinsley Sheridan,
the famous playwright and politician, if he could ever give up politics:

Sheridan: As distinct from the theatre, you mean? I don't know. There's the
             drama, of course. The temperament. And the acting, I suppose.
Burke: What would you miss about politics?
Sheridan: I'm talking about politics. (6)

In the film, Sheridan's part has been greatly reduced, Burke is nowhere to be found,
and neither are these lines. Instead, Bennett opens the film with a presentation of
one of Goffman's two classic performance spaces, the back region. What was a joke

in the stage play becomes a controlling metaphor in the film.

A gloved hand knocks on a wooden door and the camera moves into an antechamber where the royal court is dressing for the opening of Parliament. We are backstage, Goffman's favorite territory, where the actors relax before or after their ritual performances. We see the confusion, the boredom, the petty details of a large family getting ready for a tedious duty, like the annual family picnic. The mother (Queen Charlotte) keeps an eye on the children, cleaning the face of the youngest and hissing disapproval at the oldest as he swigs liquor from a flask. The father (George III) is in another room being dressed by his pages, or, as Bennett puts it, "being assembled" (6). For all the supposed solemnity of the occasion we are impressed by the chaotic, almost casual, disorder. When the call goes out for the "crown," we see a page take it out of a case, spit on it and buff it with his elbow, an amusing and titillating act of irreverence. And the king, as he is being assembled, begins to assume a different demeanor. He changes from the concerned father of fif-teen, who is happy to comfort his youngest daughter when her wooden horse is kicked over, to the father of the nation, "the genial family man banished in favour of his testy, impatient, official self" (7). Once assembled, he leads the procession at a pace more resembling a trot than a stately entrance into the House of Lords. He turns to his wife, asks "Ready?" and when she wearily answers yes, he growls, "Let's get it over with" (8). After this scene introduces us to life backstage, we're not at all surprised later to see the pages playing catch with the crown before bundling it back into its case. Shakespeare believed that the wearer of the crown had an uneasy time of it; Bennett suggests that life is just as rough for the crown itself, when no one is looking.

In the second line spoken in the film, an exchange of dialogue that survived the adaptation from stage to screen, the Prince of Wales asks his rather simple-minded brother, the Duke of York, what one of the medals on his jacket signifies. "This?" the Duke answers. "The other day I discovered I'm Bishop of Osnabruck. Amazing what one is really" (6). The young man's literal appropriation of a sinecure as a genuine component of his identity is comically naive. Nonetheless, it is Bennett's witty reminder of the fluidity of identity, its nonessentiality. You are what your name tag says you are. The claim is everything, as long as you claim it with con-viction.

The key scene in both the play and the film, the one that tells us George is regaining his wits, is not a naive assertion of identity such as the Duke of York's, but a reclamation of identity. As a therapy prescribed by his doctor, George takes the title role in a reading of Act IV of *King Lear*. By identifying himself with this "child-changed father," this "very foolish, fond old man" who is "bound / Upon a wheel of fire," George finds an objective correlative for his situation, a role into which he can once again fit—Shakespeare's great tragic king. Unlike his dim son, the king knows he's playing a role. When Thurlow, his Lord Chancellor, remarks how "affecting" the reading has been, the king answers, "It's the way I play it." And when Thurlow remarks to him, "your Majesty seems more yourself," George offers the central truth of his performance of monarch: "Do I? Yes, I do. I have always been myself even when I was ill. Only now I seem myself. That's the important thing. I have remembered how to seem. What, what?" (81–2). George III remembers once again to obey the different demands of the front and the back regions. When he is on stage as king, he must always seem kingly to his audience. His ailment has wrested away his control over his performance of monarch. Once the disease has passed into dormancy, the king can be "himself" again, at least in the public eye. The "what, what" that returns to his speech once he is "cured," signals a return of the king's uneasiness as well. In his commentary on the stage play, Bennett calls the king's verbal tic "the flag of social distress," the habit of "a nervous and self-conscious man to prevent the conversation from flagging" (xi). It's the outward indicator of the price the king pays for his plum role as monarch, the butterflies that accompany even the most seasoned actor onto the stage.

The film outstrips the play in its treatment of performance by extending the role playing to include the whole royal family, suggesting, somewhat anachronistically, that the Hanoverian royal family is little more than a theatrical construct intended to satisfy the paying customers, the commoners of England. Bennett takes George's advice to the Prince of Wales, "We must be a model family for the nation to look to" (87), from the stage version and plays upon it in the film like a musical variation. In the beginning, just after the opening of Parliament, the queen calls from her coach to the Prince of Wales in his coach, "George, smile, you lazy hound. It's what you're paid for. Smile and wave. Come on, everybody, smile and wave" (11). The same sentiments are repeated in the final scene of the film. Instead of showing just the king and queen on stage to begin the ceremony of Thanksgiving for the King's recovery at St. Paul's Cathedral, the film assembles the royal couple and ten of their children on the steps of St. Paul's to face a cheering crowd of their subjects.

King:	We must try to be more of a family. There are model farms now, model villages, even model factories. Well, we must be a model family for the nation to look to.
Queen:	(*To Duke Of York*) Yes. You must try to be more typical, Fred.
Prince Of Wales:	But Pa, I want something to *do*.
King:	Do? Well, follow in my footsteps, that is what you should do. Smile at the people. Wave to them. Let them see we're happy! That is why we are here. (74)

Seeming *is* doing in the world of the monarchy, just as seeming is being. Bennett's directions in the text describe the scene from the audience's perspective: "At the top of the steps the ROYAL FAMILY smile and wave. Who could think they are not happy?" (74).

The original viewers of both the stage play and the film had no way of knowing that the madness of George III was anything more to Alan Bennett than a richly dramatic historical event. Only late in 1999, in "Untold Stories" did Bennett publicly discuss what he had only hinted at before, that his mother had suffered from severe depression in the late 1960s and was institutionalized for eight years. As he describes the onset of his mother's illness and the doctors' inability to determine its cause or its meaning, echoes of George III's dilemma can be heard:

> A change in my mother's personality . . . had come about with relative sud-denness. In the space of a month or so she had lost all her fun and vitality, turning fretful and apprehensive and inaccessible to reason or reassurance. As the weeks passed the mood deepened, bringing with it fantasy and delusion: the house was watched, my father made to speak in a whisper because there was someone on the landing. . . . She started to sleep with her handbag under her pillow as if she were in a strange and dangerous hotel and finally one night she fled the house in her nightgown and Dad found her wandering in the street whence she could only be fetched back into the house after loud resistance. (US, 11)

Her doctors refused to see in her illness anything more serious than a garden-vari-ety bout of depression, and they dismissed as irrelevant the fact that her father had committed suicide. Their ineptitude doesn't rise to the levels of medical malpractice that Bennett shows George III enduring. But in the alternately hilarious and horri-fying scenes in the play and the film that depict the king's doctors competing to impose their "cures" on him, most of which are positively sadistic when not mere-ly inane, we can hear the echoes of a deep suspicion of medical science that Bennett acquired firsthand. While Mam did not experience the physical tortures of "cup-ping" that we see George suffer, Bennett's description of the ward he found his mother occupying conveys a horror of its own:

> [The attendant] flung open the door on Bedlam, a scene of unimagined wretchedness. What hit you first was the noise. . . . Crammed with wild and distracted women, lying or lurching about in all the wanton disarray of a Hogarth print, it was a place of terrible tumult. Some of the grey-gowned wild-eyed creatures were weeping, others shouting, while one demented wretch shrieked at short and regular intervals like a tropical bird. Almost worse was a big dull-eyed woman who sat bolt upright in her bed, oblivious to the surrounding tumult, as silent and unmoving as a stone deity. (13)

Here, Bennett realizes, as he later would emphasize in George III's case, that his mother "was mad because she looked mad" (13), seeming the same as being.

In the play and the film, Bennett draws on a theory advanced in the late 1960s by Ida Macalpine and Richard Hunter's book *George III and the Mad Business* that the king had suffered from a hereditary metabolic disorder known as porphyria, not a mental condition. Even if it were true, Bennett also reminds us that this twenti-eth-century answer, which contradicts every eighteenth-century diagnosis, does nothing to alleviate the suffering of the patient and his family. The revelation that porphyria recurs, and that George would suffer additional episodes of "madness," undercuts both of Bennett's apparently happy endings. In a similar way, when Bennett was told by his mother's doctors that "depression was not madness. It would lift. Light would return" (12), the cold comfort offered by that diagnosis did little to alleviate either her suffering or that of his father and the rest of the family. Knowing what we do about Bennett's personal acquaintance with mental illness, we can look at the changes Bennett has introduced into the film in a different and more sympathetic light. We can see the downplaying of the political and constitutional aspects of the crisis, and the greater emphasis on the domestic consequences of George III's bout with madness, as Bennett's growing recognition of the familial pain and denial that were an integral part of his own mother's illness, and not as a cynical appeal to uninformed American moviegoers. Like George III and his family gathering on the steps of St. Paul's, the Bennetts presented their apparently untroubled face to the rest of the world for forty years. The same ironic question Bennett applied to the royal family applies to his family as well. Looking at them, "Who could think they are not happy?"

NOTES

1. Bergan, 152–3.

2. Ironically, the great success of all three National Theatre plays has led to charges that Bennett has sold out to the market forces that rule the theatrical establishment. See Bull, 191, and Richard Scarr, "Alan Bennett: Political Playwright," *New Theatre Quarterly* 12, no. 48 (1996): 318–19.

3. Oscar Wilde, *The Importance of Being Earnest and Related Writings,* ed. Joseph Bristow, (London: Routledge, 1992), 66.

4. One of the many ironies of Orton's life and death was that the bill decriminalizing homosexual acts between adults was passed in July 1967, two weeks before Orton's murder.

5. Joe Orton, *The Orton Diaries*, ed. John Lahr (New York: Harper and Row Perennial Library, 1988), 251, footnote.

6. *Orton Diaries*, 148, footnote.

7. *Orton Diaries*, 248.

8. More understandably, Bennett's screenplay does not tackle Orton and Halliwell's pedophilia, which the *Diaries* devote a lot of unapologetic attention to, especially during their trips to Morocco.

9. Kenneth Grahame, *The Wind in the Willows,* (New York: Grosset and Dunlop, 1966), 117. All references to the text of Grahame's book come from this edition.

10. Turner, 27.

11. Schiff, 95.

12. De Jongh, 24.

13. Turner, 30.

14. *Independent*, Nov. 14, 1999.

15. Nicholas de Jongh, *Evening Standard*, Nov. 29, 1991; Benedict Nightingale, *Times* (London), Nov. 30, 1991.

16. See Buruma, 15–8, and Anthony Lane, *The New Yorker,* Jan. 6, 1995, 86–88.

17. See Joseph H. O'Mealy, "Royal Family Values: The Americanization of Alan Bennett's *The Madness of George III,*" *Literature/Film Quarterly* 27, no. 2 (1999): 90–6.

CHAPTER EIGHT

Conclusion: In the Van(guard)

The Clothes They Stood Up in (1996)
The Lady in the Van (1989/1999)

An American critic has noted that Alan Bennett, in addition to being a popular playwright in England, "is equally famous . . . as an author of nonfiction prose" thanks to his association with the *London Review of Books*, which publishes his annual diary and published his most famous prose work to date, *The Lady in the Van*, in 1989.[1] Bennett's current status as a semi-regular contributor to this influential literary journal might never have come about were it not for the accident of its editor, Mary-Kay Wilmers, being a near neighbor of his in Camden Town. She had observed first hand Miss Shepherd, "the lady in the van," had heard that Bennett had been keeping notes about this eccentric woman over the last two decades, and, upon her death, urged him to write up the story, with the promise that she would publish it in the *London Review*. Thus was born one of Bennett's most important links to a small but loyal Anglo-American intellectual readership, an audience familiar enough with Bennett's work to regard him as a serious literary artist.

Bennett's connection with the *London Review of Books* has also given him a chance to write prose fiction. His novella, *The Clothes They Stood Up In*, so far his only lengthy work of prose fiction, appeared in the *Review* late in 1996 and was published in book form in 1998. It tells the story of Mr. and Mrs. Ransome, upper-middle-class Londoners who discover when they return from the opera that everything they own is missing. Everything in their flat—from the furniture to the appliances, from their clothes to the cabinetry, from their books and stereo to the toilet brush and roll—has been taken away. Forced to rebuild their lives from scratch, the Ransomes respond differently to the challenge, the wife being much more open to new possibilities than her prissy husband. Because the Ransomes' marriage is emotionally arid, the wife's more adventuresome spirit appears to offer hope of change, a second chance. However, the new influences she opens herself to consist largely of American daytime television programs that dispense the jargon of self-healing and self-love, which Bennett has always considered an abuse of language.[2] Even though the Ransomes eventually discover why they have been burgled (mistaken identity) and recover their belongings (which have been reassembled with absolute precision in a storage space), they do not actually profit from this extraordinary opportunity to reinvent themselves. They return to their familiar behavior patterns, which only Mr. Ransome's death from a stroke alters, but not in any significant way.

With sharp-eyed satire mitigated by empathy, *The Clothes They Stood Up In* encapsulates many of Bennett's concerns. The Ransomes live a performative life, symbolized by the precise re-creation of their flat in the storage space, down to the casserole in the oven and Kiri Te Kanewa on the stereo. Looking at the perfect reproduction of their habitat, Mrs. Ransome concludes that her flat is really not different from "the setting for a film," which the continuity assistant would have meticulously reconstructed from photographs (*CTSUI*, 76). The emotional death at the heart of their marriage is contrasted with the exuberant sexuality of Martin and Cleo, the couple who oversee the storage space and who move into the reassembled flat as if it were their own. After they recover their property, Mr. Ransome spends many evenings surreptitiously listening to a tape he has discovered of the young couple having sex in his bed. Even though he suffers a paralytic stroke while listening to the tape, Mr. Ransome is actually killed when his wife solicitously turns up the volume on Dame Kiri singing an aria from *Così Fan Tutte*: "it is the vibration that does it . . . something happens in his head, and the frail sac into which the blood has leaked now bursts" (111). As a widow, Mrs. Ransome thinks that "the burglary and everything that has happened since has been a kind of apprenticeship" and that "now . . . I can start" (112). However, with this sentiment she merely echoes the legions of other inert Bennett characters who also imagine that they can begin again after the death of a parent or spouse or can find last-minute compensation for life's injuries and injustices. Mrs. Ransome, caught up "in the processes of bereavement and the techniques of grieving" that television has "schooled her in" (112), has substituted an ersatz emotional profundity for the shallow materialism and emotional aridity of her life with her husband. Bennett's satire on "that life which the Ransomes had the complete equipment for but had never managed to lead" (52) is gentle but unyielding.

More important to him than the opportunity to try his hand at prose, the *London Review of Books* has provided Bennett with a comfortable confessional space. The annual excerpts from his diaries, titled for example, "What I Did in 1999," have offered partial views into his life for many years, and now, with the prospect of several autobiographical installments in the *Review* of "Untold Stories," Bennett seems prepared to address the memories of his early years directly. Over the last decade, however, probably nothing about Alan Bennett the man has piqued the curiosity of the English public as much as *The Lady in the Van*. When the story was reprinted in *Writing Home*, the marketing people knew that positioning the words "Includes *The Lady in the Van*" on the cover right under the title would increase sales. Although it is true, the story of Miss Shepherd, the "lady in the van," is almost too odd to believe: Bennett allowed an elderly homeless woman whose only shelter was her van to park herself and the van in his front yard for fifteen years. He supplied her with electricity, did her grocery shopping when she was ill, and tolerated her progressively antisocial behavior and rank smells, all without any real knowledge of who she was. It's the kind of story that the English, who have long prized their own eccentrics, could identify with, even though they must also have been amazed by the magnitude of Bennett's toleration and charity.

In telling the story, Bennett recognized that he would have to establish early on his motives for sheltering Miss Shepherd, unless he wanted to be burdened with the reputation of saintliness and labeled the Mother Teresa of Camden Town. He insists that it wasn't owing to his superior character that he invited Miss Shepherd into his garden for a fifteen-year stay. "I was never under the illusion that the impulse [to shelter her] was purely charitable," he emphasizes. He'd prefer us to believe that it was an act compounded of self-interest and liberal guilt. When Miss Shepherd parked her van on the street, the Bedford attracted a constant stream of hooligans who delighted in vandalizing it and terrorizing her, so Bennett, depressed "to find such sadism and intolerance so close at hand . . . and having to be on the alert for every senseless attack," found it "impossible to work." Since no one else would deal with the problem, he first invited her to live in a lean-to in his garden and then allowed her to move her van into the yard, where she lived until her death. Bennett wants us to know that "it made me furious that I had been driven to such a pass. But I wanted a quiet life as much as, and possibly more than, she did. In the garden she was at least out of harm's way" (*WH*, 65–6) In case we haven't been convinced of the mixed motives behind Bennett's extraordinary forbearance, he chooses as an epigraph for the story William Hazlitt's definition of good nature: "Good nature, or what is often considered as such, is the most selfish of all virtues: it is nine times out of ten mere indolence of disposition" (58).

Bennett's narrative of his experiences with Miss Shepherd in his garden is culled from diary entries that begin in 1969, when she first coerces him into pushing her stalled van while she sits in the cab and makes graceful hand signals—in Bennett's memorable description, "this section of the Highway Code might have been choreographed by Petipa with Ulanova at the wheel" (62)—and end in 1990, a year after her death, when he discovers her true identity. In the intervening years Miss Shepherd graces Bennett's garden the way hermits used to inhabit the grounds of wealthy landowners in the eighteenth century, or, perhaps more accurately, the way trolls lurk under bridges in folktales, which is to say without much grace. Yet for all her reactionary religious and political opinions, her gruff and unappreciative manner, her untidy habits and revoltingly casual appreciation of hygiene, Bennett is fascinated by her, even though he cannot deny that "one seldom was able to do her a good turn without some thoughts of strangulation" (62).

After her death, Bennett is driven to uncover her story, to find "some clue as to what it was that had happened to make Miss Shepherd want to live like this," meaning in the squalor of a debris-strewn van (90). En route to discovering the facts of Miss Shepherd's turbulent life—she had once been a promising piano student, had given up the prospect of a concert career to enter the convent, but had to leave this vocation because of a series of mental breakdowns—Bennett comes to see the van as the only still and stable place in the chaos of her existence. He reaches the conclusion that "the more I laboured, the less peculiar the van seemed—its proprieties and aspirations no different from those with which I had been brought up" (90). Early in their acquaintance Bennett is disturbed by the way Miss Shepherd links the two of them in the phrase "celibates like you and me" (69). But by the end of this story, as he has done in many of his plays, Bennett has taken the peculiar and made it less so. Her brother, once Bennett locates him, immediately recognizes the irony of his and his sister's lives. He has had a respectable career and an industrious life, but "here she is, having lived like a tramp, more famous than he'll ever be" (93). Bennett too is moved less by pity for her unhappy life, and gratitude for his more fortunate one, than by a gnawing sense that Miss Shepherd has lived a more authentic life than he has. In some essential way, Miss Shepherd is the exception that tests the Goffmanian rule, the one person in his work who seems unpersuaded by the need for impression management—a female, completely unreformable, Mr. Toad. Careless of how she appears to others, unwilling to make herself agreeable for the sake of being accepted socially, she seems to reproach him:

> I mull it over too, wondering at the bold life she has had and how it contrasts with my own timid way of going on—living, as Camus said, slightly the opposite of expressing. And I see how the location of Miss Shepherd and the van in front but to the side of where I write is the location of most of the stuff I write about; that too is to the side and never what faces me. (92)

His habitual avoidance of "what faces me," what a critic has called Bennett's need "to guard his secrets,"[3] apparently bothered Bennett enough that, when he began to rework this same material into a stage play, he decided to face this failing head on.

The announcement in the fall of 1999 that Bennett had converted Miss Shepherd's story into a play aroused enormous interest and led to brisk box office business, prompted no doubt by word that Maggie Smith had been cast as Miss Shepherd, but prompted also by the public's fascination with the story. The changes Bennett has introduced in transferring the story from the page to the stage are few but significant. What seemed originally a cast of two—Bennett and Miss Shepherd—becomes a small repertory company of sixteen. Not only has Bennett dramatized the neighbors, the social worker, a couple of doctors, and his mother, who was never mentioned in the original story, but, in his splashiest innovation,

Bennett dramatizes as two characters his almost constitutional ambivalence—Alan Bennett, the participant in the Miss Shepherd saga, and Alan Bennett 2, the writer and observer. The London critics were also of two minds in their assessment of *The Lady in the Van*, some calling it the best new play of the year, a few ranking it below Bennett's best work.[4] The most perceptive of the reviews pointed out the new emphasis on autobiography—"this isn't just a play about Miss Shepherd, but a play about Alan Bennett himself, and a revealing one"[5]—and wondered at the "surprising self-exposure . . . by someone so notoriously private."[6] Nicholas de Jongh, who dismissed the play as "more a display" of Maggie Smith's theatrical tricks, laid out the paradox at the heart of Bennett's personal presence in the play: "Bennett by insisting he wants to be alone, free from prying journalists, has made himself the Greta Garbo of Gloucester Terrace. His plays and published Diaries, however, keep bringing him into intimate view."[7]

Although Bennett himself has conceded, "there is no satisfactory way of dubbing these two parts (I would not call them halves) of my personality" (*LV*, xxii), it's not hard to distinguish between the two Bennetts on stage, although their familiar costumes—matching corduroys, v-neck sweaters, suede shoes—match perfectly. The Alan Bennett who speaks with the other characters and interacts with Miss Shepherd is the good citizen, the guilt-ridden and maddened benefactor of this eccentric nuisance. Alan Bennett 2, who does not partake in the action of the play and converses only with his alter ego, is the writer, who sees in Miss Shepherd the makings of a good story and patronizes and mocks his alter ego's clumsy confusion of motives and emotions. In the course of writing the play, as Bennett explains it, he made Alan Bennett 2 "definitely more mischievous, more amoral" (xxiii) than Alan Bennett the good citizen. The play opens with Alan Bennett 2 peering at the audience through a large Georgian window, on the lookout for something or someone, miming for us Bennett's familiar definition of the writer as both detached and surveillant.

Although the two Alan Bennetts tend to have a combative relationship, each exasperated by the other's naïveté or cynicism, they join ranks when they suspect that Miss Shepherd's bolder approach to life makes their own conventional existence look empty. The charge of the unlived life, which Bennett indicted the Ransomes for in *The Clothes They Stood Up In* and accused himself of in the prose version of *The Lady in the Van*, rears its head here too. Alan Bennett 2 teases out an analogy between the unending care of aged parents and the artistic challenges of commonplace raw material that he has to be satisfied with after two decades of observing Miss Shepherd:

> Starting out as someone incidental to my life, she remained on the edge of it so long she became not incidental at all. As homebound sons and daughters looking after their parents think of it as just marking time before their lives start, so like them I learned there is no such thing as marking time, and that time marks you. In accommodating her and accommodating to her, I find twenty years of my life has gone. This broken-down old woman, her delu-

sions and the slow abridgement of her life with all its vehicular permutations . . . these have been given to me to record as others record journeys
across Tibet or Patagonia or the thighs of a dozen women. (86–7)

Apparently desperate to find any evidence to counteract this gnawing sense of wast-
ed opportunity, both Alan Bennetts comically grasp at sex to dispute Miss
Shepherd's inclusion of them in her community of "celibates" (36). First, Alan
Bennett 2 reports that he caught the eye of one of the undertaker's men at Miss
Shepherd's grave site, and "were I Joe Orton, I reflect, I would be able to turn even
this bored, impersonal glance across a grave to some sexual advantage" (84). But
he's not, and he doesn't. Then, stung by Miss Shepherd's scorn for their timidity,
"Too many scruples in the way . . . You want to take a leaf out of my book. Be
bold" (85–6), the good citizen Bennett turns back to address the audience in the
final moments of the play, as the two Bennetts prepare to exit the stage:

> Look. This has been one path through my life . . . me and Miss Shepherd. Just
> one track. I wrote things; people used to come and stay the night, and of both
> sexes. What I mean to say is, it's not as if it's the whole picture. Lots of other
> stuff happened. No end of things. (87)

Alan Bennett 2 assures him, "They know that." But when his alter ego insists one
more time, "And that's true. I'm not making it up," the "more mischievous"
Bennett 2 puts a patronizing hand on his shoulder and reassures him, "Of course
you're not" (87). This last minute deflation, which winks at the audience and calls
into question the veracity of all the sexual revelations, is the reason Bennett can
remark in his commentary that "very little of my own life is revealed" (xxii) in the
play. Yet, actually, Bennett has been bold in this play and has shown us more of his
private side than he is accustomed to, and not merely through the titillating hints
about sexual activity. The most telling revelations about his own life come from the
presence of his mother on the stage and the painful emotional connections he draws
between her and Miss Shepherd.

"Old ladies are my bread and butter" (20), Alan Bennett 2 admits frankly. And
the inclusion on stage of Mam, who has served as the prototype for many of the
women in his work, the model from whom he has drawn the hygiene-obsessed
northern women in the earlier plays, makes great theatrical sense. In several ways,
she is the perfect visual and dramatic counterpoint to Miss Shepherd. Mam is tidy
and tastefully dressed, in sharp contrast to Miss Shepherd's filthy rags and rank
odors. She is largely quiet and passive, unlike ungrateful and demanding Miss
Shepherd. And yet the similarities between the women are compelling and expose
the emotional depths of this play much more deeply than do the differences. Both
women suffer from a serious mental disorder, which leads Bennett to ruefully complain, "at the northern and southern gates of my life stands a deluded woman"
(20). Both also stake out similar emotional claims on the author, reminding him of
his ambivalence about his responsibilities to care for other people ("care" is one of

his least favorite words). Mam functions specifically as a goad to the writer's conscience. Whenever she tries to win his attention by mentioning her worries or reporting the delusions that mark her lapses into depression, she seems only to annoy him, and he dismisses her impatiently. She keeps losing ground to Miss Shepherd, whose louder eccentricities bully and distract him. Bennett recognizes the ironic parallels between the two old women, and how, having exploited one woman for his writing, he wants to avoid doing it twice—"I write about one old woman as it is. Mam. The last thing I want to do is to write about another" (15). Yet, as the audience sits watching Miss Shepherd's story, it knows how disingenuous that remark is.

One of the functions of Alan Bennett 2 is to make his alter ego face unpleasant truths. For example, when he asserts that Miss Shepherd's delusions tempt him to violence against her because she resembles his deluded mother and her own unreasonable demands, Alan Bennett resists this simple insight: "It's always Mam you compare her with. They're not the same. I don't like them even sharing the same sentence" (50).[8] The play tells a different tale. At several points, Bennett ambiguously structures the dialogue so that when the audience assumes the characters are speaking about Miss Shepherd, in actuality they are speaking about Mam, and vice versa. And yet, the play also shows that their fates are quite different. They do not share "the same sentence." Mam is consigned first to a sanitarium and then to a rest home; Miss Shepherd, the complete stranger, lives on Bennett's premises for fifteen years. Before 1999, Bennett never publicly discussed the story of his mother's final years, although he published his account of Miss Shepherd's final years within months of her death and has gone on using it through several media incarnations—print, radio, and now stage.

Bennett's silence about his mother and his openness about Miss Shepherd point up the ambivalence in his attitude to these two central figures in his life, an ambivalence that veers wildly between concern and resentment, between guilt and the impulse to violence. A small joke embedded in the play suggests that the force of Bennett's anger is not restricted to these two old women. Miss Shepherd, whose first name is Margaret, reminds Alan Bennett 2 of another infuriating Margaret—Mrs. Thatcher. Sheridan Morley spelled out the parallel in his opening night review: "Just as Bennett's life comes to be dominated by an authoritarian old woman making no sense but terrifying all those around her, so too is his nation dominated by Thatcher."[9] Bennett, however, makes the connection with more anger than wit: "Leading from the front, Mrs. Thatcher is of course in the van too, and one in my view just as full of garbage as the other" (41). Bennett's antipathy to Mrs. Thatcher and her politics comes as no surprise to readers of his diary entries during the 1980s. Here he connects the dots that join Mrs. Thatcher, Miss Shepherd, and Mam as three female loonies whose power over him he resents but cannot escape. The public and the private have come together.[10] The picture Bennett presents here of his vexed relationships with the demanding and controlling women in his life should quash for good the simplistic notion that his legacy will be the "immortalisation of the lonely, elderly woman."[11]

The honesty with which Bennett has dramatized his feelings—of being exploited as he exploits, of being craven and calculating, of being dutiful and neglectful, and most of all of feeling guilty and resentful of feeling guilty—opens up *The Lady in the Van* to autobiographical speculation and signals a different kind of relationship between Bennett and his audience. Bennett implicitly recognized this shift when he chose not to include in the stage version Camus's distinction between living and expressing, the reference he ended the prose version with. That self-incriminating doubt has been made ironic and embedded in the last line of the play—Alan Bennett 2 remarks, "Of course you're not," undercutting his alter ego's insistence that he isn't making it up about having a full life. Bennett still questions whether he has really lived as boldly as he might have, but he cannot now credibly complain that he perpetually writes only about what is "to the side" of him and never what "faces" him.

After forty years of performing and writing, what Alan Bennett increasingly sees in front of him is the darker corners of the human soul, as the second series of *Talking Heads* demonstrates through its preoccupation with obsessive sexuality and the terror at the heart of everyday life. Contributing to, and perhaps elucidating, that shadowy region is his interest in exploring the ways in which his own family history has influenced his work. Yet despite these darker shadings, the stage version of *The Lady in the Van* shows that the Alan Bennett who is writing today is in many ways the same writer who began his career forty years ago. He is still the comic writer who appreciates the absurd and sad performances of everyday English people, his own included. He is still the sympathetic observer of society's marginal figures, a writer who refuses to sentimentalize his characters by exempting them from his satiric scrutiny. He still questions the pieties handed down by the authorities about what constitutes moral and ethical behavior. And he still suspects that his own motives as a writer often are self-serving and unworthy.

An appreciation of the qualities that constitute Bennett's distinctive voice should discourage any lingering misperceptions that he is "a replacement Betjeman," the poet laureate of middlebrow nostalgia, or even worse, "literature's answer to the Queen Mother," cuddly and well-loved.[12] Properly understood, Bennett's bracing brand of comic pessimism should earn him a prominent place in the vanguard of contemporary dramatists.

NOTES

1. Wendy Lesser, "Plenty of Quirks and Tenses, but Not a Film Star in Sight" *New York Times*, Oct. 9, 1999.

2. See the speech Bennett has written for himself in *The Lady in the Van* rejecting the Social Worker's use of the term "carer": "I hate the thought. I hate the word"(*LV*, 69).

3. John Peter, *Times* (London), Dec. 12, 1999.

4. The critics for the *Daily Telegraph*, the *Daily Mail*, the *International Herald Tribune*, and the *Times* weighed in with strong praise, though the critics for the *Independent*, the *Guardian*, and the *Evening Standard* expressed some reservations about the dramatic soundness of the piece.

5. Charles Spencer, *Daily Telegraph*, Dec. 8, 1999.

6. Jane Edwardes, *Time Out*, December 15–22, 1999.

7. Nicholas de Jongh, "The Van that is purely a vehicle for Dame Maggie," *Evening Standard*, Dec. 8, 1999. Ten years earlier, de Jongh had dubbed Bennett the "Garbo of Primrose Hill." Same Garbo, different neighborhood.

8. In "Untold Stories," Bennett has revealed that "it was always the aggressiveness of [Mam's] despair and her conviction that hers was the true view of the world that was the breaking point with me and which, if I were alone with her, would fetch me to the brink of violence" (12).

9. Sheridan Morley, "Bennett's Mad, Magnificent 'Lady'," *International Herald Tribune*, Dec. 15, 1999.

10. It is possible to detect in Miss Shepherd's story the whiff of a political allegory in which the leader at the wheel of the vehicle of state, the shepherd of the national flock, is "a bigoted, blinkered, cantankerous, devious, unforgiving, self-centred, rank, rude, car-mad cow" (*LV*, 70).

11. Bergan, 187.

12. Paul Taylor, "An Englishman abroad," *Independent*, Dec. 4, 1999.

Chronology

1960–63	*Beyond the Fringe* (with Cook, Miller, Moore)
1966	*On the Margin* (TV series)
1968	*Forty Years On* (stage play)
1971	*Getting On* (stage play)
1972	*A Day Out* (TV play)
1973	*Habeas Corpus* (stage play)
1975	*Sunset across the Bay* (TV play)
1977	*The Old Country* (stage play)
	A Little Outing (TV play)
1978	*A Visit from Miss Prothero* (TV play)
	Me, I'm Afraid of Virginia Woolf (TV play)
	Green Forms, aka *Doris and Doreen* (TV play)
1979	*The Old Crowd* (TV play)
	Afternoon Off (TV play)
	One Fine Day (TV play)
	All Day on the Sands (TV play)
1980	*Enjoy* (stage play)
1982	*Intensive Care* (TV play)
	Our Winnie (TV play)
	A Woman of No Importance (TV play)
	Rolling Home (TV play)
	Marks (TV play)
	Say Something Happened (TV play)
1983	*An Englishman Abroad* (TV play)
1984	*A Private Function* (screenplay)
1986	*Kafka's Dick* (stage play)

Man and Music: Composer and Court (TV documentary)
The Insurance Man (TV play)
Uncle Clarence (radio talk)
1987   *Prick Up Your Ears* (screenplay)
1988   *Single Spies: An Englishman Abroad* and *A Question of
                 Attribution* (stage plays)
            Talking Heads (TV plays)
                 A Chip in the Sugar
                 A Lady of Letters
                 Bed among the Lentils
                 Soldiering On
                 Her Big Chance
                 A Cream Cracker under the Settee
            Dinner at Noon (TV documentary)
1989   *The Lady in the Van* (story/radio talk)
1990   *The Wind in the Willows* (stage play adaptation)
            Poetry in Motion (TV documentary)
1991   *102 Boulevard Haussmann* (TV play)
            County Arcade, Leeds (TV documentary)
            Down Cemetery Road: The Landscape of Philip Larkin (TV
                 lecture)
            A Question of Attribution (TV version)
            The Madness of George III (stage play)
1992   *Childhood* (TV documentary)
1994   *Writing Home* (collection of essays and diaries)
            Portrait or Bust (TV documentary)
            The Madness of King George (screenplay)
1995   *The Abbey* (TV documentary)
1996   *The Clothes They Stood Up in* (story)
1998   *Talking Heads 2* (TV plays)
                 Miss Fozzard Finds Her Feet
                 The Hand of God
                 Playing Sandwiches
                 The Outside Dog
                 Nights in the Gardens of Spain
                 Waiting for the Telegram
1999   "Untold Stories" (memoir)
            The Lady in the Van (stage play)

Selected Bibliography

Beckett, Samuel. *Endgame*. New York: Grove Press, 1958.

Bennett, Alan. *A Private Function*. London: Faber and Faber, 1984.

———. "Alan Bennett Chooses Four Paintings For Schools." *London Review of Books*, Apr. 2, 1998.

———. Forty Years On *and Other Plays*. London: Faber and Faber, 1991.

———. Objects of Affection *and Other Plays for Television*. London: BBC Books, 1982.

———. *Office Suite*. London: Faber and Faber, 1981.

———. *Plays Two*. London: Faber and Faber, 1998.

———. *Prick Up Your Ears: The Screenplay*. London: Faber and Faber, 1987.

———. *Talking Heads*. London: BBC Books, 1988.

———. *Talking Heads 2*. London: BBC Books, 1998.

———. "Talking Shop." *Radio Times,* October 10–16, 1998.

———. *The Clothes They Stood Up in*. London: Profile Books, 1998.

———. *The Lady in the Van*. London: Faber and Faber, 2000.

———. *The Madness of George III*. London: Faber and Faber, 1992.

———. *The Madness of King George*. London: Faber and Faber, 1995.

———. *The Wind in the Willows*. London: Faber and Faber, 1991.

———. *The Writer in Disguise*. London: Faber and Faber, 1985.

———. *Two Kafka Plays*. London: Faber and Faber, 1987.

———. "Untold Stories." *London Review of Books,* September 30, 1999, 11–16.

———. *Writing Home*. London: Faber and Faber, 1994.

Bennett, Alan, Peter Cook, Jonathan Miller, and Dudley Moore. *Beyond the Fringe: A Revue*. New York: Samuel French, 1963.

———. *The Complete Beyond the Fringe*. Edited by Roger Wilmut. London: Methuen, 1987.

Bentley, Eric. "Farce." *The Life of the Drama*. New York: Atheneum, 1965.

Bergan, Ronald. *Beyond the Fringe . . . And Beyond: A Critical Biography of Alan Bennett, Peter Cook, Jonathan Miller and Dudley Moore*. London: Virgin, 1989.

Brantley, Ben. "Swimming in Irony." *New York Times Book Review*, October 1, 1995.

Bull, John. *Stage Right: Crisis and Recovery in British Contemporary Mainstream Theatre*. New York: St. Martin's Press, 1994.

Buruma, Ian. "The Great Art of Embarrassment." *New York Review of Books*, February 16, 1995.

De Jongh, Nicholas. "In Search of the Garbo of Primrose Hill." *The Guardian*. "Review," December 13, 1990.

Goffman, Erving. *The Presentation of Self in Everyday Life*. London: Penguin Books, 1990.

———. *Frame Analysis*. New York: Harper and Row, 1974.

Grahame, Kenneth. *The Wind in the Willows* (1908). New York: Grosset and Dunlap, 1966.

Guinness, Alec. *My Name Escapes Me*. New York: Viking, 1997.

———. *A Positively Final Appearance*. New York: Viking, 1999.

Innes, Christopher. *Modern British Drama 1890–1990*. Cambridge: Cambridge University Press, 1992.

Lahr, John. "Madjesty." *Light Fantastic*. New York: Delta, 1997.

———. *Prick Up Your Ears: The Biography of Joe Orton*. New York: Vintage, 1987.

Lane, Anthony. "Power Mad." *The New Yorker*, January 6, 1995.

Lesser, Wendy. "Plenty of Quirks and Tenses, but Not a Film Star in Sight." *The New York Times*, October 9, 1999.

Macalpine, Ida and Richard Hunter. *George III and the Mad Business*. London: Allen Lane The Penguin Press, 1969.

Mackinnon, Lachlan. "Life on a Sunday Afternoon." *Times Literary Supplement*, November 13, 1998.

Manning, Philip. *Erving Goffman and Modern Sociology*. Stanford, Calif.: Stanford University Press, 1992.

Morgan, Kenneth O. *The People's Peace: British History 1945–1990*. Oxford: Oxford University Press, 1990.

O'Mealy, Joseph H. "Royal Family Values: The Americanization of Alan Bennett's *The Madness of George III*." *Literature/Film Quarterly*, 27, no. 2 (1999): 90–96.

Orton, Joe. *The Orton Diaries*. Edited by John Lahr. New York: Harper and Row Perennial Library, 1988.

Painter, George. *Marcel Proust: A Biography*. London: Chatto and Windus, 1989.

Scarr, Richard. "Alan Bennett: Political Playwright." *New Theatre Quarterly* 12, no. 48 (1996): 309–22.

Schiff, Stephen. "The Poet of Embarrassment." *The New Yorker*. Sept. 6, 1993.

Turner, Daphne. *Alan Bennett: In a Manner of Speaking*. London: Faber and Faber, 1997.

White, Edmund. *Marcel Proust*. New York: Viking, 1999.

Wilmut, Roger. *From Fringe to Flying Circus*. London: Eyre Methuen, 1980.

Wolfe, Peter. *Understanding Alan Bennett*. Columbia: University of South Carolina Press, 1999.

Wu, Duncan. *Six Contemporary Playwrights*. New York: St. Martin's Press, 1995.

Index